LEST WE REMEMBER

What Oxford's war memorial tells us about the British Empire and why that matters

DUNCAN TAYLOR

Lest We Remember
© Duncan Taylor 2024

This book is sold subject to the condition that it shall not, by way of trade or otherwise, be lent, resold, hired out, converted to another format or otherwise circulated without the publishers' prior conjunction in any other format other than that in which it is published.

The right of the author to be identified as the author of this work has been asserted in accordance with the Copyright, Designs and Patents Act 1988.

ISBN 978-1-910779-43-9

Typeset and cover design
by Oxford eBooks Ltd.

www.oxford-ebooks.com

TABLE OF CONTENTS

Illustrations .... *vi*

Picture credits .... *vii*

Recessional .... *viii*

Introduction *1*

The Tirah Memorial – Inscription *10*

PART I *13*

    1: The North West Frontier 15

    2: A Good Thrashing... 35

    3: Struggling On 51

    4: Unbeaten 75

INTERLUDE *93*

    5: Foundations 95

PART II *101*

    6: African Pearl.. 103

    7: Mission Fever... 113

    8: Annexation 131

    9: Desolation and Death 143

    10: Remembering 175

    11: Forgetting 189

    12: Reckoning 203

Afterword... *219*

Acknowledgments *220*

Notes... *221*

Bibliography *243*

Index *267*

About the author *277*

ILLUSTRATIONS

Figure 1. The Tirah Memorial (Jackson's Oxford Journal, 10.7.1900) 4

Figure 2. The Tirah Memorial in 2024 12

Figure 3. Colonel Robert Warburton 22

Figure 4. Sir William Lockhart 36

Figure 5. Medical Staff at the Field Gymkhana 52

Figure 6. Left to right - Col. Plowden, Lt. Owen, Lt. Feilden 62

Figure 7. Burning a village in the Maidan Valley 77

Figure 8. An Afridi village with the distinctive fortified tower 77

Figure 9. Jirgah with Orakzai. Lockhart centre right back to camera 84

Figure 10. Major A.B. Thruston 104

Figure 11. British East Africa 1892 108

Figure 12. The punishment of Pvt. Rajat Faragella 124

Figure 13. Colvile in later life, knighted and a major-general 144

Figure 14. Sudanese Troops 1897 153

Figure 15. The engagement at Lubwa 168

Figure 16. Kabalega (left) and Mwanga heading into exile. 171

Figure 17. The original memorial plaque at the fort at Lubwa, Uganda 174

Figure 18. Thruston wearing the Star of Africa 174

Figure 19. Proposal for memorial design, 1920 174

Figure 20. The agreed design, 1920 192

Figure 21. Pitt Rivers display of Bunyoro royal artefacts 210

Front cover: King Mwanga of Bunyoro .... (fig.16)

Back cover: King Kabalega of Bunyoro .... (fig.16)

PICTURE CREDITS

Figure 1. Content provided by The British Library Board. All rights reserved. With thanks to The British Newspaper Archive (www.britishnewspaperarchive.co.uk).

Figure 2. Author

Figures 5 & 6. With permission of The Soldiers of Oxfordshire Museum

Fig 12 & 16. The Bodleian Libraries, University of Oxford, [MSS. Afr. s. 1494, MSS], [page 15]; Micr. Af. 597.

Figures 18 & 19. Reproduced with thanks to The British Newspaper Archive

Figure 20. Author – with permission of the Pitt Rivers Museum.

RECESSIONAL

God of our fathers, known of old,
Lord of our far-flung battle-line,
Beneath whose awful Hand we hold
Dominion over palm and pine
Lord God of Hosts be with us yet,
Lest we forget – lest we forget!

The tumult and the shouting dies;
The Captains and the Kings depart:
Still stands Thine ancient sacrifice,
An humble and a contrite heart.
Lord God of Hosts, be with us yet,
Lest we forget – lest we forget!

Far-called, our navies melt away;
On dune and headland sinks the fire:
Lo, all our pomp of yesterday
Is one with Nineveh and Tyre!
Judge of the Nations, spare us yet,
Lest we forget – lest we forget!

If, drunk with sight of power, we loose
Wild tongues that have not Thee in awe,
Such boastings as the Gentiles use,
Or lesser breeds without the Law
Lord God of Hosts, be with us yet,
Lest we forget – lest we forget!

> For heathen heart that puts her trust
> In reeking tube and iron shard,
> All valiant dust that builds on dust,
> And guarding, calls not Thee to guard,
> For frantic boast and foolish word
> Thy mercy on Thy People, Lord!

*

Rudyard Kipling

Written for the diamond jubilee of Queen Victoria, 1897

INTRODUCTION

It is a bleak November day. A blustery wind snatches at the gowns of the clerics and academics gathered under a grey and soon to be drizzling sky. Standing alongside them, city dignitaries wearing their chains of office, elderly men wearing medals, some with berets, and a halted procession of uniformed soldiers and cadets with lowered flags. A sombre crowd of onlookers line the broad thoroughfare of St Giles, closed to traffic for the occasion. Remembrance Sunday is a serious affair in the ancient university city of Oxford, as it is in the countless other towns and villages in Britain where similar ceremonies take place. Like its many counterparts the monument which forms the focus of the ceremony is immaculately kept, surrounded by closely mown grass and well-trimmed hedges with wreaths laid at its base. The stone is unblemished and the text as clear as the day it was dedicated over one hundred years ago. It is a fitting tribute to those who died in the 1914-18 and subsequent World War, and the care and reverence which the monument attracts is testament to the hold on the collective memory that those wars still have.

However, it is not the only, nor the first public war memorial in the city. Closer to the centre and less than a mile away stands another. It was unveiled just 21 years before its neighbour and commemorates the men of the Oxfordshire Light Infantry who died in the service of their country in 1897-98, only 16 years before the outbreak of the First World War. It occupies an altogether different place in the city's memory and affections. There are no services of remembrance held at this monument, no laying of wreaths, no prayers for those who died for queen and country. The stone is worn, the writing only partly legible, and sitting at its base instead of wreaths are people eating fast food, drinking cups of coffee or from cans, smoking and watching the world go by. It's a major magnet for pigeons which use it as a convenient perch with all the usual consequences. Although it forms the centrepiece of the square in which it sits, and is nearly 27 feet tall, it is an overlooked feature, the main focus being the imposing new shopping centre which forms one side of this civic space. It is an ignored and unloved monument which provides a convenient seat for passing shoppers and other characters drawn to city centres. There are few who know what or who it commemorates, and even less who care. It has become not so much a monument to remembering as a monument to forgetting.

Things were decidedly different on the day of its unveiling at the dawn of the new century in July 1900. A large crowd had gathered to watch the band of the garrison and 50 men march to the site to form a guard of honour. The rector of the parish was there in his surplice, and the mayor and aldermen processed in full dress-robes and regalia from the splendid new town hall completed just three years previously. In his speech the mayor pointed out that this was the first time a military monument had been erected in the city, and said that he and the corporation were proud that the land for it, 'one of the finest sites in Oxford', had been donated by the city council to commemorate their compatriots who had fought in the Tirah region of north west India. He eulogised the sixty-two men whose names were inscribed on the stone who "had not feared to face death itself in honour of, and to the glory of their God, their Queen and their country"; at these words the crowd broke into spontaneous applause and continued to clap long after the memorial was unveiled by Miss Morrell, the mayor's daughter.

The rector then addressed the crowd, praising the devotion, courage and self-sacrifice of the Englishmen recorded there. He thought that the monument in such a prominent place in the city 'would help to remind all passers-by at what great cost the Empire that they boasted and were proud of had been won and was being held.' He had no doubt it 'would speak of duty, and honour and patriotism to all who pass by'. In particular he hoped that it would be noticed by boys on their way to school that 'the great roll-call of British heroes was not yet completed, and that their names might yet be entered on it ...'. Little did he know that by the time they reached manhood the schoolboys he had in mind would be pitched into the trenches of the First World War and all too many names added to the roll. Proceedings were brought to a close by the firing of a salute and the singing of the national anthem, and were only slightly marred by a private in the front-rank fainting and falling to the ground.[1]

There was no doubt in anyone's mind on that day that it was fitting and right to remember the men who had died while serving as part of the British imperial force in the Tirah campaign on the northwest frontier of India. Nor could there have been any doubt in their minds that the Empire which they celebrated would continue long into the future and would continue to need defending.

Figure 1. The Tirah Memorial 1900.

There is one man whose name indirectly connects both monuments and the three wars which they mark. He was born in Oxfordshire and as a young man pulled strings to get himself attached as a journalist with the Tirah expeditionary force. He was a man in a hurry who was desperate for recognition and on occasion given to foolhardy acts of staged bravery in order to get it, as he confided to his mother and as his peers sometimes noted.[2] He was eager to be awarded a medal, and when none was forthcoming wrote to a senior officer pleading for what he termed his entitlement 'to a medal and 2 clasps for my gallantry, for the hardships and dangers I have encountered. I am possessed of a keen desire to mount the ribbon on my breast'.[3] His request was granted, and he wore it along with his other subsequent decorations to the end of his life. His career had advanced considerably by the time of the 1914-18 war when he was appointed first lord of the admiralty, and it had progressed even further in in the Second World War when he held the post of prime minister.

Winston Churchill would surely have been surprised and perhaps appalled by the different treatment and hold in the public memory accorded to the two monuments described above. Not only had he participated in the Tirah Campaign, he was a passionate imperialist with a deeply rooted belief in the British Empire to which he retained an unwavering commitment. In 1897, at the time that the news reached England of the uprising in Tirah he was giving a speech in Bath in which he extolled the virtues of the Empire, derided 'croakers' who disparaged or doubted its benefit, and argued strongly for its continued expansion so that Britain might continue the "course marked out for us by an all-wise hand and carry out our mission of bearing peace, civilisation and good government to the uttermost ends of the earth".[4] As prime minister, when facing calls for Indian independence, he declared, "I have not become the King's first minister to preside over the liquidation of the British Empire". In perhaps his most iconic speech delivered during the Battle of Britain he concluded emphatically, referring to the Empire and not to Britain alone: "If the British Empire and its Commonwealth should last for a thousand years, men will still say, 'this was their finest hour'". Similarly in his famous and rousing speech declaring "we shall fight on the beaches.... we shall never surrender", he concluded with the line, if "this Island or a large part of it were subjugated and starving, …then our Empire beyond the seas…would carry on the struggle". As historian David Edgerton has argued, Churchill's conception of "we" encompassed the Empire and was not confined to just his island compatriots.[5] He regarded the two World Wars in which he played such a conspicuous part as being waged by and for the British Empire, rather than by and for Britain itself.

Although the scale of the war in Tirah in 1897 was clearly vastly smaller than that of the two World Wars, all three wars were nevertheless imperial wars in which Britain fought alongside its colonial troops to defend its imperial territories. There is a seamless transition from the Indian troops fighting alongside their British counterparts in the Tirah campaign in the mountains of Afghanistan in 1897, to the Indian troops who did the same in Egypt and East Africa in the First World War, and in north Africa and Malaya in the Second World War. In what still remains the largest defeat in British military history, the 62,000 British troops who surrendered to the Japanese at Singapore in 1942 were not defending the shores of the British Isles, but the British Empire and British economic interests in the east. The majority of those surrendering were not even British: more than half were Indian and a quarter were Australian.[6] The contribution of the Empire territories in the two global wars was enormous and crucial to Britain's ability to remain engaged in the battle against Germany and Japan until the entry of the U.S.A. and USSR as allies. The scale of colonial troops and support in the two world wars remains under-appreciated by many. By 1945 two and a quarter million Indians and an estimated half a million Africans were serving in the armed forces.[7] They were widely deployed throughout the Empire, for instance 12,500 African troops fought in Burma. Nor were their losses insignificant: it is thought around 15,000 British African troops were killed in combat. In addition, an estimated 15,000 colonial subjects were working in the merchant marine, and countless numbers were working to produce the raw materials needed to wage war and to supply Britain itself.[8]

There is a therefore a continuum or parallels between the imperial wars which Britain fought in the nineteenth century and the larger scale conflicts it fought in the twentieth century. There are striking similarities in the territories in which it fought, in the troops with which it fought, in the method of financing the wars, and also it can be argued in the reasons for pursuing warfare. Britain was after all an imperial power reigned over by the emperor of India throughout the period.

But this continuum is not reflected in the collective memory of these wars, nor in the attitude to the respective monuments which commemorate their dead. The Tirah Monument is far from alone. There are thousands of memorials, statues, inscriptions and other reminders of Britain's imperial past in our towns and cities. Very occasionally they attract attention and approbation, such as the statue of Cecil Rhodes in Oxford which campaigners have sought to remove, or that of Colston in Bristol which ended up in the city harbour. But usually, like the Tirah Memorial they stand ignored and lost in the fabric of our streets. Like the Tirah Memorial, they no longer strike a chord in the collective memory.

*

There are things that we remember and things that we forget. We cannot remember all that has passed, and by remembering some things we are forgetting others. Remembering and forgetting are two sides of the same coin. History is about remembering the past, about retrieving and preserving things from the record of past events, but it is also about forgetting. It is about leaving some things out from the record.

In previous times history was largely written by educated men of the higher social classes, often with a military or clerical background. Their focus fell on men like themselves and on the topics that were of interest to them such as battles or internecine quarrels. Historical omissions included the history of great swathes of humanity such as women, or indigenous peoples, or the experiences of children; and enormous cultural spaces were passed over or ignored such as popular pastimes or entertainments, rather than those of the elite in society. What we choose to remember tells us not only about the past then, but also about ourselves in the present; what our concerns are, what we care about, how we like to picture ourselves in the scope of time. History is not only a window into the past but also a mirror which reflects back at us. The tales we tell about the past are selective; they include some things and omit others; we make a choice about what to include and what to exclude. This is as true for us on an individual level as it is for communities or society as a whole. There are things we are proud of in our pasts, and things we regret, or are ashamed of which we prefer to pass over and leave unsaid:

the elision in a CV, the unmentioned ex-partner, the time we made a fool of ourselves or let somebody down. No nation or community likes to be reminded of or to remember the more uncomfortable aspects of its past. Virtually all nations present a glorious history to their members and project this to the wider world. It is fundamental to group cohesion that we tell a good story about ourselves.

Public memorials are part of a process of remembering, of commemorating, of affirming and projecting a version of ourselves. They signal what we care about. The erecting of monuments in stone and bronze also implicitly aims to give permanence to that which is being commemorated. These are not intended as temporary structures or temporary repositories of memory, but represent an attempt to preserve in the collective memory events of significance to those who commissioned them. The etching of names on stone is one the most basic and universal ways of trying to preserve the memory of lives lived, of people lost. Any graveyard or monument in any country in the world will tell as much.

This book seeks to find the reason why one particular monument to soldiers who died in the service of their country in 1897 has fallen into physical neglect, when its counterpart to those who died in 1914-18 continues to be publicly reverenced. In doing so it explores the context and the wider issues connected with the military campaigns in 1897 which helps to explain the contradiction. The Tirah Memorial tells us about our nation's past, about the men who died and the campaign they served in, and about the pride the city felt in their endeavours. But the monument's now degraded state and the public indifference shown towards it also tells us about how we now view that past. It speaks of us as well as speaking of them. It is time to recover the memory of what has been forgotten.

THE TIRAH MEMORIAL – INSCRIPTION

THIS MONUMENT WAS ERECTED
BY THE OFFICERS NON-COM-
MISSIONED OFFICERS & MEN
OF THE SECOND BATTALION
OXFORDSHIRE LIGHT INFANTRY
IN MEMORY OF THEIR COM-
RADES WHO DIED BETWEEN
THE 15TH OF AUGUST 1897 AND
THE 4TH OF NOVEMBER 1898

KILLED BY MUTINEERS IN UGANDA
Brevet-Major A. B. THRUSTON

DIED OF DISEASE ON ACTIVE SERVICE
LIEUT. J. L. POWYS
LIEUT. D. R. NAPIER
LIEUT. H.W.B. TRENCH
2ND LIEUT. J. G. FITZGERALD

DIED OF WOUNDS
SERGEANT-MAJOR H. DEMPSEY
KILLED IN ACTION
SERGEANT J. S. HOPKINS
LANCE CORPORAL W. BELL
PRIVATE W. BUTLER

DIED OF DISEASE
LANCE-CORPORAL W. MARTIN

BUGLERS
A. J. BETTS
T. BULL
C. COX

PRIVATES
W. ADAWAY
J. H. BEER
A. E. BISSONI
G. BOND
G. BAYNES
A. CROSS
H. E. COOK
F. CALLIS
G. COMLEY
W. DORMER
W. J. DEATH
C. DIX
G. DAY
F. EVERETT
E. FERRIS
W. FORTNAM
H. GARDNER
W.J GODLIMAN
S. GREEN
G. HICKS
J. HOARE
J. HULL
G. HUGHES
F. S. KNIBBS

Figure 2: The Tirah Memorial in 2024

PART I

The North-West Frontier

1: THE NORTH WEST FRONTIER

It was the last thing he wanted to do. And at such short notice! The valuable pictures and books to be packed away; trying to get the servants to understand how to protect his clothes against the ravages of white ants in his absence; his campaign tent and bed to be retrieved, and the impossibility of deciding what to take and what to leave out when only 80lb allowance had been made for his luggage. If that were not enough to deal with, it was August, the hottest time of the year, when he would much rather be relaxing in his long chair on the verandah, drinking tea and reading a book - as indeed he was when the telegram arrived which turned everything upside down - and to top it all his groom refused to accompany him and absconded at the last moment!

It wasn't the lead-in to retirement that Lieutenant-Colonel Richard Thomsett had in mind and was rather enjoying at his bungalow in Bareilly in north west India. He looked back longingly at the lost and better days of his youth in the British Raj when,

> *'Polly Travers would give us a rattling good Irish ditty...when poor Griffen of the 9th often led the way at paper chases; when Colonel Hudson brought down the house with 'Nanny Lee', and Colonel Carter charmed everyone with his fine baritone voice and rendering of 'Rose Marie'; when Kingcrat and Mozelle displayed their prowess on the turf, when Hutchins of the 4th Huzzars won the*

> *Kadir Cup, and Marmaduke Tippets had not yet been forgotten, and Thomas of the 9th showed them the way to do the new waltz, although he swore he did not know "God Save the Queen' from any other tune, except the hats came off!"*[1]

More recent changes had not been to his liking. There was too much tennis, too many afternoon tea parties where people smoked cigarettes and one had to be polite in front of the ladies; and come to that, too many young ladies - and all seemingly bad at playing the violin! He missed the conviviality of the old mess life. Above all though, he believed that things had not been so good since the Indian Mutiny. Rather than benefiting from the superior education and civilisation of the British, the native Indians seemed to have become resentful and thought that they too were entitled to the same. It was not uncommon for Indians to 'forget' to salaam or bow to their master, he had noticed, and senior Indian civil servants now kept their umbrellas up when passing Englishmen and no longer dismounted as a mark of respect when out riding.

Although the fools at HQ had given him only a matter of days to report, it was nevertheless flattering to find himself appointed principal medical officer of a column on the expeditionary force forming at Rawal Pindi. And what a force it was! Rumours had been circulating for weeks about yet another frontier expedition, but this was far more than just a few battalions and battery or two of mountain artillery as had happened dozens of times before. Something big was clearly brewing but as to what it was, he was in the dark. More immediate matters had to be dealt with and his long experience told him to ignore the baggage allowance and prepare for the cold and wet conditions which no doubt lay ahead. Two pairs of boots, two pairs of puttees, two waterproof sheets (one for his horse), three flannel shirts, three pairs of warm socks and a pair of gloves; a serge coat, a greatcoat, and a waterproof coat; a pair of flannel trousers and slippers for the evening, and of course riding breeches for daytime; an enamel canteen, spare horseshoes and nails, and a few of Lazenby's compressed soup tablets were the bare essentials. A couple of bottles of brandy, a dozen tins of Bovril and a dozen of condensed milk, and two pounds of arrowroot for filtering water would be a useful addition to supplement the daily rations. There certainly wasn't need to take whisky and soda, nor the numerous tinned provisions and even Marie biscuits which junior officers now deemed indispensable to campaigning! It was of course also necessary to kit out his servant, but a sheepskin coat, a pair of warm pyjamas, puttees, a blanket and thin boots would be more than sufficient and even appreciated.

Thomsett's poor opinion of HQ was confirmed when he reported for duty after a trying week of delayed trains and bad weather, only to be informed that the unit to which he had been summoned did not exist, and never had done. Moreover, no one knew the whereabouts of the general to whom he was to report. Eventually reunited with his luggage and horse, he spent time acquiring yet more kit including a tent for his office, the necessary furniture for it and stationery, but although he was moved up to Peshawar in late August it was to be many, many frustrating weeks before he was to meet with his general and acquire troops and a unit. Despite the urgency with which he had been summoned, the organisation and mustering of the troops continued to be chaotic, and it was not to be until October, worrying late in the season, that the assembled column finally marched from Peshawar towards the mountains of Afghanistan.[2]

*

Lt. Col. Thomsett was one of a number of military men who published accounts of their experience after the campaign in the Tirah in 1897-8. The Tirah region which straddles modern-day Pakistan and Afghanistan comprises five valleys around the source of the river Bara. Readers may be familiar with the names of these from more recent wars in the region including Maidan and Bara. The Tirah expedition was a mobilisation designed to quash a rebellion by Pashtun peoples and assert British authority and pre-eminence in the region. This was but the latest in a long line of expeditions and wars which the British had fought there.

The Peshawar column of which Thomsett was chief surgeon was one of three which comprised the Tirah expedition and was the one to which all but one of the men recorded on Oxford's memorial were attached. The second battalion of the Oxfordshire Light Infantry made a strong impression on Thomsett. As they marched in the advanced guard, he noted that they had 'a fine swing' and 'looked very fit as they trudged along solemnly and quietly'.[3] The Peshawar column was the reserve unit and was named after the city where it was to be based until called forward as needed. The two other columns were the main offensive force. The multi-national and multi-ethnic composition of the column is apparent from the list of divisional troops marching with the Oxfordshire regiment: the 2nd Royal Inniskillin Fusiliers, 9th Gurkha Rifles, 45th Sikhs, 9th Bengal Lancers, No 5 Co Bengal Sappers and Miners, 2nd King's Own Yorkshire Light Infantry, 1st Duke of Cornwall's Light Infantry, 27th Bombay Light Infantry, 2nd Hyderabad Infantry, Jodhpur Imperial Service Lancers, Kurram Moveable Column, Bengal Infantry, Nabha Imperial Service Infantry, 6th Bengal Cavalry and Central India Horse, and the Rawalpindi

Reserve Brigade.[4] The total roll-call of the column amounted to nearly 100 British officers, 1,800 European troops and just short of 2,900 Indian ranks, but there was nearly an equal number of non-uniformed support staff and followers, as well as 4,000 animals.[5] It was no small undertaking.

But this was just the reserve column, the others were even larger. In total over 1,000 British officers, over 10,000 British troops, nearly 500 Indian officers and 22,000 Indian troops, along with several hundred clerks and hospital orderlies, and an estimated 20,000 non-uniformed followers mustered on the dusty plains preparing for the assault.[6] This was, and was designed to be, an overwhelming force, a nineteenth century equivalent of the 'shock and awe' strategy subsequently employed by the U.S.A. in Iraq. Through a combination of modern technology and sheer size it was expected that it would swiftly intimidate and overcome its opponents.

The terrain into which the army was heading was extremely challenging. It lacked railways and roads, and much of it was literally uncharted territory, the topography of which the British had no knowledge. Despite having modern technology in the form of the latest rifles and artillery – the latter of which the enemy lacked - the transport of so large a number of men and their provisions in such mountainous and undeveloped territory presented a major logistical challenge, and the method used would have been familiar to armies operating centuries, even millennia previously. Eighteen thousand mules and ponies and 9,400 horses were just the initial complement of transport animals. Later 13,000 camels and an unknown but enormous number of additional ponies, donkeys, and bullocks were employed as the supply lines lengthened.[7] To this must be added animals for consumption so that the total amount of animals far outnumbered people.

The British forces in India did not have anything like this number of animals to draw on, and consequently forcibly commandeered them from the local populations. As many as 103,000 animals were impressed but of these only 70,000 were found to be fit for service.[8] This was partly because people understandably preferred to surrender their weaker, older and more sickly animals, but also because the sheer scale of the roundup proved impossible to manage. Animals were left for days in railway carriages without food or water; there was insufficient fodder when they arrived at camp; an outbreak of foot and mouth disease was initially left uncontained; insufficient mule drivers were assigned, leading to them being unable to cope with the number under their charge; animals were not branded and so it was not possible to identify to which unit they belonged and consequently many straying animals were left without food and care. The neglect continued as the force advanced with reports of many animals lying dead or dying for want of food or blankets at night. When the force finally reached its destination, it had to abandon camp and move due to the high number of dead animals which were contaminating the site.[9] This ineptitude was widely reported and criticised at the time and was symptomatic of the chaotic organisation which characterised the start of the offensive.

It was not only animals that were falling sick. Both the climate and the conditions in camp were beginning to have an effect on the men. This particularly affected British troops who were more susceptible to falling ill. From the Peshawar column alone, one British officer, 122 European ranks and 23 Indian ranks were too ill to proceed further than Peshawar before the campaign even began.[10] An Oxfordshire sergeant writing home mentioned that a quarter of the 800 or so men he was with had been hospitalised suffering from 'ague and fever'. This probably refers to malaria and was of sufficient concern to Thomsett to order the issuing of daily doses of quinine as a prophylactic measure.[11]

It was not clear to the men trapped in the endless wait at Peshawar what the reasons were for the delay. Some recorded their frustration but stoically accepted that high command must have a reason of which they were unaware; one rumour was that they were waiting for colder weather. One officer speculated on an intriguing reason for the delay which was that the government was trying to broker a peace deal to pre-empt the military campaign. The rumour centred around the person of Colonel Robert Warburton who had recently retired but was still in India awaiting his departure home to Britain. Warburton had been a political officer in the Khyber region for 18 years and was widely respected by the indigenous peoples. Warburton was uniquely placed to reach terms as he was mixed race: his mother was a member of the Afridi clan, a niece of the emir of Afghanistan who had met his British father when the latter was in charge of the emir's artillery. They were married in 1840 and Warburton junior recognised that such a union would be impossible in the late nineteenth century when racial attitudes towards mixed marriages had hardened; he described their marriage certificate as 'a curious old document'.[12] Following the death of his father Warburton was assiduous in striving to support his mother who found herself penniless when the legacy that her husband left to her was swallowed up in a bank crash. He was fluent in the local languages which he had learned as a child, and although a British military officer was able to travel with just a walking stick for protection and was warmly received wherever he went. It seems likely that Warburton accepted the offer to return to negotiate, but before he could do so it was announced in the British press that he was not returning and military hostilities commenced.[13] It appears that those who favoured an emphatic and forceful military response to the rebellion had outmanoeuvred those who preferred a more stealthy and traditional settlement.

Figure 3. Colonel Robert Warburton

*

On the face of it there seemed little reason for imperial Britain to care about Afghanistan. Unlike many of its other territories it was not a rich country, it was not blessed with abundant raw materials that could be shipped for processing back to Britain; it did not offer fertile new lands to colonise with emigrant farmers; nor was there great British domestic pressure to convert the population to Christianity as there was in Africa. It could never conceivably be a cash cow which would enrich the conqueror. Moreover, it was, as it remains, a notoriously difficult mountainous terrain, inhabited by an infamously belligerent and divided population. In short, it offered much trouble and little gain.

How very different from India which lay to its south and east. Here any trouble was more than outweighed by potential and actual gain. To understand why the men whose names are on the Tirah Memorial were in Afghanistan at all, why India was so important to the British, and why they felt insecure in their position there in the late nineteenth century, we first need to consider Britain's history in the subcontinent.

*

British merchants had been present in India since around 1600 when Queen Elizabeth I sold the rights to trade there to a group of 200 men, but the British state itself did not become involved in the governance of the country until 1784. Prior to this it outsourced governance of the region to a private company to which it also granted a monopoly so leaving it with no competitors. From small beginnings as a trading company, the East India Company grew to become in effect a state in its own right. It appointed its own governor general, levied and collected taxes from the indigenous population, employed its own army and civil administrators, imposed its own legal and judicial system, minted its own money, and of course had its own flag to fly over the territories it controlled.* And all under the oversight of a board of twenty-four directors answerable to their shareholders alone.

Unsurprisingly, this was a massively profitable enterprise for the company whose members grew exceedingly rich, and in some cases staggeringly so. The company operated in effect as a giant extortion racket, constantly increasing the level of taxes, and inflicting violence and torture on those unable to pay. By the late eighteenth century as many as two thirds of those ruled by the British had fled their lands, unable to pay the taxes required of them and fearful of the consequences that would follow.[14] None of these taxes were invested in India itself but were used to pay the company's costs and dividends to its members. Fabulous bribes were accepted by company officials from Indian princes to leave them alone, but these were often pocketed and ignored as the company's army conquered more and more territory to further enrich its shareholders.

British contemporaries recognised the rapacious and venal extent to which members of the company were stripping India of its wealth, and outrage reached a sufficient pitch for one governor, Hastings, to be impeached by parliament for corruption on a grand scale and abuse of his powers. The newly enriched were also lampooned in the press, and satirised in literature such as Thackeray's 'Vanity Fair', and the nickname of 'nabobs' stuck to them.

Robert Clive, otherwise known as Clive of India, serves as an example. Although beginning as a clerk in the East India Company he transferred to its army and eventually led the military campaign against India's richest state of Bengal and

---

* A background of red and white stripes, with the union flag positioned upper left.

its French East Indian Company allies. Victory at the battle of Plessey in 1757 catapulted him to stupendous wealth as he plundered the newly conquered territory and returned to England with a fortune. 'Loot' and 'looting' entered the English language from Hindustani as a result of his endeavours. Not content with returning to England as one of Europe's richest men, he went back to India and in the space of two years managed to garner another sum estimated at twice the value of the first.[15] His statue can still be found standing between the Foreign Office and Treasury in Whitehall.

Initially then, India was the means by which a relatively small group of well-connected British men became very, very rich, and in which the living standards of Indians declined precipitously, while the freedom of their Indian rulers was curtailed. As time progressed however the stranglehold of Britain increased and British industrialists were able to use their wealth and influence to introduce legislation in Britain to their advantage. Ultimately whole sectors of Indian industry were destroyed and production shifted to Britain with the consequent financial benefit affecting a much wider spectrum of the British Isles' population.

For instance, before the arrival of the British, India led the world in the production of cotton cloth not only in terms of quantity but also in quality. Indian muslins, a light and decorative cloth, were highly sought after for fashionable purposes, whilst calicoes were in demand because they were cheaper than alternative manufactures. Bengali weavers traded their products to all of Europe, to Egypt, Iran, China and Japan, and so successful were they that India's share of the textile trade has been estimated at a quarter of the global total in the early eighteenth century.[16] The East India Company established itself as a monopoly buyer of key segments of this manufacture and cut off direct access to overseas markets for Indian manufacturers, and so was able to force down the price paid for cloth, while maintaining or increasing the sale price and profits. This was done both by the creation of laws such as that which made it a felony for weavers to sell their cloth on the open market, and through the use of violence including whipping.[17]

As the industrial revolution began its early stages in Britain, British manufacturers found they were unable to compete both on price and quality with Indian manufacture, and so sought and gained protectionist measures. British tariffs were raised on Indian produced cloth on twelve occasions at the turn of the eighteenth century reaching up to 80% of the import value, while tariffs in India were dismantled, so forcing open the huge subcontinental market to British produced goods. The Indian textile business was squeezed nearly out of existence. Within the space of a few decades India became an importer of cloth and an exporter of raw cotton for use in British factories. Having eliminated the competition, British exports of cloth boomed as it supplied the huge market of its global Empire. No single market was as important to Britain as India. By the turn of the twentieth century India accounted for a remarkable third of all its exports. It had become a hugely valuable market for British industry.[18]

A similar tale could be told for other industries such as ship-building, shipping, salt, and steel production. The salt industry, which once employed 150,000 people, had all but ceased by 1860 due to a deliberate policy of levying higher taxes on Indian production to favour British imports. Without a level playing field, and lacking investment, India was unable to compete, and fell from being an exporter of higher added-value manufactured goods to an importer of manufactures and exporter of raw materials. From having an estimated 25% share of global GDP in 1750 (about the same as the U.S.A. today) it had fallen to less than 2% in 1900.[19] The mills and factories of Britain were kept busy at the expense of Indians who lost their livelihoods, and in many cases their lives as a result.

*

The British came to call the rebellion that broke out against company rule in 1857 'The Indian Mutiny', as if it just was a case of troops who refused to obey orders. In popular retelling this was due to an unintentional mix-up with the ingredients in the cartridges they were required to bite into before deploying - which contained animal fats barred by their religions. Resentment ran much wider and deeper than this however, and civil revolt spread rapidly across the whole country. The East India Company's rule was seriously threatened and British authority was only restored with great difficulty after atrocities were committed on all sides. The revolt shook British power to the core and sweeping reforms followed. The principal of these was the ousting of the British East India Company as governors of India, and the British state's direct annexation of its territory. Queen Victoria became queen, and eventually empress of India. Even she recognised that this was more than a mutiny, referring to it as a 'bloody civil war', and in time it would come to be called the Great Rebellion or the First War of Independence.

The immiseration of India continued under this new management as the newly formed Indian government moved in lock step with the commercial interests of Britain. Nowhere was this more apparent than in the production and trading of opium. The commercial cultivation of poppies and the manufacture and sale of opium was an extraordinarily profitable and important industry which was developed and promoted by Britain throughout the nineteenth and into the early twentieth century. It was a trade moreover that was under the direct control of the Indian government and revenue service, which established a monopoly, and through a mixture of incentives, coercion and corruption forced peasant farmers to switch from growing foodstuffs to cultivating opium. The land given over to it in the state of Bengal alone grew from 90,000 acres in 1830 to 176,000 ten years later, and then to over half a million acres by the end of the century.[20] In mid-century there were one and a quarter million people engaged in its cultivation, farming an area larger than Italy.[21]

The main market for this drug was neither India nor Britain, but an unwilling China. The consumption of opium was illegal in China and the authorities there struggled in vain to control the contraband trade sponsored by the British. The governor of Canton went so far as to write a personal appeal to Queen Victoria to cease the trade in which he railed against 'people who only care to profit themselves, and disregard their harm to others'.[22] Finally, Governor Lin and the Chinese government became so exasperated that they seized and publicly destroyed a large quantity of British traders' opium. The British government reacted with fury, demanding reparations and the right to trade opium, and waged a three-year war with China to this end, despite having secured a payment of six million pounds as reparation. In 1856 Britain doubled down, and along with French forces launched a second war which was to last for four years until China was finally forced to agree to open its markets to European trade and allow the free passage of opium. It was during this war that the 1,000 year-old imperial summer palace outside Beijing was looted and torched, and its pillaged contents transferred to European homes and institutions.

The harm that this trade was inflicting on the Chinese population did not go unnoticed. By 1900 it has been estimated that there were up to forty million opium addicts in China, one-in-ten of the population.[23] The Chinese opposition has already been described, but in Britain itself there was a huge popular backlash spearheaded by missionaries, and in India the enforced use of land for poppy cultivation and the tight control on prices were one of the underlying causes of the Great Rebellion of 1857. The British and British-Indian governments nevertheless continued to operate as a narco-state into the twentieth century.

To understand why the British were so determined to go to war over the trade, one only has to consider the revenues that it produced. The British government in India gained directly from the traffic through taxes on opium which accounted for as much as a quarter of all its tax revenue (a similar proportion to income tax in the UK today) and was the second largest source of revenue after land tax. A royal commission in 1898 concluded that the government of India would be unviable without this revenue stream, which had grown from near zero at the beginning of the 1800s to one hundred million rupees by the end of the century.[24]

It was not only the government that benefited, but also the merchants engaged in the trade who earned enormous profits. The money from opium trading, for example, allowed the East India Company to cover all of the interest costs on the considerable debts which it had incurred to expand in the subcontinent. Companies such as Jardine Mathieson, and Swire and Co exported opium from India to China, and then used the funds generated to buy tea for shipping back to Britain.

The Cutty Sark, now moored in Greenwich, was one of many such ships engaged in this trade, the underlying finance of which was from the sale of narcotics. It is not an exaggeration that without trafficking opium, Britons would not have been consuming tea from China, as China was largely self-sufficient and had little need for imports or trade with the outside 'barbarian' world. One historian has assessed the importance of opium to be so great that it formed the 'keystone' of the British Indian Empire through generating public revenue for the government and generating funds for capital investment by the private sector.[25]

The British design of fostering, or even forcing opium addiction among the Chinese population was not the only reason for the relative decline of China during this period. Nor, it has been argued, was the presence of the British in India the only cause of the economic turmoil and relative decline which it experienced. It is of course true that investment poured back into India from Britain, a very great deal of it. In 1885 India accounted for a fifth of all Britain's overseas foreign investment.[26] Investments in irrigation, communications and above all railways had a dramatic effect on trade, the economy and society. There was a rush to invest in this booming market, as well there might be when the returns were guaranteed by the British government and paid for by Indian tax payers. Gauging that investors would consider the initial returns too low and the risks too high, the government guaranteed returns of at least five percent to investors in railway bonds. Later the Indian government itself began to fund railway construction, not least to enable the speedy transfer of troops through the territory.[27] This construction was financed through loans from the British government repayable with interest funded from the Indian taxpayer. The development of railways was not an act of benevolence, but based on a hard calculus of profit and loss to enable the cheaper and quicker shipping of raw materials for export, and imported goods to market.

History is messy. Monocausal explanations, whilst appealing, are rarely if ever sufficient to explain what happened in the past. The extent to which Britain's colonial engagement benefited India is a topic of ongoing debate amongst historians. There are some who argue that it stopped India's development dead, while others argue that the long-term benefits were significant. What none dispute however is that in the short term the economic shock resulted in a severe dislocation of the existing economy and social relations - if we can talk of decades as being short term. Similarly, there is debate over the extent to which British rule in India affected the course of the nation's industrial decline: whether it was the decisive factor in the decay of the textile and shipping industries, or whether it was just one factor amongst many - albeit an important one. What none doubt however is that the British became richer as a result of their conquest and domination of India. By the end of the nineteenth century it was clearly vital for British interests to protect the investments it had made, and the large export market which it had forced open and upon which so much of its domestic industry and employment depended.

However, the importance of India for the British went beyond financial considerations. There was another respect in which India and its peoples were undoubtedly the lynchpin of Empire. The East India Company had recruited Indians into its military forces from its inception. Known variously as native troops or sepoys, they always formed the majority of troops in the British Indian army which had grown to 250,00 men by the mid-nineteenth century, and 325,000 by the end of the century.[28]

After the 1857 Great Rebellion there were major reforms to the army, and in particular a stress on recruiting more Europeans, as well as Sikhs and Gurkhas as these were groups which had not joined in the Rebellion. This strategy also fitted with a widely accepted racially based theory that men from mountainous and highland areas had a more martial spirit than those from lowland areas who were considered to be more effete and physically weaker. Although admiring the manliness and courage of the indigenous highlanders, the British also believed that such men were incapable of fighting successfully unless they were led by British officers who were their racial superiors with a greater mental capacity.[29] Indeed, one British officer considered that they were brave precisely because they lacked intelligence.[30]

Illiterate, poor, rural recruits were the preferred soldier, and men from urban areas were avoided. This is significant as after the Rebellion garrisons were established outside all major towns as part of a policy of military control of the civil population. A commission in 1879 explicitly recognised that the viability of the British government in India depended on military force, and that an early and strong response to disorder was necessary to cow the population.[31] The army came to absorb an extraordinary half of all Indian government revenue, and fully one third of it was deployed on internal security work.[32] It was not an army that was principally raised to defend external borders, but to defend the domestic security of the colonial regime. By any measure India was a despotic military state under British rule.

The importance of the Indian army to Britain was greater than just retaining its control of India however. It was also an army which was widely deployed outside the sub-continent and formed a mainstay of British imperial campaigns across the globe up to and including the Second World War. During the nineteenth century troops from the army fought in China, Ethiopia, Malaya, Malta, Egypt, the Sudan, Burma, Tibet and also East Africa as outlined in the second part of this book. All of its soldiers, including those posted from Britain to India, were paid for by the Indian government, and so from taxes on Indian peasants as well as opium trade revenues. Without the Indian army there would have been no British Empire.

By the late nineteenth century British India encompassed an area much larger than today's India and incorporated what are now the independent states of Bangladesh, Pakistan, Myanmar and Sri Lanka. It had a population of 300 million people accounting for three quarters of the total population of the British Empire. It was Britain's single biggest imperial export market, and single biggest location for overseas investment. The wealth which it generated, and the soldiers for which it paid enabled Britain to maintain a global military presence and protect its trade networks. Not for nothing was India known as the jewel in the crown of the British Empire. It was imperative that nothing should be allowed to threaten it.

2: A GOOD THRASHING

As the troops languished in the heat and chaos of base camps at Peshawar waiting to commence their campaign, General Sir William Lockhart, knight commander of the Order of the Bath, knight commander of the Star of India, was enjoying a period of well-earned leave in the pleasant climate of a European summer. Born in Renfrewshire, Scotland he followed both his elder brothers into the Indian army joining the Bengal Infantry when he reached the age of 17. One of his early engagements was during the Great Rebellion and he had seen repeated further active service in Burma, Bhutan, Abyssinia, Indonesia and crucially in the Hindu Kush where he had commanded a survey expedition. He was subsequently charged with undertaking several punitive expeditions on India's north west border. He had progressed to become every inch the senior Indian army officer with an impressive array of medals, and an equally impressive and expansive moustache. He was the obvious choice to command the campaign to Tirah and received a telegram summoning him back from leave in early September, finally arriving at the forward headquarters on 4th October 1897. Lockhart however was not a well man. He had been invalided to England nine years previously, but had returned to India before his recovery was complete. Repeated bouts of malaria left him physically exhausted and would tax his strength during the coming campaign.

Lockhart was certainly an optimist. He envisaged a ten-day campaign and had booked his return trip to Europe for mid-November confident that matters would be resolved well ahead of his planned departure.[1] The objective of the campaign he outlined as being to exact reparations for the damage to life and property of the British caused by unprovoked aggression.[2]

Figure 4. Sir William Lockhart

This was by no means a new or unusual objective of the British in India and was put more bluntly by a fellow officer in his account.

> *The history of the British Empire has repeatedly shown that (savage neighbours) sooner or later become unendurable and undergo a gradual process of loss of independence and absorption into the control of civilisation. In the case of tribes... fiercely jealous of any threat against freedom, which chiefly means the liberty to carry on internecine feuds with one another and generally to make life a burden to themselves and their neighbours, this extension of the blessing of civilisation must of necessity be attended with much bloodshed and suffering.*

Or in simpler terms, they 'require a thrashing to keep them in order'.[3] This was not the first time Britain had endeavoured to give a thrashing to the troublesome inhabitants of the region. Nor would it be the last.

*

The British had first become involved in Afghanistan in the 1830s when a local ruler named Dost Khan sought their alliance in a dispute with his brother. The lukewarm British response led him instead to turn for help to Russia which triggered a panicked response by the British who launched a full-blown invasion of Afghanistan with 20,000 troops. They first captured Kandahar, and then Kabul in 1839 deposing Dost Khan in the process. However, the British triumph was short lived and they were forced to abandon the capital and garrison in 1842 in an infamous retreat from which just one European successfully reached safety. Others were taken captive and ransomed, and many Indians were killed or sold into slavery by their captors.

A further British assault retook Kabul, but this time Dost

Khan was recognised as the legitimate ruler. After much difficulty and at great cost the British had what they wanted, which was not direct annexation or control of the country, but to establish a compliant regime under a sympathetic ruler which would act a buffer state between India and Russia. All was relatively settled until the death of Dost Khan in 1863 when a civil war broke out amongst his sons which was to last for six years during which all parties were trying to manoeuvre for support amongst either the British or Russians - or both.

Britain's policy in Afghanistan was driven by three factors: firstly, the perceived need to guard against external threats to India from Russia and its allies; secondly, by the need to maintain internal security in India through preventing incursions across the border by armed gangs; and thirdly to prevent political or Islamic religious unrest from spreading into the subcontinent from the frontier areas. These three aims were not necessarily mutually exclusive.

Britain's fear of Russian transgression was probably exaggerated but it was not without foundation. Like other European powers, not least Britain, Russia had been aggressively expanding its territory, moving through the Caucasus into Georgia and Azerbaijan, and eastwards into Bokhara, Samarkand and Tashkent. British wariness of Russian moves to foment internal unrest in India was apparently confirmed by the publication of a book by a Russian colonel in 1857 in which he argued that the Great Rebellion had failed due to a lack of organisation and outside support, and that Indians who were sick to death of British rule were waiting for 'a physician from the north'. This book had traction as it followed soon after the Crimean War (1853-6) in which Russia occupied parts of modern-day Romania, Bulgaria and Armenia which lay within the Ottoman Empire. This fear of Russian incursion into British Empire territory was not just confined to government circles, but was widely held in all classes of British society where a Russiaphobic paranoia became embedded. Whether the Russian threat was more imagined than real, it nevertheless felt real to people at the time and was a key factor in determining British policy.

In 1849 the British East India Company annexed the Sikh province of Punjab. The 11 year old Maharajah Duleep Singh was separated from his mother who was acting as regent. She was held as a prisoner and he would not see her again for 16 years. He was forced to hand over his kingdom and then exiled. The Punjab bordered the northwest territories controlled by Pashtun peoples who were not formally under the suzerainty of neighbouring Afghanistan. Raiding across the border by Pashtuns into the now British controlled Punjab led to a series of military retaliations into Waziristan in 1865, 1868, and 1869; and further north in 1850, 1853, 1855, 1878 and 1879.[4] It was not for want of trying therefore, but little progress had been made in subduing or controlling the border territories. In response a new British government led by Disraeli moved to adopt a more assertive 'forward policy' to protect the north-west frontier of India, which sought to defend the border through gaining the support of neighbouring states and peoples, and projecting British force into their territory on a more established basis. Rather than a purely defensive and reactive policy, this was intended as a shift to a proactive and forestalling strategy. To this end the Indian viceroy sent a diplomatic mission to the emir of Afghanistan in Kabul with a request to allow the permanent stationing of a British resident in Kabul. The mission was refused access to the country and returned without success. The perceived offence was made worse as the emir had allowed and received an embassy from

Russia. The incensed Viceroy Bulwer-Lytton declared that Afghanistan was nothing but "an earthen pipkin between two metal pots" and launched a second full invasion in 1878 with 56,000 men.[5] Kabul was again taken, the emir fled and his successor agreed to the stationing of a British agent and to conduct his foreign affairs in line 'with the wishes and advice' of the British government.[6]

However, as with the previous invasion, the presence of British troops in Kabul rather than settling matters only served to inflame the local population. When mutinous soldiers had their demands for overdue pay refused, rioting broke out during which the British embassy was burned to the ground and its 200 occupants killed while the emir failed to intervene. As in the previous Afghan war the British were forced to fight their way back to Kabul and re-established control which they did, but only after committing atrocities in revenge. There was no further attempt to station a British resident.

One outcome of this war was an agreement reached between the emir and Britain to demarcate respective areas of control, and to establish a commission to agree upon a definitive borderline between the respective territories of Afghanistan and north west India. In 1893 the border was defined as the Durand line named after the British chief negotiator, and the British proceeded to reenforce it with a chain of forts which they occupied with troops. Unfortunately, no one thought to consult those who lived on the newly agreed border and violent protests and raids continued, the situation being aggravated because social and ethnic communities now found themselves divided by the new boundary. The British response was to launch yet more punitive raids in order to assert their authority, confiscating cattle, burning crops, destroying villages, poisoning wells and irrigation systems, and refusing to take prisoners. Churchill was shocked at the savagery of the punitive expeditions in which he participated, and on one occasion he recorded the burning alive of a prisoner.[7] Although the British assured the resident people that they had no intention of annexing their territory, the Pashtuns nevertheless observed the building of forts in their lands and the fate of the previously independent but now annexed neighbouring Punjab and drew their own conclusion.

*

Although the whole of Afghanistan was in play, the prime concern of the British was with the Khyber Pass which runs through a range of mountains and connects Kabul in Afghanistan with Peshawar, now in Pakistan. This passage through a gorge with sides reaching up to 1,000 feet in height narrows at one point to as little as 100 yards for a distance of four miles. It has long been recognised as a key gateway into India with the oldest recorded passage of an army in the fifth century BCE. The British were acutely aware of their vulnerability at this point and understood that whoever controlled the Khyber Pass also controlled access into India from the north. In line with their policy of not annexing and directly controlling Afghanistan, the British did not garrison the Pass with their own troops but instead paid and armed paramilitary mercenaries to police and defend it. The Khyber Rifles as they were known, were drawn from a sub-group of the ethnic Pashtuns called Afridis, who were themselves among the very people adversely affected by the implementation of the new border policy. Despite this, the approach was broadly successful and maintained the status quo in the Pass until 1897. To understand why the Afridis could help enforce British rule and at the same time oppose the new border it is necessary to understand the fluid identities and allegiances of the peoples of Afghanistan.

Part of Britain's difficulties arose from their felt need to divide what they considered the uncivilised world into neat hierarchies based on race and geography. The bedrock of this understanding was a belief that the majority of north Europeans represented a higher stage of civilisation. (The notable caveat were the Irish who were often represented as little better than apes.) This view was expressed by J.R. Seeley, the regius professor of modern history at Cambridge University, in a series of lectures in 1881-2 later published as an influential book called 'The Expansion of England' which continued to be published until the 1950s.[8] From the sweeping assertion that 'There can be no question about the general fact that the ruling race in British India has a higher and more vigorous civilisation than the native races', he went on to analyse the racial characteristics and classification of the people of the subcontinent, concluding that there were three races. The most primitive were darker skinned and should be classed as 'not civilised' and 'barbarous'. The next above them in civilisational terms, were the Muslims, some 50 million in India who had immigrated at different times from outside the country. These formed a 'sort of semi-civilisation, certain strong virtues but of a primitive kind, in short an equipment of ideas and views not sufficient for the modern forms of society'. Finally, there was the Aryan race which showed the greatest aptitude for civilisation and had begun to develop it a long time ago, creating poetry and philosophy and the beginnings of science. It was believed that part of the Aryan race had migrated to Europe in the distant past and that modern Europeans were derived from this group; a belief borne out by analysis of language similarities amongst other pseudoscientific and academic investigations. Hitler was later to seize on this to develop his racially constructed world view. Seeley believed that in some ways the Indian variant still resembled the gifted European race, but alas, for unknown reasons it had failed to develop in India itself. He concluded:

> *On the whole then we find in India three stages of civilisation, first that of the hill-tribes which is barbarism, then that which is perhaps sufficiently described as the Mussulman (Muslim) stage, and thirdly the arrested and half-crushed civilisation of a gifted race..*[9]

This intellectual underpinning lay behind persistent attempts to sub-delineate people into tribes. In the case of Afghanistan, the social relations and groupings present were extremely difficult to chart in this way and led to a bewildering plethora of groups and to misconceptions about allegiances as a result. The boundaries between the ascribed tribal groups were not clear; they intermingled and shifted. The Afridi group for instance had recruits in the British Indian army, but also fought against it, and also had groups of members who fought against other members.[10] It was an impenetrable social system to which the British assigned clans within tribes, and then into further sub-divisions of sub-clans and eventually to extended families and branches of families. Even with such a comprehensive mental map however, this conceptualisation of Afghan society was unable to cope with the fluid and fissiparous nature of the political and social situation. Infighting and vendettas extended to families against families, and to individual men against individual men. In terms of their internal political structure, the groups ranged from those with a despotic chief, to those which lacked any leader or leadership and where matters were decided in communal council or jirgahs.[11] The reality was that there was no neat, clear-cut chart of tribes in the way that the European's template demanded. It is against this background that we can understand why the Pashtuns who guarded the Khyber Pass saw no conflict in fighting for the British against family and kinsmen in return for being paid to do so.

Subject to the above qualifications, the British-Indian campaign was waged against two principal groups: the Afridi and the Orakzai. British conceptions of the characteristics of these Muslim, hill-dwelling peoples were complicated and reflected the half-way house status ascribed to them by Seeley in his analysis. They were both positive and negative. A colonel for instance wrote of them as being 'bred and born amongst steep and rugged hills, and dark and dangerous ravines, inured to extremes of hot and cold, accustomed from childhood to carry arms and to be on their guard against the wiles of the treacherous kinsmen by whom they are surrounded', and thought that 'it is small wonder they are hardy, alert, self-reliant and active, full or resource, keen as hawks, and cruel as leopards'.[12] Animal similes abounded with other observers comparing them to a veritable zoo of creatures including tigers, sharks, vultures, panthers, and wolves.[13] Another colonel characterised them variously as 'marauding cut-throats', 'exceptionally fine mountaineers', 'admirable marksmen', and 'ferocious adversaries'.[14] Of course, this assessment reflected back on the British themselves: here was a manful foe, no push-over that could be mown down and subdued with a Maxim gun, the forerunner of the machine gun, as they rushed forward ill-armed in their naivety. To engage and defeat them would take courage, superior skill and intelligence, and superior codes of honour. Whilst the Afridi and Orakzai were characterised as worthy adversaries in terms of courage and fighting skill, they were also deemed to be treacherous and cruel and to not play by the rules. In this latter respect they were inferior beings outside of the bounds of civilisation and could be treated accordingly.

*

Given the long standing and seemingly unchanging nature of internal rivalry and feuding among the Pashtun peoples, it came as a considerable shock to the British authorities when they united and rose up as one in 1897. An attack by an estimated 10,000 Afridis overran two British forts situated at the Khyber Pass in late August and so gained control of this vital artery. Shortly afterwards the Orakzais attacked and captured another pass. The 'forward policy' had proven to be a catastrophic failure, and the principle of 'divide and rule' had been ineffective. It was with considerable alarm that the British government realised that the whole of the north west frontier of India was under immediate threat. Foremost in the minds of the British was the danger that this unrest would spread and spark another major rebellion in India itself. Facing a force of Afridis and their neighbouring Orakzais of perhaps as many as 55,000 it was clear that urgent and decisive action was called for.

The question arises, as it arose at the time, as to what had united the previously irreconcilable indigenous groups, and how had this been achieved with such stealth as to catch the authorities unaware.[15] In fact, there wasn't very far to look as their demands were published and were available to the extent that they appeared in British regional newspapers.[16] The petitioners called for a meeting or jirgah with the British powers to discuss these, but this was rejected.[17] They were due a 'thrashing' to teach them a lesson instead.

Their demands were threefold. Firstly, they wanted a reduction in the tax on salt which was sharply increased by the British in 1896 to the extent that its price quadrupled. Salt was of course a basic necessity, but it was also one of the main sources of trading income for the Afridis whose territory included salt mines.[18] Secondly, they wanted the withdrawal of British troops from the vicinity of a holy site in the upper Swat valley and other specified areas; and thirdly a section of the Orakzais demanded that the British return women who had run away to British territory, this being the previous practice. This last demand remains obscure and it is not clear if these women were willing partners of Anglo-Indian forces or how many there were.

The British were convinced that these reasons, whilst not without merit, were not the real or underlying cause for such a major uprising. Instead, they feared and suspected a wider Muslim plot to destabilise the region and the whole of India. The British Indian Empire contained more Muslims than any other country in the world, and Queen Victoria ruled over more Muslim subjects than she did British Christians. With their transnational religion it was believed that Muslims were uniquely placed to undermine and even overthrow British rule. It was noted that a new consciousness of themselves as Muslims had become apparent following the Turkish (Islamic) defeat of (Christian Orthodox) Greece in 1896. Before he was summoned to Peshawar, Lieutenant-Colonel Thomsett discerned that Muslims had started to wear the fez, the distinctive hat associated with Turkish nationalists. He described their apparent sense of disgruntlement and warned his fellow Britons to be on their guard against violent attacks, although he did admit this antipathy might have something to do with the burning down of their mosque by Hindu police.[19]

Another officer wondered if people should be 'surprised if the Pathan (Pashtun) with his inordinate vanity and religious fanaticism imagined that a Musselman (Muslim) millennium was near at hand, that the days of the Raj were numbered and that the people of God were once more to come into their inheritance and rule in the land of Hindustan as conquerors'.[20] In contrast to the steadfast British, the rebellious factions were described as fanatics and religious zealots, or in the words of the Punjabi government, 'priest-ridden fanatics, and bigoted followers of the prophet'.[21] Henry Walter Bellew, a British medical officer with extensive experience in Afghanistan described the inhabitants as 'extremely bigoted and entirely controlled by their priests and (at) all times ready for a jihad or holy war'.[22] The young reporter Winston Churchill ascribed the cause of the rising to a 'mad mullah...A wild enthusiast, convinced alike of his Divine mission and miraculous powers, he preached a crusade of jehad against the infidel'.[23]

It was reasoned therefore that somebody must have preyed on this sentiment and incited the revolt, a hidden hand, a fanatical leader. With the Mahdi-led uprising in Sudan still in the recent past, the idea of a Islamic fundamentalist mad mullah or mad fakir was widely used and took hold in the British popular press and imagination, becoming a way of personifying and justifying retribution against an unreasonable and irrational foe trapped in a medieval mindset.

These fears were not without some substance. In late July a religious mendicant had proclaimed that the end of British rule was imminent, and that he had holy powers to stop up their guns and that the stones he threw had the same effect as a gun on the enemies of Islam. This was not as incredible as it first appears as British troops had previously been forced to fall back on using blank ammunition when their supplies of live ammunition ran out.[24] He attracted a following of 5,000 who went on to attack a British held fort, but were eventually repulsed once reinforcements arrived. This was one of a number of similar attacks in the following weeks.[25] Mullahs were also instrumental in reconciling the Afridi and Orakzai so allowing them to join in coalition against the government.[26] However, it seems unlikely that there was some underlying mastermind, whether mad or sane, who was directing affairs. In particular suspicions about the role of the emir of Afghanistan proved hard to pin down, and no evidence was found to suggest he was behind the insurrection, although suspicions remained.[27] Likewise evidence of Russian incitement was sought for, but remained sketchy at best.

It is true that the grievances of the Afridi and Orakzai ran wider and deeper than the three demands they submitted. They said as much in a petition to the emir of Afghanistan, although we must allow that they were appealing to him for help and so presumably saying what he would want to hear, or towards which he would be sympathetic,

> *The British government has been from olden times gradually encroaching upon our country, and even upon Afghan territory, and has erected forts at various points within our border.... We will never consent to tender our allegiance to the British government, and become their subjects. We will never give up the reins of authority of our country to the hands of the (British) government... We have now under the guidance of God, opened the door of jehad in the face of the said government.*[28]

Whilst there was clearly a religiously inspired aspect to their actions therefore, fundamentally their objection was to British governance and to the policies which had been introduced. They wanted to retain their independence in their own lands, or in other words their sovereignty.

*

Faced with the dual threat of a Muslim revolt and possible Russian interference, the British decided they had to act decisively and emphatically to re-establish their pre-eminence and control of the north west frontier provinces. In the language of the time, it was essential to restore British 'prestige'. Prestige formed a large part of the self-conception of the British and their role in the late Empire. This was true at an individual level where British personnel were expected to behave in accordance with certain codes of dress and conduct in front of the indigenous population; to display a superior and authoritative air in their demeanour and actions. It was also true at the level of the state. The British formed a tiny minority in the territories they occupied and it was believed that maintaining British prestige was the *sine qua non* of ongoing control. This was envisaged as being a mixture of being admired, respected and looked up to. But it was also a euphemism for instilling fear in the subject populations.

General Lockhart decided that the best way of restoring this exalted national status and regaining control of the Khyber Pass was to occupy the heartlands of Afridi territory in the high reaches of the Maidan Valley. Having done so, he would announce the terms of surrender with which the Afridis and Orakzais were to comply. By this audacious action he intended to deliver a knock-out psychological blow as it was the proud boast of the Afridis that no invading force had ever entered this territory and it had never even been seen by Europeans. The British endowed it with an almost mythical status, picturing its fertility and regarding it as holy territory for the Afridis with the mosque at Bagh as the centre of their belief system and power. Lockhart expected that by making this emphatic assertion of British supremacy over their lands with an overwhelming force, by displaying the right to go wherever they liked whenever they liked, that the Afridis would buckle and submit to the terms of reparation which he would impose.[29]

The Maidan was the summer home of the Afridis who practised transhumance, decamping to winter accommodation in the lower grounds of the Bara valley and areas bordering the Peshawar valley. It had very rich soil and was extensively terraced with numerous farmsteads growing grains, walnuts and other fruits. It also offered grazing for the herds which moved with the human population on the seasonal migration. The reason it had not been visited by outsiders was not because it was an uninviting place, but because it was so remote and inaccessible. The approach to it was through 'narrow, torturous and precipitous' gorges barely wide enough for a single file of men, which were flanked by boulder strewn hills.[30] It sits at an elevation of some 9,000 feet and in winter is snowbound with high winds and freezing temperatures. The autumn is wet with sleet and plentiful mud.

The size of the column which was to occupy this tract, and the late start in the season were therefore to present considerable challenges in the weeks ahead.

3: STRUGGLING ON

Lt-.Col. Thomsett had got used to the mud and slush which seemed to be permanently in his tent. The cold he could cope with, in fact it was quite a relief not needing to have a punkah at night as he had at Peshawar.* And while no one could enjoy their clothes being damp the whole time, his servant was doing his best for him in the circumstances. No, what was really wearying Thomsett, and was frankly unnerving, was the shooting into camp at night, or 'sniping' as he had learned it was called. It hadn't been like this on previous campaigns, when the enemy was armed with blunderbusses and knives and one could retire safe in the knowledge that one would wake up in the morning. But now the tribesmen had modern weapons and were putting them to horribly effective use. He had considered sleeping under his bed as some of his colleagues recommended, but then some of them had gone so far as to surround their tents with stone walls, and even to dig pits into the ground to sleep in! He couldn't even light a candle at night for fear of attracting the messengers of death that kept him awake as they whizzed past. Some nights he had barely slept at all.

Still, he found that life in camp really wasn't so bad on the whole. The food was good - they were still receiving fresh fruit and vegetables. He had also made friends with an excellent Indian medical officer who seemed to have an inexhaustible supply of sweets and delicacies. He had found him to be good company and liked to relax with him at the end of the day. Surgeon Lieutenant-Colonel Ahmed enjoyed universal respect

---

* A 'punkah' was Anglo-Indian slang for the attendant who pulled a rope to waft a ceiling mounted fan.

across all religions and ranks and was well known in the region. Thomsett couldn't help but think it might be a better idea to send him to parley with the Afridis rather than sending an army against them.

There was fun to be had too. There were some fine story tellers, and some excellent jokes told of an evening. The signalling officer's baritone was a thing of wonder and his rendition of one or two choice ditties caused gales of laughter. A memorable afternoon had been spent at a gymkhana laid on by one of the native regiments at which the dhooly bearers' race was particularly amusing.*

Figure 5: Medical Staff at the Field Gymkhana

On a more serious note, he had decided to refrain from drinking alcohol and smoking until Christmas. Not that there was anything wrong with drinking - far from it, he enjoyed it. It did you good and set you up for the day to have a peg of whisky and soda with breakfast - which was also a necessary

---

* A 'dhooly' is a stretcher.

stimulant at other meals to give one an appetite. He had found it also beneficial after hard exercise. In his experience there was no harm in drinking alcohol if one was thirsty, but one had to be on one's guard against taking 'nips' between meals as people were inclined to do. Besides which, it was so difficult to get hold of in the present situation.

Thomsett had also reassessed the amount of kit he had bought along in light of the difficulties with transport. So far, he had managed to keep hold of the five mules and two horses with which he had set out, but it had been an extraordinarily difficult journey and they were still only seven miles from their start. He had decided it would be sensible to send as much as he could spare back to base in Peshawar.[1]

*

After an eight-week delay, during which the Afridis had taken advantage of British dilatoriness to withdraw from fighting to gather their harvest, the British-Indian army finally began to advance on 4th October 1897.[2] The logistical problems which it faced at base camp had not been overcome and it immediately fell into supply difficulties which it would never resolve throughout the campaign. The paths were so narrow that any mishap with an animal or its load could lead to queues of up to fifteen miles.[3] On occasion ponies which were too slow were pushed over steep slopes to clear the way for the following baggage train, a 'most comical sight' according to one officer.[4] Progress would undoubtedly have been quicker had the British officers not taken along with them so much equipment for their domestic comfort. This was the recommended minimum for 24 officers: six tables with detachable tops; 24 collapsible chairs; six bottles of port, six bottles of champagne, six bottles of brandy (for use in cases of sickness); two small kegs of whisky (88 bottles equivalent); eight cooking pots, two kettles, four frying pans; knives, spoons etc for cooking; 24 each of soup plates, 9-inch plates, tumblers, forks, knives and desert spoons; three vegetable dishes, two joint dishes, three milk jugs, two tea-pots, six serving spoons, six large forks and one set of carving knife and fork. Eighteen days provisions included but was not limited to 36 x 1lb tins of milk; 72 of jam; 72 each of tongue and sausages; 36 of bacon - and six bottles of Worcester sauce. All of this required ten mules to carry it, one alone for the whisky. To serve their mess they required a total of 12 servants including three waiters, two cooks, one water-carrier, one washer, and three grooms.[5] Given that this was for just 24 out of the 1,500 officers on the campaign it can readily be seen how the transport, which was usually progressing in single file, was impeded.

On the first day the Oxfordshire Light Infantry set out at six in the morning and the first of them arrived at their destination seven miles distant at three in the afternoon; the rear guard however did not reach them until 12 hours later at three the following morning having been marching for 21 hours.[6] Not only this, but the loading and ordering of the baggage was chaotically managed so that troops would arrive at the end of their day's march and have no food, water or shelter until hours later, or not at all. On one occasion it was reported their baggage did not arrive until five days later.[7] Long periods could be spent in the heat without water. An Oxfordshire sergeant recounted how he and his horses had no water for 26 hours and when they did find some it was dark and brackish but not unpleasant. Within half an hour however, he 'shook like a leaf and felt very queer'; the following day he felt worse with 'fever and ague' and fainted while riding his horse, tumbling down a slope but escaping serious injury.[8] His was not an isolated case; men often were forced to drink from muddy puddles and to sleep out in the open.[9] The animals too lacked fodder and water with many becoming sick and dying.[10] The camps were not organised in advance so that the units did not know where they were to station themselves and men wandered disorientated, looking for their allotted place and luggage. All of this understandably had a negative effect on the health and the morale of the advancing force.

The armed forces were accompanied by around 20,000 people usually referred to as followers. A better word for them might be enablers as the army would not have been able to survive, let alone progress, without them and their role is usually overlooked. In particular they were able to provide provisions for sale. These were often the only ones available to the troops as their allocation had not arrived with them. There was a bazaar where troops could spend the money that was distributed to them, and also a coffee shop attached to the Oxfordshire Light Infantry which was regarded as literally life-saving by its lieutenant-colonel. 'Many times, the coffee shop was drawn upon… when nothing else was procurable and without which the men would have starved'.[11] Lt. Col. Thomsett also refers to an enterprising Muslim who had set up a soda factory in a tent.[12] There were also artisans such as cobblers, and no doubt all the other trades and crafts which support daily life were also present.[13] Even when the lead column reached the remote heights of the Maidan valley, Indian merchants were bringing whisky, tinned-milk, butter, cheese and eggs to the camp for sale. One officer considered that these were expensive, but not unreasonably so considering the risks the men were running in bringing them so far and into such hostile territory. These provisions were enormously welcome and a great boost to morale as the standard military allocated fare was limited to tinned beef and biscuits.[14] In addition to these entrepreneurs were the innumerable hired porters required to move the column along. Indian civilians were both benefitting from, and aiding the British-led forces.

Added to the supply problems was the misery of sniping to which they were subjected. The Afridis were renown as excellent marksmen, often trained by the British and equipped with British rifles with which they had either been issued, or had captured or purchased. They were also expert in using the natural features of the landscape to conceal themselves, and constructed low stone parapets, called piquets, to shelter behind. Perched on the slopes above the advancing column they could choose their moment to effect the most damage. They realised early on the vulnerability of the baggage train which afforded an easy target and impeded successful progress of the troops. They also used dusk, after the British had set up camp, to fire into the camps, in particular singling out officers who were easily identifiable by their dress. The officers presented themselves as sitting ducks as they sat down to their dinners; one was hit in the arm which was then amputated, and another shot dead through the cheek as he was eating.[15] Forty casualties occurred in one day in this manner.[16] This was a shrewd strategy and one to which the British had no effective response. Their troops were trained to fight in massed formation in open battle and were inexperienced in dealing with guerrilla warfare of this type. As an example, early in the campaign a troop of soldiers finding themselves outnumbered withdrew and formed into squares some six to eight deep. Rather than providing protection this simply made them an easier target to hit, whilst at the same time restricting their ability to fire back.[17] They could hardly be blamed for taking this course of action: it was what they had been trained to do. High command quickly realised that radically different tactics would be required for the current offensive. A stream of increasingly insistent memorandums were issued from headquarters insisting that 'barrack square and parade ground points of drill are out of place on a hill side where the object is, if at all possible, to get away from the enemy before they close on you.'[18] Whilst the British had artillery which their Pashtun opponents lacked, in practice its effectiveness was limited. By the time it was in position the snipers who were the intended target had withdrawn; the Pashtuns also realised that they could avoid its effects by sheltering in the many deep ravines which characterised the terrain.

*

Death at the hands of snipers was to be the fate of the three men of the Oxfordshire Light Infantry whose names are on the Tirah Monument marked as killed in action: Sergeant J. S. Hopkins, Lance Corporal W. Bell and Private W. Butler. They met their deaths on 30th December 1897 on what had started out as a routine day for the Oxfordshire Light Infantry stationed in the Khyber Pass. Their task was to leave their camp at nine in the morning in order to search for food for their animals and destroy as many villages as they could. Since this work was obviously likely to be resisted by the inhabitants who generally fled to the hills at the approach of the British forces, it was necessary to post flanking picquets of soldiers to deter attacks on the main body of troops who were engaged in the task. Typically, these had around 20 men in each. With their task completed the main force retired to their camp at 2.30pm and afterwards the picquets began to withdraw in an organised fashion with a rear-guard covering the withdrawal. It was an action they had undertaken many times and with which they were familiar.

This occasion was to be different however. For some reason one of the fortified villages they had to pass had not been destroyed. It appeared that there had been some mix-up in orders with the particular place being missed off the orders of an adjacent regiment. When the withdrawing party of about 40 men were some 300 yards from the tower in the village they came under fire. Three unnamed men were hit and wounded.

All were able to scramble to safety into a ravine or 'nullah' which punctuate the country. Two of the wounded men were able to walk down this to reach the surgeon accompanying the party where their wounds were dressed and they proceeded to safety in a nearby house. The third had his wounds dressed by the senior officer present, Colonel Plowden. The wounded man then followed his other two comrades down the nullah to safety.

Normally the nullah would have provided a safe haven but in this instance, it was overlooked by a ruined Buddhist building from where the company now came under fire from enemy snipers. They had no choice but to run across open ground to try to reach safety. While making the attempt Lance-Corporal Bell was hit in the head and died immediately. Three officers, Colonel Plowden, Lieutenant Owen and Lieutenant Feilden dragged his corpse back into the nullah while under fire.

At this point accounts of what occurred differ. A number of men were wounded including Colonel Plowden, Lieutenant Owen and Sergeant-Major Dempsey. Plowden is described variously as having been shot in the abdomen, in the left hip, in the ribs, or as having suffered a less severe wound as the bullet entered his body only after it had been deflected by the hilt of his sword. Wherever it struck, he contracted pneumonia the next day but eventually recovered and rejoined the regiment. Owen was hit in the arm probably with a new type of exploding 'dum-dum' bullet which shattered the bone. He also received hits in his water bottle and revolver holster. He too would recover and rejoin active service. The third man, Harry Dempsey, was hit in the stomach with the bullet lodging in his spine – he managed to roll over the lip of the nullah but was still lying injured and exposed to enemy fire. He would subsequently spend months in hospital and it was hoped would make a full recovery. However, he contracted food poisoning from eating a tin of contaminated peas, and although he partially recovered from its effects died on March 19th. He left behind a wife and small child.[19] Plowden and Owen along with two other wounded men were helped to safety away from the nullah. Once there, an enterprising and courageous bugler called Crowhurst asked if he might use Colonel Plowden's superb Arab pony to attempt to ride to camp to alert the general to the situation. This permission was readily granted and he galloped under fire to complete his mission. He too according to one account was severely wounded, but according to another was unharmed.[20]

Among the soldiers who were wounded was a Private Butler who was hit in the leg. The wound was dressed by Lieutenant Carter who then proceeded to carry Butler on his back across open ground towards safety. It was while doing this that Butler was shot in the head and killed, the force of the blow knocking Carter to the ground. Carter was rescued by Feilden whilst Butler's corpse was left in open ground. Feilden received a shot through his helmet and a shot also grazed his knee, but was left unharmed.

The situation was now extremely serious. Captain Parr, Lieutenants Feilden and Carter and eight unwounded men were trapped in the nullah along with four wounded and one dead comrade. Private Smith and Sergeant-Major Dempsey were lying wounded in an exposed position. Those in the nullah were only partially safe from fire, and any movement, even raising of the head, exposed them to danger.

Captain Parr ordered Lieutenant Carter to make a dash to a nearby house where Lieutenant Davies and some men were waiting to withdraw to camp, unaware of the disaster unfolding just three quarters of a mile away. On receiving the news from the understandably breathless and barely coherent Carter, Davies took some men and after successfully covering the open ground with just a bullet wound to the sole of one man's boot, they joined the party in the nullah. The increased numbers did not however do anything to alleviate the situation and the men in the nullah were alarmed to hear the enemy creeping closer and closer. They were in a position to clearly hear their foes' voices and were disturbed by their periodic yelling which was characteristic of a jackal according to one listener. All they could do was shout back in response in an attempt to keep their courage up. Even more alarmingly the enemy became close enough to enable them to throw stones over the edge of the nullah in the hope of hitting the sheltering soldiers and making them expose themselves to sniper fire. The men sheltering in the nullah were sure they were about to be rushed upon and killed.

What happened next is obscure despite several detailed accounts being given afterwards. Battle is no doubt a confusing and even bewildering experience and it is perhaps not surprising if accounts vary of the events which occur during it. However, the differences in the retelling whilst subtle are significant.

According to Lieutenant Davies, they were fired on by a man just ten yards away who had crept up behind them.

'We turned round and charged across the nullah and up the further bank. I got to a spot just above the [wounded] sergeant major [Dempsey]'. Davies then records in his journal that he fired two shots from his revolver at a fleeing enemy tribesman but that he had forgotten to remove the safety catch and so the man got away unharmed. Colonel Plowden was not present by this stage because of his injury but his seniority gave his account added weight and entered the official record. He similarly reported that Davies and Parr led the charge out of the nullah. However, early press reports penned by a reporter with the regiment describe the enemy getting sufficiently close so that 'with one last yell, they rushed in to the nullah' at which point a counter charge commenced. This is not too dissimilar from the recollection of Davies. However, a later report in The Times of India recorded that as the enemy came near to the nullah that a party was formed with fixed bayonets for a charge who 'dashed up the bank with a cheer'.[21]

Lieutenant Frith who was with Davies has a different recollection of events. He had no reason to detract from his superior's account and indeed had the highest regard for Davies writing home to his mother,

> *Davies is a regular "Ripper". I was astonished at his iron nerves and calmness in danger. In the middle of a very hot fire he turned round and said "Have a cigarette Frith" His example was a great help to me. In fact every soldier admired him.*[22]

According to Frith, rather than spontaneously leading a charge in response to being fired on from behind, Davies after careful consideration 'ordered a few of us to charge up this high bank' which was exposed to fire from three sides. The implication is that Davies was not among the first of those charging out of the nullah. Frith concludes his account laconically with the reflection, 'Well we didn't gain much by that. Only me and Davies were left unwounded'.

Whether it was a spontaneous, reactive charge, or a premeditated ordered charge, the outcome was grim. A further man, Sergeant Hopkins was shot dead as he ran forward. Captain Parr was severely wounded as he approached the top of the nullah and fell back into the arms of Frith. Captain Parr survived however and lived to be present at the unveiling of the Tirah Memorial in Oxford in 1900. An unnamed private received a minor wound, while Colour-Sergeant Jones was severely wounded in the thigh.

Figure 6: Left to right - Col. Plowden, Lt. Owen, Lt. Feilden

The charge was effective however in pushing the enemy back, and with dusk falling it became possible to rescue the wounded. Lieutenant Davies dragged Col. Sgt. Jones back into the nullah hurting him horribly in the process, and then told him to crawl down the nullah to safety. Davies records that he then returned to the wounded Dempsey to drag him in too, but Dempsey begged him to fetch more men to carry him as he could not stand being dragged. Sergeant-Major Dempsey was eventually fetched in by Lieutenant Frith, Sergeant Smith and two other unnamed privates. Sergeant Smith was severely wounded in the neck while doing so. Another injured man, private Smith, who had been lying in the open exposed to fire was found to be shot in the arm only and was able to walk with assistance; he too was bought to safety. The final man to be wounded that day was another private, Warner, who received bullet wounds in both thighs as he escorted the injured to the rear.

In the space of a few hours the brigade had incurred three wounded commissioned officers, one sergeant-major and five sergeants wounded, one sergeant killed, one corporal killed, one private killed, and five privates wounded, but with no losses on the other side. It was a disastrous engagement where, despite obvious bravery, they had been unable to fight back effectively against the enemy.

*

It is notable that the British accounts lay so much stress on the need to help and retrieve the wounded, and to a lesser extent the dead. The reason for not making a withdrawal is repeatedly given as the need to stay with the wounded and not leave them behind. Plowden, Owen, Bell, Smith and Warner are all recorded as being injured or killed while helping the wounded. Carter not only carried the injured Butler but also a further three men more successfully to safety. Care is needed though in taking these accounts at face value. For instance, whilst Bell is recorded as killed while helping the wounded in the official record and in newspaper reports, it is clear from contemporary diaries that he was shot dead only after the wounded had been cleared from the field. There are Christ like overtones to the idea of laying one's life on the line to help the wounded - for greater love hath no man that he lay down his life for his friend. It is also true that doing so was likely to receive commendation, even a medal, which was another incentive. Certainly, Davies' action in dragging Jones seems to a certain extent to be questionable. If Jones could crawl, why did he have to be dragged causing him agony? Death or an injury can also be sanitised or justified as being heroic if the victim is cast in the role of helping the wounded, and it may be out of kindness or consideration for family that the best gloss was put on what was a hopelessly imbalanced and ultimately futile engagement.

However, this reasoning can be pushed too far. These men had a real fear of the fate of the wounded, and by implication of their own safety, if they fell into enemy hands. As one officer explained in a letter to his son at school in England,

> *...there was not an inch of cover to be obtained for 50 yards, and the difficulty was the wounded men. You see among civilized people the wounded could have been left out, but with these savages every wounded man left out is tortured and cut about in the most revolting manner.*[23]

This is confirmed in the diary of Sergeant Crutch from the Oxfordshire Light Infantry who was attached to General Lockhart as a signalling officer. Whilst occupying the Maidan Valley he recounted how after blowing up and destroying 53 villages in one day, a detachment of the Northamptonshire regiment became cut off. Two officers and 15 men were killed, 'the majority of them mutilated and presenting a shocking sight when bought into camp the following morning'.[24] Similarly, during the retreat through the Bara valley he encountered 'a ghastly sight, three Sikhs found in the morning killed and mutilated and one half burned'.[25] It was widely believed that no prisoners were taken, and the fate, at best, of wounded men left behind would be death at the hands of the enemy. In the words of the young reporter Churchill, 'It is a point of honour on the Indian frontier not to leave wounded men behind. Death by inches and hideous mutilations are the invariable measure meted out to all who fall in battle into the hands of the Pashtun tribesmen'.[26] It was also crucial to retrieve any weapons and ammunition the fallen had with them in order to prevent them being captured and used against the British forces themselves. Their motivation for retrieving their comrades was therefore very strong and entirely rational.

However, atrocities were not only committed by 'savages' but also by the 'civilized' people. Sergeant Crutch also records following in the wake of a British assault and coming across 'a most fearful spectacle' of a half-burned Afridi, 'the stench which hung around this particular spot was almost unbearable'.[27] It has previously been mentioned that Churchill knew of the burning alive of a prisoner and he freely admitted that the British did not take prisoners wounded or otherwise. He wrote that he had seen several things 'which had not been very pretty' but that he had 'not soiled my hands with any dirty work'.[28]

And yet even this reciprocal horror does not entirely describe the extent of the fate which could befall prisoners or wounded soldiers. The Pashtun response was more discriminating than contemporary British accounts and beliefs held it to be. Lieutenant Davies later recorded in his journal of an incident where five Bengal Lancers were captured by Afridis but were then released unharmed, 'the cavalry being pathans

[Pashtuns], the prisoners were not killed at once by the Afridis, as they would have been if they had been Hindoos'.[29] Likewise, the Afridi were sparing of Gurkha troops who Sergeant Crutch reports were stripped on one occasion after their capture and sent back to the camp even though 'they could easily have killed them'. He also noted that this was the usual fate of captured mule and other animal drivers. On one occasion Crutch records that a driver had been beaten and 'more or less mildly mutilated to the great amusement of the Afridis' before being sent back – perhaps a coded reference to enforced circumcision.[30] Even European captives did not necessarily suffer the fate which was widely expected for them. Officers in particular were valuable and could be ransomed. A Sergeant John Walker was wounded and captured, but rather than being killed and mutilated (not necessarily in that order), he was taken captive, his wounds attended to, and treated kindly according to his own account. Whilst held he was able to receive tea, sugar, newspapers, writing material and even a letter from his general which were passed to him via the British political officers who remained in contact throughout his captivity and negotiated his ransom and release after one month of confinement. He was one of five captured soldiers at the time.[31] In this context it is notable that the Afridis did not fire at the wounded men who were left exposed on open ground during the engagement described above. The Afridi's worst excesses seems to have been more targeted, at Sikh troops in particular - who were equally bestial in their methods towards the Afridis.

Another thing which stands out from the varied accounts of the day's events is the framing or presentation of the action and its participants. Officers are always named but the names of the wounded privates are given only occasionally and then incidentally. We do not know exactly who the first three men to be shot on that day were for instance. The ordinary soldiers are literally written out of the historical record and leave little trace. This recounting is a long way from the foregrounding of ordinary 'Tommies' which would follow the 1914-18 war just 21 years later. Here it is the officers who are heroes, the rank and file are blurred background figures. The Tommies are not the only ones missing from the contemporary accounts. The full party that day comprised not only British soldiers of the Oxfordshire Light Infantry but also included four Indian stretcher-bearers, and Indian grooms for the hospital and officers' horses. Their role and fate is unaccounted for. Likewise, another key actor who is referred to in passing was the party's interpreter named as 'Timour the Tarter' who led a party to seek help from the general in the rear.[32] We don't know if he succeeded and if he did whether he arrived at camp before the dashing bugler Crowhurst. Further tantalising whisps of history are present in the archive. Among the men fighting that day were some of the 119 who had arrived from England just eight days previously. Readers would have been reassured from front line reports that they had behaved as well as their more seasoned compatriots. However, they would remain unaware that these men had not come alone, but were entered in military records as accompanied by four boys, three women and eight children.[33] We do not know the relationship of these people to the men fighting, nor their whereabouts once they reached India, nor if any were related to those wounded or killed. It is possible however that they were related to some of the men fighting in the Khyber Pass on that day.

The focus of the historical record is on the nobler actions of such people's superiors, who are cast as gallant, calm, decisive and above all self-sacrificing. Lieutenant Carter carrying four wounded to safety; the admirable sang froid and stiff upper lip of Davies; the miraculous near miss of the bullets through Feilden's helmet or onto Plowden's protecting sword. All of these incidents could come straight out of the pages of an imperial adventure story and are surely written about with a consciousness of this template. We have already seen how the confused events around the charge out of the nullah mutated into a version in The Times which better fitted the imperial heroic trope with the troops running up the bank 'with a cheer'. The tendency to heroicise loss is also evident on the Tirah Memorial in Oxford where Sergeant-Major Dempsey is not listed under those dying of disease (from his tin of peas) but as 'died of wounds'. He is the only man on the monument to be listed in this way.

This framing was not just imposed upon them by florid-prosed journalists keen to get a story in their papers. It was also sought after by the officers themselves. Davies describes himself heroically leading a charge, revolver in hand shooting a fleeing enemy. It is a picture book imperial military scene. He may well have forgotten to take off the safety catch of his revolver in the heat of battle as he says; with his life endangered it would no doubt be easy to make such an error. However, his explanation also allows for an answer to the potentially embarrassing question as to why he did not fire his pistol, and taken with the account of Frith suggests he may have exaggerated his role. Davies' account also seems to be crafted with an eye to its reception, to show himself in the best light to his superiors. Davies' endeavours to promote his role in the day's engagement are instructive. He kept a rough diary which he then copied into a hardback journal. He then copied the relevant entry again and sent it to his father, a general, in England. His father then wrote further multiple copies which he sent to his many friends and well-placed contacts promoting his son's actions. This is akin to self-promotion on social media in today's world. Davies was but one of many young officers, like Churchill himself, who were thirsty for recognition, for medals, for advancement in their careers and who were acutely conscious that their way forward lay in engagements such as this. Courageously leading a charge, or heroically rescuing wounded while under fire were the means to this end. There are notable parallels between Davies' account of his actions and that of Winston Churchill's reports of his own actions published in the British press. Churchill too found himself facing a group of tribesmen with his revolver failing to have an effect, and Churchill too dragged a complaining soldier to safety who begged his would-be rescuer to let him struggle on alone.[34] Davies' subsequent deflation at the lack of success of his endeavours is palpable. He wrote increasingly despondent letters to his father - who he addressed as 'Dear General'. He rued that there was unlikely to be a resurrection of fighting in the spring and speculated on where else he could be posted to secure opportunities to fight and distinguish himself. In reference to the lack of recognition of his own part in the engagement of 30th December, Davies describes his general as a 'surly old chap, not giving to saying much', and plots how he could secure a place at staff college if there is to be no further fighting for him.

*

The engagement of the Oxfordshire Light Infantry on 30th December is a microcosm of the difficulties faced by the British in the wider war. It was recognised as such by Colonel Plowden who reflecting on the day wrote that it 'may be taken as a specimen of the sort of fighting that every regiment has experienced during the Campaign'. He continued,

> *Rearguards and detachments surrounded; fighting against an invisible foe; hampered with wounded; often far from support; and depressed with the knowledge that one's fire is making no impression on the enemy – such is the fighting that has fallen to the lot our men. Warfare of this kind, I need hardly say, requires the finest qualities of leadership on the part of officers, and discipline on the part of the rank and file, and I can testify to the fact that these qualities have been conspicuously shown by our officers, and the discipline of the rank and file has equalled that of the armies who won for us the Empire we are fighting to defend.*[35]

The ever-perceptive Sergeant Crutch penned in his diary somewhat more succinctly that, 'the enemy were never idle but would not fight in the open, or give us a chance to retaliate, so we levelled their houses, eat (sic) and burnt up their grain, and destroyed their trees'.[36]

It infuriated the British that their enemy would not make a stand and fight in a set-piece battle. To many this only confirmed the stereotype they had of the Pashtuns as being sly and lacking civilised values. They preferred what one British officer characterised as 'unheroic skulking behind rocks' to gallantly standing up face-to-face in the open.[37] Their tactics rather were to withdraw in the face of their enemy's advance, and using their knowledge of the local geography and their mountain skills, move behind and to the flanks of the advancing troops and attack them where they were more vulnerable. One officer wrote of regret that there had never been the opportunity for 'a good stand-up fight, a brilliant charge, an honest cheerful engagement', and how dispiriting it was to realise that they had 'rarely...inflicted on the enemy losses heavier, or even as heavy, as those we suffered ourselves'.[38] Churchill lamented that there was no fort or canon to capture, nor capital city to attack, and that it was impossible for regular troops 'to catch or kill an impalpable cloud of skirmishers'.[39]

It is in this context that the reception of the fight to take the Dargai heights must be understood. Rather like the evacuation from Dunkirk which was to follow four decades later, what was a military debacle came to be presented as a triumph.

The settlement of Dargai sits on top of a spur that holds a dominating position over the road which passes below. The ascent to it was so precipitous that pack animals were not able to negotiate its narrow tracks, and the ground leading up to its cliffs was sloping, open terrain which offered no cover for approaching troops. When the Second Column found their way blocked by Afridis and Orakzais holding the heights it presented a formidable challenge, and it took many hours for troops of mainly Sikhs and Gurkhas to gain ground and reach near to the summit. The Afridis were able to inflict casualties on the attacking forces before deciding to retreat and leave the heights to the British. However, the British commanding officer felt that they were not a sufficiently strong force and were insufficiently provisioned to remain in place. He had a point. Some of the men had been without water for 19 hours and there was none to be had safely within the immediate vicinity.[40] The decision was taken to withdraw and leave the heights, which were then occupied again by an even larger body of Pashtuns. As the imperial troops withdrew they came under attack and suffered further heavy casualties. The assault had been a futile operation with the British having taken losses but with no gain made.

There was no option but to try to retake the heights and a second offensive was launched two days later. Repeated attempts to take the summit were repulsed and troops found themselves pinned down, unable to advance or retreat. The situation seemed hopeless and the commander of one regiment signalled that it was futile to try further.[41] Fresh troops in the form of the Gordon Highlanders, a Scottish regiment, were deployed along a different route and following a rousing speech from their colonel stormed and took the heights with the Afridis again falling back with minimal casualties. It was an act of great courage and turned what had seemed a hopeless situation into a victory.

The portrayal and reception of this attack was electric. Here at last was something recognisable as a battle and evidence of progress in the military campaign which had begun to attract criticism from some politicians and commentators. More than this though, it was an opportunity to celebrate perceived British values of perseverance, sangfroid, bravery and gallantry. In the words of one officer, it represented the 'high water mark of British courage' when 'the pluck of British soldiers once more won against great odds'; it was 'a glorious victory won after hours of playing the man', and he had no doubt that 'Britain gloried in the proud, unconquerable spirit which sacrificed itself in her cause and for her honour.'[42]

Winston Churchill was not the only reporter embedded with the military. To their relief the accompanying press reporters finally had a story that would strike a chord and sell papers. The editor of The Daily Express was not wrong when he coined that newspapers don't make wars, but wars make newspapers. The demand by editors for stories was intense as the newly emerged mass popular press vied for readership. This 'story' had it all: a narrative arc with a happy and triumphant ending, an exotic and thrilling landscape, the triumph of noble actions, and the affirmation of masculine, British characteristics. The reporting accorded with the narratives in literature of the Empire as a stage for manly virtues and adventure such as appeared in 'Boys' Own' or other periodicals and novels of the time. Acts of personal courage were singled out, for example that of a major who while lying injured on the ground cheered on his men to the assault; or the private who risked his life to aid an injured lieutenant, who on regaining consciousness and in a reciprocal act of heroism and sacrifice ordered the private to leave him to his fate; or the 'thrilling incident' when a soldier dashed across open ground dodging bullets to reach safety 'amid loud huzzas and congratulations' from his colleagues. A feat he repeated two more times before being shot and dying in agony three days later.[43] Public imagination was caught in a way that few imperial events had ever achieved before, or would do again.

The tremendous interest in the Gordon Highlanders' role led to numerous paintings being commissioned, poems published - including by the poet laureate - and the production of commemorative pottery and Christmas cards. Madame Tussauds rushed to produce a tableau of the storming of the heights.[44] The lionisation of the Scottish regiment was boundless. Foremost among those celebrated for his courage was a Scottish piper who, whist still under fire, continued to play his bagpipes after being shot in the ankle. Interest in this figure was only increased by it taking time to identify the individual concerned. Piper Findlater went on to achieve extraordinary celebrity, being presented with the Victoria Cross by the queen empress herself as he recovered in hospital, and later receiving a pension and position in her household so allowing him to retire to his croft. His image was displayed everywhere and he played several times a night at the London theatres, going on to tour throughout Britain, the United States and Canada.

However, despite the popular fervour surrounding this particular action, the enduring reality of the campaign was very different. As the weeks dragged on, the Indian-British forces became increasingly weary, cold, ill-provisioned and sick; unable to successfully engage with, let alone inflict defeat on their enemy.

4: UNBEATEN

The ultimate objective of the campaign, the fabled Maidan Valley high up in the Tirah, was finally reached by the first British Empire forces on the last day of October 1897. The first white men to have ever set eyes on it were struck by its fertility, by the large number of solidly built homesteads which dotted it, by the carefully constructed and cultivated terraces, and by the lack of trees which came as a surprise to them. Trees were not the only thing that was absent however. So too were the Afridis. They had decamped from their summer quarters a little earlier than usual to avoid the British forces and returned to their winter lands in the Bara valley. This was not what the expedition had expected to find and it left General Lockhart's strategy void of meaning. His plan was predicated on the belief that once the Maidan was occupied, the Afridi would submit. They didn't. There were no people present with which to engage and to whom terms could be dictated.

The occupiers also soon found that the valley was not quite as deserted as first appeared and immediately became subject to attacks on their extended baggage trains. On the very first night the baggage failed to arrive and over 200 Sikh troops' kit was stolen. The men were left to sleep uncovered in the cold, and some units would spend the next several weeks without tents or cover of any kind during the night, lying exposed to the autumn rains which eventually gave way to snow.

Initially the valley which measures some seven by three miles seemed like a land of plenty and the troops were able to forage for stores of maize, barley, onions, walnuts and honey which had been left by the hurriedly departing inhabitants. There seemed to be plenty of food for their animals too. However, as they progressed the stores became thinner and foraging parties became the subject of attack when they were dispersed and distant from camp. Added to this the Afridis continued their highly effective sniping into the camp at night-time. There was no doubt in the British mind now that they were being outwitted and outfought. Thomsett thought that the British were ill suited to fight in this sort of terrain and that it might be better left to Gurkhas and Sikhs; and the formerly ebullient Times' correspondent despaired that while the Afridis were perfectly happy in their winter home in the lower valleys, their young fighters had within two weeks managed to purloin 20 of the most modern rifles from the British along with the latest bullets, and 200 head of transport animals with all their baggage, 'while all we have done in the way of reprisals is burn their summer residences and seize what forage as they have left behind'.[1] The campaign felt futile and the weather continued to deteriorate adding to their demoralisation. Within days of their arrival thick ice was forming on water overnight, and snow would follow before they left.

Faced with the absence of a population to overawe with their might, the British imperial troops set about the task of destroying houses and anything else they could. The distinctive fortified homes were not easy to demolish, and explosives were needed to level their strong towers. Timber was removed to burn for heat in the camps, and everything which could be removed was taken away. Fruit trees had the bark ring-stripped so causing them to slowly die. Progressing in this manner they eventually came to the mosque at Bagh described excitedly by The Times newspaper correspondent as the base of the mullah who had ordered jihad against the British and the site of the Afridi parliament.[2] It had been envisaged 'as a sort of capital to Maidan', a kernel at the heart of the Afridi highlands which might yield treasures as well as victory.³ They were sorely disappointed with what they found which was described as little more than a mud hut with some crude carvings.⁴

Figure 7. Burning a village in the Maidan Valley

Figure 8. An Afridi village with the distinctive fortified tower

Accounts from the time describe a particular disappointment with not finding anything they could loot as high hopes had been invested in the mosque's imagined riches.⁵ Although looting was restricted to an extent by international treaties, it remained endemic and was considered an essential perk of military campaigning. Loot could range from items taken as souvenirs to valuable artefacts which could be sold on return to 'civilisation'. It would be only a few months later that British soldiers in Benin in west Africa hit the jackpot in this respect when they plundered the famous bronzes, some of which are only now being repatriated. In contrast to the experience of their compatriots in Africa, one disappointed officer in the Tirah recorded that 'beyond an occasional worn out and worm-eaten copy of the Koran, or a jezail or a pathan knife, there was nothing in the way of loot worth taking home as a memento of the campaign'.[6] Despite this protestation, handwritten Qurans were highly prized and sought out in the deserted houses; Thomsett was deeply gratified to receive one as a gift from a recovering patient.[7] The soldiers clearly recognised a value to these holy texts.

*

The cold and wet conditions were beginning to have a significant impact on the health of the invading men who fell ill in increasing numbers. Considerable forethought had been given to the medical arrangements for this campaign with a relatively new system of hospitalisation trialled at scale for the first time. It was recognised that a more mobile warfare required a different approach, and that a series of medical relay stations would be required to get sick and wounded men to the rear for treatment. The planning for these was meticulous as were the calculations required to estimate the number of patients to be expected and the support required for them in terms of transport, medical and other supplies and personnel. These measures involved some duplication as patients were divided along racial lines with Indian troops and officers separated from Europeans.[8] Assessments made after the war concluded that the system had been a success and that fatalities were in line with expectations. The method was subsequently used in the South African and First World Wars.

The resources given over to the men's health were well aimed as troops were under far more danger from disease than they were from the enemy. This is borne out by the names of those on Oxford's Tirah Memorial where all but four of the 60 men listed as dying on the north west frontier did so because of disease. These were only the men who had actually died of disease and the number who fell sick was far higher. Over the course of the winter 1,000 men were hospitalised due to injuries sustained, but 11,000 were admitted due to disease of whom fully two-thirds never recovered sufficiently to rejoin their units.[9] Although there were more Indian troops by a factor of approximately two to one, the hospitalisation rate was higher for Europeans as they were less able to withstand the climatic conditions and had less immunity to the associated illnesses.

The cause of this disease was principally poor sanitary conditions, especially contaminated water which led to high rates of dysentery and typhoid fever. It was known that impure water was the cause of these diseases but it proved impossible in practice to do much about it in the field. An example has already been given of men having to drink muddy water as their supplies of clean water had not arrived. Likewise, instructions were issued to avoid both bathing and drinking in the same river water, and there was an awareness that animals were polluting the drinking water. In practice the men could not boil water before drinking it as they often lacked the means to do so, and the sparsely available filtration equipment was clumsy, slow and not considered to be particularly effective.

The rate of decline of those affected could be alarmingly rapid. Lieutenant J.G Fitzgerald of the Oxfordshire Light Infantry is one of those whose names is commemorated in the city; he was admitted to hospital on 30th November and died 20 days later. Ten days after this, another Lieutenant, H.W.B. Trench, died of typhoid and pneumonia after suffering a fortnight's illness. He was aged 24. They are just two of the 600 British troops who died of disease.[10]

These rates of hospitalisation and mortality were considered unavoidable, and in line with the estimates made at the outset. They would be even higher in the South African or Boer War which followed two years later when an astonishing 96% of men fell ill at some point, and 100,000 were hospitalised for bowel infections.[11] The number of killed and wounded at 6,425 was far outstripped by those who died of disease at 11,237.[12] Again, the cause was poor sanitation and drinking water.

Throughout the nineteenth and eighteenth centuries vastly more soldiers and sailors died of disease than of injuries sustained in fighting, and this prompted a turn in medical science towards considering how such diseases could be prevented in the first place, rather than just trying to treat and alleviate the symptoms. An early vaccine against typhoid was developed by 1896 but it was not widely available at the time of the Tirah campaign. Notably, it was first tested on Indian soldiers in South Africa before it was offered to British troops.[13] Indeed, India became a focus for scientists testing vaccines among the local population in the late nineteenth century and became a centre for the production of vaccines for use throughout the Empire.[14]

This concern to prevent diseases led to a debate around their causes. Two opposing schools of thought were that on the one hand that they were due to poor environmental conditions such as bad ventilation or sanitation; and on the other hand that disease spread by infectious germs which had recently been identified by scientists. Florence Nightingale, a superb statistician and inventor of the infographic, was a passionate believer in the benefits of improved environments, and scathing about the validity of the theory that germs were vectors of disease to the extent that she was one of the original anti-vaxers. This new focus on environmental causes of disease and concern for public health resulted in the first sanitary act being introduced in Liverpool in 1846, but it would be another 50 years before the British introduced similar measures for their Indian subjects.[15]

It is widely recognised that one of the benefits of western imperialism was the introduction and dissemination of western medicine. What is less often appreciated is that this was a reciprocal process with British and other Europeans learning a great deal from foreign contact which enabled them to progress medical science. As well as using native populations as the subjects for experimentation, Europeans were keenly interested in local medicinal plants and their use. As early as the seventeenth century a physician with the East India Company called Samuel Browne collected and sent samples of such plants back to Britain where they remain in the Natural History Museum. Medicines derived from Indian plants were stocked and advertised by apothecaries, and prescribed by doctors.[16] A similar interest was taken in Chinese medicine. A cabinet stocked with surgical instruments and medicines was sent back to Hans Sloane in Britain who shared the knowledge it contained with members of the Royal Society. The use of quinine as a prophylactic against malaria is another example and has already been mentioned in connection with the Tirah campaign. This is derived from the bark of the Chinchona tree native to South America.

*

Although we know something about the lives of the four lieutenants who died of disease and are remembered on the Tirah Memorial we know very little about the lance-corporal, three buglers and 24 privates who met the same fate. The lieutenants came from a higher echelon of society, were privately educated at Marlborough and Cheltenham Colleges and had progressed through the officer training school at Sandhurst to reach their rank. They were in the early days of their military careers, with at least one of them following his father into the Indian army. Given their rank and status, short obituaries were published in relevant military journals and newspapers.

The lives of the privates are much more elusive, and their reasons for joining up were likely to have been significantly different. The global economy experienced what was termed at the time as the 'great depression' from 1876 through to the end of the century. Britain was especially hard hit by this with losses recorded in financial and manufacturing businesses, but it hit hardest in agriculture where grain prices suffered a dramatic fall following the development of prairie lands for arable farming in Canada and north America. Many rural people flocked to find work in cities exacerbating the slum conditions found there. Joining the army was an obvious route out of poverty but it was not a popular one, nor the first choice of most of those who signed up. According to one contemporary observer it was 'the least desirable and worst paid of employments'.[17]

Thanks to the research of Stephanie Jenkins it has been possible to recover something of the lives of three of the privates on the Tirah Memorial. That is has been possible to discover records for only three of the men speaks of the lack of regard and status that such men held. William Godliman was in a reform school working as a farm labourer at the age of 13; when he was 20 he signed up with the Oxfordshire Light Infantry and was awarded the India Medal in 1895. He died of typhoid shortly after the conclusion of the Tirah campaign aged 23. George Radbourn was recorded working as a ploughboy aged ten, joined the military aged 25 and was immediately sent to India where he died of typhoid a few weeks after Godliman. Thomas Wiggins was an agricultural labourer who joined up at 17, giving his age as 19, and was also immediately sent to India. He died of typhoid aged 21.[18] These were men who had probably joined up from a situation of hopelessness or desperation, and were fighting in a war far from home in extremely difficult conditions. Referring back to the words of Oxford's mayor at the Tirah Memorial's unveiling, they might well have not 'feared to face death itself in honour of and to the glory of their God, their Queen and their country'. But dying of typhoid is a curious way to serve one's country.

*

General Lockhart had been chosen to lead the campaign for his diplomatic skills as well as for his soldiering abilities. He had experience of punitive raids against Pashtun and other factions, but also of negotiating terms of reparations and surrender. Moreover, he was backed up by an extensive political or intelligence staff who maintained contact with the various interests and looked for a way through to resolution of the action.[19] To this end he had called for a meeting with the elders of the warring parties in the traditional manner at a jirgah. The Orakzais responded that they were ready to come to terms, but only a minority of Afridis did so, and the intended full jirgah failed to take place. Meanwhile winter was closing in and the continuing presence of the occupying forces in the highlands was untenable. Lockhart had no choice but to withdraw. Making the most of a bad situation he issued a warning and invitation to the recalcitrant Afridis.

> *I am going away from these highlands of Maidan because the snow is coming and I do not wish my troops to be exposed to the cold of winter. But I am not going to leave your country. On the contrary I am going to remain in your country until you fully comply with the terms of government, and it is my intention to attack you in your other settlements during the winter. Whatever your evil advisers may tell you, I say that the Afridis attacking the English is like flies assailing a lion, and, as an old friend of many of you, my advice to you is to submit, and let your wives and families return from the cold mountains to their homes'.*[20]

Figure 9. Jirgah with Orakzai. Lockhart centre right back to camera

To add force to this statement he made what would prove to be a disastrous decision to retreat via the Bara valley, the winter quarters of the Afridi, in one last attempt to assert authority over them with the presence of British imperial forces in their territory. This would surely make them see the futility of 'prolonging a struggle so disastrous to themselves'.[21]

The retreat through the ten-mile long Bara valley began on 7th December and it was decided to take the minimal amount of baggage to expedite the passage back down to Peshawar, and to avoid some of the attacks that had been so prevalent and so effective against the supply transport. This included taking no tents. For three days and two nights all went well and there was no attack on the withdrawing column. But this was because the local factions had been paid off by the political officers to allow safe passage. They had not been so successful with the hardline factions further down the valley, and over the following four days the column found itself having to traverse extremely difficult terrain under continuous attack. They frequently had to cross the fast-flowing and freezing waters of the river Bara to make progress, wading waist deep, sometimes recrossing it ten times to cover a mile of forward progress. At night without tents they and the animals endured heavy rain and sleet, and the ground became impassibly muddy due to the enormous traffic. This particularly impacted on the pack animals which slipped, shed their loads, and became stuck. They too suffered from cold and fear as they were also the target of sniping. The impact on their handlers was even greater however, with some of them driven to the borders of insanity. The men recruited from Madras who along with the others lacked the necessary clothes and blankets, were also completely unused to cold and became numb with fear and cold, unable to carry out their tasks.[22] When wider stretches of the valley were encountered a rush forward happened as each tried to get ahead to escape, sometimes abandoning their loads and mules in the process. When narrower stretches were reached the passage became blocked by everyone trying to get through and not get left at the rear. The stretcher-bearers too abandoned their loads of wounded men as they became physically unable to continue. Consequently, when a soldier was wounded, it required an additional four enlisted soldiers to carry him on a stretcher and another to carry his rifle to prevent it falling into enemy hands. In all six men were taken from fighting for every incapacitated soldier, so adding to the burden of the remaining troops. Some of the rear-guard porters were stripped of their clothes and left to die of exposure by the enemy, while others seized the rum casks and drank themselves to death. The Afridis were relentless in their attacks, both during the day and at night, which seemed to increase in frequency and severity as the retreating forces became more and more debilitated. There had been no losses on the scale of this journey since the Great Rebellion of 1857 or even the First Afghan War.[23]

When the surviving men finally reached camp the reaction of their waiting comrades to their condition was one of shock and disbelief. Lt. Col. Thomsett wrote that the sight 'almost beggared description', as he watched for six hours their passing by. The men had bare legs red from exposure, lacking socks or puttees, and wearing broken boots looked 'gaunt and rugged, with their faces and hands almost black, and many of them devouring hunches of bread which had just been handed to them as they entered our camp'. He noticed that there was little to no organisation evident, and that the sick were mixed up with the able and were suffering agonies from their handling. The Times' correspondent noted that 'It was more a despairing sight than a military spectacle', the men were all 'drawn, pinched, dishevelled and thoroughly worn out'. Many remarked that it looked more like the retreat from Moscow of Napoleon's army.[24]

*

Recriminations began almost immediately. Although Churchill wrote defensively of the campaign in a letter to The Times of India that 'the army receives the humble submissions of the most ferocious savages in Asia', he was more forthcoming in a letter to his mother in which he wrote, 'the whole expedition was a mistake as it relied on tribesmen giving in when their country was invaded and their property destroyed. This they have not done …. It is because we have no real means – except by prolonged occupation – of putting the screw on these tribesmen and making them give in that it is a mistake to make the attempt'.[25] He was not the only future prime minister to be enraged at the outcome. Neville Chamberlain, who had himself served on the north-west frontier, published a highly satirical letter lauding that 'henceforth profound peace is to reign along the frontier'.[26] Officers involved in the campaign also turned on their leaders, publishing highly critical accounts of the supply situation and top-heavy command structure. One officer admitted that their foe was 'a nation of skilled marksmen, masters of guerrilla warfare, amply provided with arms and ammunition, inhabiting a country as difficult as any in the world [who] for months… set at defiance the might of the British Empire'.[27] The domestic press was also scathing with one article sufficiently alarmed to question the financial viability of the Indian Government as a consequence of the cost of the expedition, and highlighting that the British nation would have been quick to condemn the type of actions undertaken in its name if they had been carried out by Russia in central Asia.[28]

Lockhart's final despatch tried to put a positive spin on the outcome,

> *The troops under my command have marched everywhere within the Orakzai and Afridi limits, and the whole of Tirah has now for the first time been accurately surveyed. Our enemies wherever encountered have been punished, and their losses are stated on unimpeachable evidence to have been extremely severe. The towers and walls of almost every fortified village in the country have been levelled to the ground, and the winter supply of grain, fodder, and fuel of both tribes has been consumed by the force. The Orakzai have been completely subdued and have complied with the terms prescribed for them, but the Afridis still hold out, although I have strong hopes that they may before long submit*.[29]

Nevertheless, it appeared to everyone, not least the Afridis themselves, like a British defeat. The uncomfortable fact was that the British certainly couldn't have been said to have won, nor to have demonstrated superior leadership, tactics or technology, or to have achieved the elusive aim of restoring their prestige. It was clear that they had underestimated the enemy and overestimated their own effectiveness. Arguably, rather than restoring prestige they had undermined it still further. The flies had seen off the lion.

*

The political officers continued their work over the weeks following the withdrawal and peace of a sort was eventually brokered with the Afridis in early spring. They agreed to return rifles and pay reparations in cash, and in return the British did not return to their territory in the Maidan as had been threatened. However, all was not quite what it seemed as it was widely believed, probably correctly, that the recalcitrant Afridis had been paid by a mysteriously funded third party for surrendering their rifles. In other words, they had been paid off. The political officers were good at their job and both sides could end the conflict claiming victory.

The Khyber Pass was garrisoned by British-Indian troops for a few years until 1901 when the new viceroy returned to the status quo ante of employing the Pashtun-derived Kyhber Rifles to do the job. British forces continued to be engaged in fighting Pashtun factions with wearying regularity: in 1900, 1902, 1908, 1914-15, 1917, 1919-22, 1927, 1930-31, 1935, and 1936-39; even well into the 1940s they were endeavouring to track down the 'fakir' or leader of a jihad launched against imperial troops.[30] In 1947 with the British withdrawal from governance of India, the Pashtun people were not given their preferred option of a nation state of their own and voted to join with the new country of Pakistan. More recently British troops invaded Afghanistan in November 2001, and whilst the majority left in 2014, the final troops were not withdrawn until 2021.

There are obvious parallels between the Tirah campaign and more recent wars in Afghanistan, not least the names of the places where the action took place. To these can be added the use of an intended overwhelming military force with superior technology to defeat the enemy, along with the failure of this approach in the face of masterful use of the terrain and guerrilla tactics. The use of intelligence and the exploitation of divisions within society to recruit different factions both in support of, and in opposition to the invading army is also familiar. So too is a fear of a masterminding 'mad mullah' type figure, in the more recent case Osama bin Laden. Likewise, a fear of the threat and reality of global jihad becoming embedded was a major concern for western powers. Finally, the attempt to govern through local politicians, and the recruitment of indigenous para-military forces was no more successful in the twenty- first century than it was in the nineteenth.

The cost of the Tirah operation was £2.4 million which was borne by the Indian government. The British imperial forces suffered losses of 1,437 men of whom 287 were killed. It is not possible to ascertain losses for camp followers, although at least one report stated that they had higher incidences of dysentery so they may be higher than those of the regular troops. Similarly, the losses of the defending inhabitants cannot be ascertained, but losses in fighting were considerably below those of the British forces.[31]

There is a curious coda to this particular imperial war when the departing General Lockhart was accompanied to the train station by a crowd of 500 cheering but previously hostile Afridis who insisted on pulling his carriage. This can be interpreted in various ways. To some it was a demonstration of their respect for the general and evidence that British prestige was triumphant after all, showing the 'thorough goodwill of the tribesmen' towards their British masters.[32] To others it showed that the Pashtuns acknowledged the British as their honourable equals and that it was a sort of after-match handshake with the opposing team.[33] The Afridis could equally be seen however as cheering the departure of their defeated foe in an ironic, even mocking manner, and celebrating the retention of their cherished independence.

In 1898, one year after the huge national celebrations for

Queen Victoria's jubilee, Britain was still an uninvited and largely unwanted foreign presence in India, imposing a military state without reference to the local population's wishes, and benefitting from an enormous market for its production. Britain continued to exploit the sub-continent's mineral resources especially coal, and had established large scale commercial plantations for growing coffee, tea, sugar, indigo and jute; the enormous oil and timber resources of Burma had also been swallowed into the imperial Indian domain when the country was given as a new year gift to Queen Victoria.[34]

To secure all of this against perceived external Russian and Islamic threats, Britain invaded neighbouring Pashtun lands to assert its hegemony, and faced a population which fought back tenaciously and ultimately successfully to preserve their independence.

*

Lt. Col. Thomsett could not have been happier. The weather had warmed up, he had enjoyed his first bath in months, had managed to catch up with some old friends, and now by a stroke of luck had got himself a lift back to his longed-for home and its inviting verandah. Just as he was about to depart Thomsett was approached by a dark eyed Afridi from the Khyber Pass. He gratefully accepted a bunch of violets from what he described as 'the most beautiful boy I have ever seen', his former punkah coolie.

INTERLUDE

5: FOUNDATIONS

The Tirah Memorial in Oxford is built on land which had previously formed the churchyard of the parish church of St Peter-le-Bailey. During excavations for its foundations a large number of what were delicately termed 'animal bones' were recovered, some of the larger ones being transferred to a nearby cemetery. In order to supply a solid base in this cluttered ground for what was to be a heavy and tall structure above, it was found to be necessary to dig foundations of over 20 feet in depth, almost the same height as the monument itself.[1] The foundations are embedded deep but hidden in the city, as too is the legacy of Empire.

*

The Oxford University Press is a prestigious publisher which began printing around 1478, shortly after the introduction of the new technology into the country. Today it employs more than 6,000 people and has offices in over 50 countries. It is the largest university press in the world and its revenue is an important income stream for the university, part of which is used to fund bursaries for students. As would be expected with such a long history, the company has had its ups and downs through the years and on occasion came perilously close to folding. However, the Press had one major advantage over its rivals which was an agreement reached in the seventeenth century to the rights to print the new King James' Bible. With the growth in missionary and evangelical activity in the nineteenth century increasing the demand for bibles and related literature this was to catapult the hitherto sleepy regional firm to stupendous growth.

In 1796 the press sold just over 136,000 copies of the Bible, in 1846 sales were just short of one and a half million and by the end of the century were approaching three million. The largest customer for these by far was the British and Foreign Bible Society which by 1865 accounted for more two thirds of the OUP's output. These were then shipped out to South Africa and other British colonies for schooling the heathen. In 1894 its warehouse was described as a 'great centre of industrial activity' from where 'many millions of copies of the Holy Scriptures have been distributed to every quarter of the civilised and uncivilised world'.[2] The number of employees needed to cope with this growth, and the profits flowing back to the University, increased accordingly. The Oxford University Press had become the vast company with the international presence it still retains.

It also led to the firm's senior partner, Thomas Coombe, becoming a very wealthy man. He was a supporter of the so-called 'high church' movement which favoured a traditional Catholic style liturgy and decoration in churches, and he and his wife encouraged and patronised artists who looked to an older style for their inspiration in accordance with his principles. The Pre-Raphaelite school of painters benefited greatly from his interest. Artists such as John Everett Millais, William Holman Hunt and Dante Gabriel Rossetti were hosted by the Coombes at Christmas. The Coombes were enthusiastic buyers of their early work and John Everett Millais painted the family's portrait. On the death of his widow the Coombe's collection of their works was bequeathed to the Ashmolean Museum where it remains displayed in its own gallery.

A little further along the street in the inner suburb of Jericho where the press had its factory, was another company which benefited from the imperial market. Lucy's ironworks was established as an iron-monger around 1760 but had grown to become a great guzzler of coal and producer of cast iron at its Jericho foundry established in 1825. It produced iron street furniture among other products, and its lampposts were exported to Port Elizabeth and Johannesburg in South Africa.[3] Lucy's has left lamppost manufacturing far behind, but still thrives, employing 1,500 and operating in 70 countries.

To the north of Oxford in Banbury, the firm of Barrows & Co. was also operating an iron-foundry where it produced a range of products including threshing machines and mobile steam engines. The company was a major exporter to Australia, India and South America and also contracted with the government War Office and India Office. In 1881 it was providing employment for 100 men and boys.[4]

Another similar firm, The Oxford Steam Plough Company operated from a site in Cowley in Oxford. These steam-driven engines worked in pairs and were considerably quicker and more efficient than using horses to plough. The company sold its engines in Canada and was later bought up by John Allen who developed a prototype armoured train for use in the South African Boer War (1899-1902), as well as supplying the war office with traction engines and trucks for use there in hauling munitions.[5]

Frank Cooper's distinctive 'Oxford Marmalade' is still sold although it is no longer produced in Oxford. The first jars are said to have been produced in 1874 by Mrs Cooper and management of the business passed to her and Frank's son in 1894. By 1901 sales were sufficiently robust that it moved to a purpose-built factory near the train station from where it received coal, sugar and oranges which were then processed and shipped out to all corners of the Empire. The marmalade acquired an exalted status with royal endorsement, and became emblematic of the British abroad with a tin even accompanying the iconic explorer Scott on his ill-fated expedition to the Antarctic.

The nearby town of Witney to the west of the city is particularly proud of its heritage in producing blankets. The works of the firm of Early and Co. dominated the town in the late nineteenth century where it employed 400 people. The wool it used came from Australia, New Zealand, and east India, and it sold its blankets widely into the Empire including Bermuda, Newfoundland and Australia.[6] The Board of Ordnance was also a major customer.[7] Early's is a text-book example of the imperial model of sourcing raw materials from the Empire and exporting back value-added manufacture. Its success would enable members of the Early family to engage more directly in the Empire by setting up a branch in South Africa and buying property and farmland there.[8]

Oxford and its shire are not renown as industrial centres. These few examples show how even in a relative industrial backwater, and in rurally based communities, jobs and profits were derived from Britain's imperial world. Its reach and depth was much greater in the northern industrial areas of the country which stood at their zenith, and in the financial City of London - the pulsing, beating heart of Empire.

The beneficial flows of wealth lapped far beyond the workers' terraces or conservatively minded Anglican patrons of the arts. The University itself was to be the beneficiary on a grand scale from the generosity of the arch-imperialist Cecil Rhodes, whose now controversial statue surveys the High Street. As well as funding the building at Oriel College from which his effigy gazes down, he also established the Rhodes Trust, a philanthropic fund to train future leaders of the British Empire.

Oriel's connections with Empire are surpassed only by that of Balliol College. Established in 1263 it burst to prominence in the late nineteenth century as a powerhouse of Empire, particularly in relation to India, producing scores of men who went to work in Indian administration. By 1884 fully half of those training for the Indian civil service were at Balliol.[9] The college was also at the forefront of attracting and educating Indian students and in establishing a University department for the study of the subcontinent. The fees for educating its Indian members and the salaries of its graduates in India were paid for by the Indian government (whose tax base relied heavily on trade in opium as we have seen). Balliol also produced three successive viceroys of India and can count among its alumnae Sir Michael O' Dwyer who sanctioned the Amritsar massacre of unarmed civilians in 1919. The university was therefore not just a passive beneficiary of legacies but was actively engaged in the dissemination and enabling of Empire.

Economic historians remain divided about whether the Empire was a net benefit or cost to Britain. And if it was, the extent to which it was. Frustratingly, for them, it was both a net cost and a net benefit, but at different times and in different places, so making any overall assessment all but impossible. What is clear however is that at the micro-level people in Oxford, Oxfordshire and Britain got up to go to work in the mornings, or picked up their paintbrushes at their easels, or sat down to their studies because of the opportunities and markets that had been opened up to them by the men commemorated on the Tirah Memorial – including Major Thruston, who we are about to meet.

PART II

The Dark Continent

6: AFRICAN PEARL

It's a long way from the biting cold of the Afghan mountains to the steamy heat of the Ugandan tropics, as the men of the 27th Bombay Light Infantry found out. In January 1898 they were suddenly pulled from their deployment alongside the Oxfordshire Light Infantry in the Peshawar Column stationed in the Khyber Pass, and assigned to fight in Uganda. The reason for their unexpected arrival in Africa is bound up with the fate of the first name inscribed on the Tirah Memorial in central Oxford who it is recorded was 'killed by mutineers in Uganda'

Arthur Blyford Thruston had not even wanted to be a soldier. As a boy he was described as 'delicate, quiet and rather serious', and he himself admitted that he lacked courage at school where he excelled in ancient languages and classics. He was a proficient artist too. In later life he reflected that he would have preferred to continue his studies at university going on to win a fellowship, or to be an inspector of schools leisurely travelling around England, or a parson with a comfortable living.[1] But the choice was not his to make and he went to officer training college at the age of 17.

On passing out he joined the Oxfordshire Light Infantry as a lieutenant and served with them in Limerick, Gibraltar and Egypt where he caught typhoid fever and was sufficiently ill to be invalided home. After recovering he returned to join his regiment in Bangalore where he learned Hindi, but was struck down by severe illness, probably malaria, and was again invalided home to Cowley barracks in Oxford in 1887 aged 22.

Two bouts of serious illness and his travels had changed him profoundly. He read widely about Hinduism and Buddhism, and was impressed by them as he would later be by Islam. He studied Turkish and Arabic and passed interpreter exams in both. As time went on, he spent more time away from England and became increasingly cynical both about his compatriots and what he was fighting for. He evolved very far from the two-dimensional, cartoonish figure we might imagine emerging from those two great factories of imperial leadership, Marlborough College and Sandhurst.

Figure 10. Major A.B. Thruston wearing the tarboosh as an officer of the Egyptian army

He also became tougher, characterised by a wiry frame and formidable skill at both horse and camel riding. In 1890 he joined the Egyptian army and developed a great admiration for the Sudanese troops under his command. He resigned his commission in disgust when he was ordered to abandon a fort he had laboured to build in the heat alongside his men, and the leaving of which left him in breach of the promise he had made to the local population that the British would stay to defend them against Islamic fundamentalists.

He returned to England thinking that his career was over, and was surprised when he was asked to join a commission to Uganda. He journeyed there for the first time in 1893 when he was aged 28, and was involved in a campaign against a prominent leader called Kabalega. However, his health again failed and he returned to England the following year where he was promoted to the rank of major, and received the Star of Zanzibar and the Africa medal. After recovering he undertook a course of surveying and was then sent to the north-west provinces of India. From there he was posted back to Egypt in charge of Arab troops which he led in actions against the Islamic fundamentalists, or dervishes as they were then called, who were harassing the British presence in Sudan. He then returned to Uganda as second in command of the Uganda Rifles, a body of Sudanese to whom he became very close, and for whom he had great admiration. Unlike most of his fellow officers, he was not only fluent in their language and sympathetic to their religion, but had come to respect them and their culture, and to doubt and even openly challenge the principles which he, as an officer of her majesty's Empire had been inculcated since birth. He was the last person anyone expected to be killed by his own troops, a belief shared by himself, and most surprisingly by his troops who had sworn their loyalty to him just days before he was taken and shot dead. He was 32.

To understand the reasons for this we need to retrace the reasons why he and the British were in Uganda.

*

The modern country of Uganda is a creation of the British in 1890. It incorporated four pre-existing and separate kingdoms of Buganda, Bunyoro, Ankole and Toro.[2] Buganda, the land of the Baganda people, was the largest of these in terms of area and had a long history of warring and raiding with the neighbouring and second largest kingdom of Bunyoro, the homeland of the Banyoro people. The former was about twice the size of Ireland, and the latter about the same size; Toro was about a quarter of its size and the remaining territory smaller still.[3]

Uganda sits around and to the northern end of Lake Victoria and to the east of Lake Albert. Today it is bordered to the east by Kenya, to the north by South Sudan, to the west by the Democratic Republic of the Congo, and to the south by Rwanda and Tanzania. Before this division into national territories the region was more amorphously encompassed in a British Protectorate, that is to say it was not ruled directly by Britain, but its kings had 'agreed' to their foreign affairs being conducted by Britain, and to take its 'advice' on matters of governance and diplomacy. The Protectorate of British East Africa covered the island of Zanzibar (incorporated in 1890), Buganda (1894) and Bunyoro, Toro, Ankole and present-day Kenya (1895). In other words, it ran from the coast to the shores of Lake Albert. Prior to this it had been claimed by Britain as part of its African sphere of influence, a concept which was brokered among European powers to accord them exclusive control and oversight of particular, but loosely defined territories. A German sphere of influence existed to the south in modern day Tanzania, a French sphere in northern Africa and in parts of west Africa, and the Belgium king was the personal owner of the Congo including present day Rwanda.

In terms of the terrain and climate, Uganda was reached by transit from Mombasa on the east coast of Kenya. There was no railway, no meaningful roads, and passage was made with caravans comprised mainly of very large numbers of hired porters who walked. The first 200 miles from the coast consisted of 'dreary, tangled and thorny scrub' and was malarial but not excessively so; thereafter it climbed steadily to the highlands of Kikuyu, in modern day Kenya, which were much colder and considered to be an excellent climate for Europeans.[4] The route then descended to Masai country where the people were hostile, before rising to its highest point in the Mau mountains, and then again descending into Buganda which was a mixture of open hills and swampy ground, and was highly malarial. The journey was both long and taxing. Only around 12 miles a day was the usual rate of progress and the journey from Mombasa to Buganda consequently took a minimum of two and a half months, and could be up to four. Most of the provisions for sustenance during the march had to be carried in the caravan as there was no source of food, and often no suitably clean water during the passage. Deaths and illness among the porters were common, and Europeans, although at times mounted on donkeys, suffered similarly from dysentery, lung infections, malaria and ulcers which given the climate could quickly develop from scratches.

There was nothing intrinsic to Uganda that attracted the British. Despite it later somewhat optimistically being promoted as 'the pearl of Africa', early surveys could see no benefit in it other than being a potential market for British manufactures at some distant point in the future. In 1898 the British Treasury complained at the cost of retaining Uganda, a territory which had yet to yield any significant revenue.[5] Attempts to develop large scale commercial farming for cash export crops had failed. This is reflected in figures for exports which show that in 1903, 80% of their value was in the form of elephant tusks, although this was in decline as stocks were 'exhausted' in the words of an official report.[6] The author of the report also thought that 'it would be ridiculous to recommend a European to settle in East Africa'.[7]

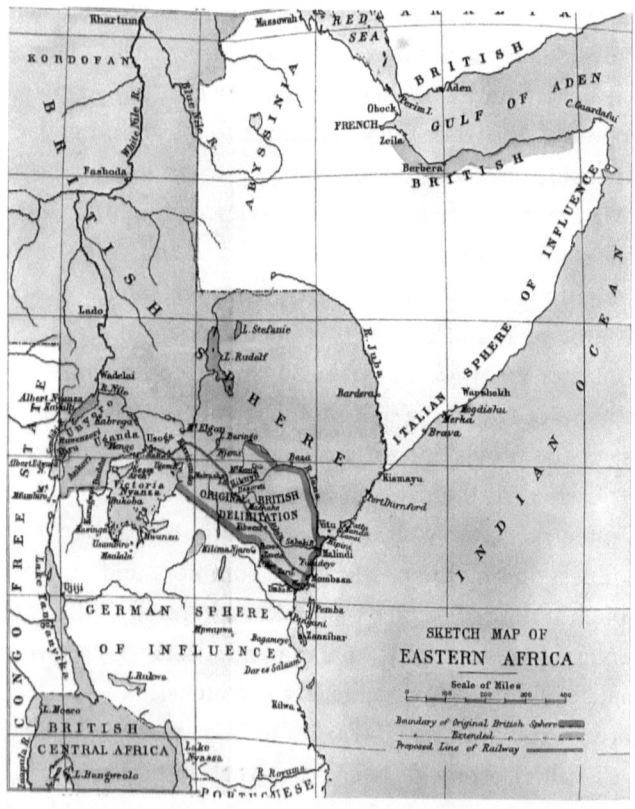

Figure 11. British East Africa 1892

Compared to other parts of its Empire, British interest in the region was relatively recent. The first white men had not appeared there until 1862. The reason for this was that it was nearly impossible for them to survive the endemic diseases found in a region which was popularly known as 'the white man's graveyard'. Malaria, dysentery, blackwater fever and cholera took an alarming toll on those venturing into central Africa. An expedition led by Mungo Park along the river Niger in 1805 returned with just four left alive of the 44 Europeans who had departed.[8] Thirty-six years later a steamship expedition along the same river resulted in 130 Europeans falling severely ill, and 50 dying out of the 145 who sailed.[9] It wasn't to be until 1854 that a journey was completed along the Niger with no loss of European life.

Advances made in preventing, rather than treating, diseases gradually came to reduce these terrible odds, particularly after 1870 when medicines in soluble or tablet form became available for the traveller.[10] Whilst medicine enabled Europeans to penetrate into central Africa, and would be used by them to gain converts in their missionary endeavours among Africans, Europeans also introduced new diseases to the interior of the continent which had a devastating effect on local populations, including measles, plague, whooping-cough and venereal disease.[11]

Even with modern medicines however, the climate was still considered unsuitable for Europeans to settle permanently as it was 'enervating' and malarial.[12] At the start of the twentieth century European children were removed from the country at the earliest opportunity, and it was believed that long term settlement would lead to degenerative racial decline among the white settlers.[13] Even as late as 1922 an informed writer advised that children should be removed when they approached adolescence on the grounds that 'constant association with the natives, who are, in regard to sexual instincts, as yet but little higher than animals, is bound insidiously to sow seeds of moral corruption.'[14] Uganda was not therefore thought suitable for establishing a white settler colony as had been the case in north America, Australia, New Zealand and South Africa.

The settlement point is an important one as it was widely believed that Britain needed to export its surplus population by planting colonies overseas. There was a Malthusian belief that it could not sustain its level of population growth for want of a sufficient food supply, and that failure to address this would lead to catastrophe. Ever mindful of the threat of political unrest and dissension there was a particular class of people that were deemed to be most suitable for this one-way trip to what were seen as virgin lands ripe for exploitation. Speaking at a meeting of the Society for the Propagation of the Gospel held at the Clarendon Hotel in Oxford in 1884, the bishop of Carlisle remarked that those colonising were not dukes and country squires but 'the poor who were pinched out and pressed out'. 'The very principle of colonisation', he was reported as saying, 'was that a man could leave his home here - perhaps a very rough and uncomfortable one - and find a grand improvement in his position and livelihood as he never could have had if he had remained in the old country - that was why he recommended men to go to a new country where there was plenty of room for all those who chose to go'. He asked his audience if they were prepared to see the University Parks ploughed over and given to the growing of corn, and to laughter explained the necessity of expanding overseas. If his audience would care to look at an atlas they would see 'dear old England, that tight little island, like a spot in the northern part of the map' while there were 'great continents to the east and west which might lose a little chip from one corner as big as England and never know the difference'. He had no doubt that Great Britain would 'throw out her swarms of people to take possession of the whole face of the earth and subdue it to a great extent to the dominion of their Sovereign the Queen'.[15] This need to export people was not confined to Britain. East Africa was seen by the British as an 'America' for the Hindu from British held India, a boundless empty land waiting for colonisation, and Indian emigration was encouraged as the British moved people around the chess board of their Empire without reference to the host populations.[16]

In summary Uganda was difficult to reach, lacked resources to exploit and was unsuitable for settlement by Europeans. What it did have, and what made it irresistible in the eyes of many, was far more valuable: human souls.

7: MISSION FEVER

No one had ever seen anything quite like it.

The splendidly ornate town hall opened just two years previously was packed from morning till night with a mixture of the curious, the ignorant, the learned and earnest proselytisers. The main room had been ingeniously divided into various 'courts' where one could view the objects, each with a label attached to explain what it was and its use. The East African court contained,

> the possessions of a martyred Christian bishop, 'King Lokonge's throne, a chief's throne made from the vertebrae of a whale, bark clothing from Uganda, Luganda bible in a biscuit tin, an east African 'piano' the music which is produced by striking a number of wooden balls with a stick, a model of a Wanika hut, a gold mounted Arab sword presented to commander Ogle by the sultan of Zanzibar, an Arab sword with a silver studded hilt taken at the capture of a slave dhow, and a number of banners full of shot holes bearing Arabic inscriptions and verses from the Koran, a medicine man's harp obtained with great difficulty by Sir John Kirk used in incantations, a number of silver nose, foot, finger and toe-rings, an autographed letter of General Gordon's with portrait, native cloth, various articles of domestic use, a preserved python, cone and leaves of the silver tree, assegai and drum used in the last Kaffir war, necklace from Basutoland, bone comb, spears and shields of the

> *Angoni tribe, Royal spears from Uganda, Mengo chief's staves, Masai war head-dress, drum, spear and shield, the executioner's robe from Uganda, and a number of instruments illustrating the horrors of the slave trade such as bilboes, manacles, chain, whip and slave yoke, the latter weighing about 30lbs, an iron collar which was taken off a slave, and a slave driver's stick of hippo hide.[1]*

And that was just the East African court. There were further areas given over to West Africa, India, China, Australasia, North America, South America and Japan, as well as a Mohammedan court covering the countries of Palestine, Egypt and Persia. In all over 3,000 objects could be viewed. It was such a large exhibition that it spilled over into the galleries and adjoining rooms and was described by the bishop of Oxford in his opening speech before the heads of colleges and town worthies as a strange, wonderful, interesting and amusing collection.[2]

The ticket price secured more than just looking at strange and unfamiliar objects. There were regular concerts on the enormous, new Willis organ, and violin, cello and piano recitals along with song recitals by notable amateurs. 'Lantern lectures' with projections on a screen, as well as more regular lectures were held; a room was given over to paintings and photographs of China; a sale of work by various ladies from the surrounding counties as well as Oxford itself was held in the assembly room. In front of the organ a full-sized replica of the women's quarters in a Bengali gentleman's house had been erected, in which women of the Zenana Missionary Society used life sized models to explain the life and customs of the women in the zenanas of north India. Similarly, a Miss Sach discoursed on the costumes of the Palestinians using live models.³

Each day of the six-day event began with a speech by an eminent figure such as the vice-chancellor of the University, the dean of the cathedral or the lord high chancellor of England. There is no record of the number of attendees, but it was an enormous success and raised over £550 in the first three days. As well as the large number purchasing tickets, there were a striking number involved in putting on the exhibition with 800 stewards in attendance, as well as the numerous people who had lent items for display, and the many performers in different guises. For this was not a commercial venture but an event held to celebrate and raise funds for the centenary of the Society for the Propagation of the Gospel.⁴

This exhibition tells us how deeply the Empire had penetrated into people's lives and homes by the end of the nineteenth century. All of the items were privately owned, none were from museum collections, and they were loaned by people living in a small geographical area. There was clearly an enormous interest and curiosity about colonial cultures which veered towards the macabre at times. However, the public were not just being invited to view them as entertainment or for education, they were not there just as neutral observers of foreign cultures, they were also being encouraged to become engaged in the imperialising mission, whether as direct actors or by providing funds. It was the proud boast of the organisers that over 1,600 British students, men and women, had signed a declaration to become missionaries. The exhibition's 'great object... was to show the great and vast needs of the heathen world', according to the opening remarks of the minister. The Christian duty of British subjects was to spread the word of the gospels and reap a harvest of souls.⁵

This evangelical fervour was no niche or side stream in

contemporary society, but flowed broad and deep. Stimulated by evangelical movements in the United States there was an upsurge in religious enthusiasm in the last decades of the nineteenth century which reenergised existing missionary societies. This was led by non-conformist churches and later gained traction with the established Church of England. The Society for the Propagation of the Gospel, which had organised the Oxford exhibition, was one of a number of similar organisations including the Church Missionary Society which played a crucial role in Uganda as we shall see.

Interest in missionary activity in Africa was closely tied up with popular campaigns against the slave trade. Although Britain had abolished slavery within its territories in 1830 it remained widespread in central Africa led by Arab traders, who it was thought were trafficking as many as 70,000 people a year.[6] Arab traders were of course Muslim, so another layer of antagonism was added to the mix which further fired enthusiasm for the cause of missionary activity.

Above all though, it was the huge celebrity status of a Scottish missionary, David Livingstone, that drove large numbers of people to want to emulate him, or to support those who did. His protégé was an American journalist called Henry Morton Stanley - who had famously greeted the long-lost explorer with the wonderful understatement "Dr Livingstone, I presume?" - and would go on to become nearly as famous himself. A letter from Stanley published in *The Daily Telegraph* in November 1875 lit the blue touch paper under the desire to proselytise Uganda. In it he described Uganda in glowing terms and enjoined,

> *Oh that some pious practical missionary would come here, what a field and harvest ripe for the sickle of Civilisation! ...nowhere in all the Pagan*

> *world is there a more promising field for a mission than in Uganda! ... Here gentlemen is your opportunity -embrace it! The people on the shores of Nyanza [Lake Victoria] call upon you. ...I assure you that in one year you will have more converts to Christianity than all other missions united can number*[7]

The Church Missionary Society raised £5,000 within days of this being published and eight white missionaries arrived some eighteen months later in 1877. This was the start of many such missions to the country and to Africa more widely, the progress of which was reported in the press and also at meetings held in towns and villages throughout the country. For instance, Oxford hosted The British and Foreign Bible Society to two talks on the same day by the bishop of Sierra Leone. Six of the parish churches in the city, including those in the poorest areas, raised £739 for the Church Missionary Society in one year. At their annual meeting which 'had a good attendance', they were addressed by a Mr Hughes 'who had worked for eighteen years in that hotbed of Mohammedanism, Affghanistan [sic], where he carried his life in his hand'.[8] Mission mania had taken hold.

British imperial expansion into Uganda was initially driven not by the government, nor for commercial gain. It was not a top-down imperialism, but bottom-up, pushed along by a religious and philanthropic public. The British government would follow, not lead, the cultural and spiritual imperialism of the missionaries.

*

British missions were Protestant. Protestantism had been shaken into life in the fifteenth century with a core principle that the laity should have direct access to the gospels, rather than them being written in a language they didn't understand and requiring the mediation of a priest. In order to be able to read the gospels three things are required: firstly, the ability to read; secondly, a written language that can be read; and thirdly, writing on a page to read. And herein lay a gargantuan task for missionaries. Many of the groups they were proselytising had no written alphabet and so their first task was to create one. This was not as easy as it might seem as the languages that they were dealing with were not fixed but changed across generations to the extent that a speaker of fifty years ago was unintelligible to modern speakers, according to one missionary.[9] Numerous dialects were also present. As the missionaries struggled to find notation for spoken sounds with which they were unfamiliar, and as they formalised and standardised this notation across different speakers and across time, they thus found themselves creating what was in effect a new language. And by creating new languages they inadvertently created new identities in the societies they encountered. The shaping of linguistic groups led to the development of a sense of cohesion and heritage, and by extension of opposition to other linguistic groups when competing for resources.[10] This process was not peculiar to colonial missions and was also under way in Europe as nation states sought to create homogeneity among their populations – French for instance was enforced as the language of instruction in Breton schools in 1890.[11] Italy had been unified only since 1861 and similarly set about spreading a common language.

Having formalised a written language, the missionaries then needed to translate the bible. Here organisations such as The British and Foreign Bible Society stepped into the breach. By the end of the century the Society, along with similar organisations, was producing the Bible in 410 different languages.[12] This was an enormous task requiring hundreds of translators. These bibles then had to be printed and distributed before the final link in the chain could be completed, which was to teach the heathen to read.

African society had not lacked education before the arrival of Europeans. Children were trained and learned tasks and how to operate as adults in society.[13] There is more to education than literacy and successful developed societies have existed without it such as the Inca. The aim of the missionaries was not to boost economic development through literacy, nor to boost the career prospects of their pupils though better education, but was much more limited to teaching reading so that the gospels could be accessed. The close association of this link can be seen in Protestant converts being referred to as 'readers' by their fellow countrymen. Neither writing nor arithmetic were taught in the early schools. A similar restricted scope had been implemented in England in the recent past where a leading educational reformer, Hannah Moore, advised not to allow the poor to learn to write. Despite having acknowledged that the Baganda were 'of a higher intellectual type...eager to learn..(and)..show a remarkable aptitude for learning', it would not be until 1901 that the government recommended that missionaries teach writing, arithmetic and English to the more intelligent pupils so that they might serve as junior clerks in their own country.[14] There was no provision for education outside of the voluntary activities of the missions.

The formalising of languages outlined above operated alongside, and was reenforced by, the European compulsion to categorise nature and peoples. As the European empires expanded from the eighteenth century onwards there was a scientific scramble to identify, classify and label the many new life forms that were being encountered by Europeans for the first time. Private and museum collections from this period still dominate institutions such as the many natural history and ethnographic museums. The urge to taxonomise and compartmentalise knowledge in this way extended to the conception of the peoples that the expanding empires encountered and subjugated.

Out of this grew a near obsession with identifying tribes. The word 'tribe' implies unity among a group, a degree of cohesion among its members perhaps based on atavistic religions or ties of blood; it implies some delineation or boundary to its membership, and a leader to which it defers. In short, a conceptually manageable sub-division which could aid understanding, and in practical terms could be used for management and governance of subject peoples in the Empire. If a tribe and its leader could be identified, he could be bought off, deposed, or made an ally, or indeed an enemy against whom other tribes could be recruited. It was on this basis that the British came to apply the principle of 'divide and rule' by which they sought to exaggerate, stoke, or even create divisions among populations and so position themselves as impartial rulers who alone could prevent their descent into anarchy.

What was perceived as the non-civilised world was divided up in this way and each tribe was ascribed different characteristics and qualities. They could be noble or simple, barbarous or peaceful, treacherous or friendly, and so on. Racial science along with theories about the hereditary effects of climate led to identification of the Fante, for instance, as weak and cowardly because they lived in swampy lowland areas, whereas those living in highland areas or deserts were perceived as manly, strong and aggressive.[15] The conception of tribes thus also carried with it a sense of inferior and superior which became integral to this way of thinking about the world.

Although there were pre-existing ethnic groups, the

boundaries of so-called tribal society were much more fluid than Europeans understood, both in terms of group cohesion and in terms of territory.[16] People did not necessarily think of themselves as belonging to a tribe and were often baffled by the question as to which tribe they were part of. It is perhaps the equivalent today of being asked which community you belong to. This was not confined to Africa; inhabitants of modern-day northern Greece were similarly unable to understand the question as to which nation they belonged at this time. The Acholi who inhabit northern Uganda and southern Sudan provide a good example of this creation of new identities by colonialists. They were a divided group governed by sixty chiefdoms and spoke a range of languages and dialects. There was no such thing as Acholi people, as they understood and referred to their identity from their respective chiefdoms. The British abolished these and labelled them Acholi.[17] This was not the only ethnic group to be created by the British, and others which had been loosely structured became united for the first time, such as the Kikuyu in Kenya, or the Bagisu in Uganda.

As British rule became embedded the requirement to be part of a tribe became a necessity. Applicants for government jobs were required to state their tribe, as did the census; justice was administered through newly created tribal courts, and education was organised along ethnic lines.[18] As Europeans charted the geography of Africa, filling in the blank spaces on their maps, they imagined into being indigenous groups which were spatially bounded, ranked into hierarchies determined by race, and stratified by layers of chiefs. They fixed what had been mutable and often unclear identities and created new fault lines and divisions in society.[19]

Despite the limited scope of education in literacy, there

was a firm belief that technical or craft education could be of enormous benefit to Africans. The advance of commerce was seen as an indistinguishable and necessary adjunct to the successful advance of Christianity. Livingstone argued that what we would now call economic development was the necessary ground out of which Christianity would grow, and that religious conversion as such was of secondary importance. He believed that it was poverty and the associated social factors that held back conversion, not a lack of will on the part of Africans themselves. He campaigned strongly for the establishment of commercial enterprises, and assessed the economic and commercial potential of territories he explored with this end in mind. Missionaries were accompanied by men experienced in construction and cultivation, and initially concentrated on establishing large scale commercial cotton plantations using indigenous labour. It was thought that cotton would provide an export crop which would lift Africans out of what was perceived as poverty. Hand in hand with this went the need to investigate the viability of navigable rivers to reach the coast, and the feasibility of steamships to carry cargo for export. Railways were another use of steam technology to penetrate the interior and open it up for commerce. Along with western medicine and commerce, Christianity formed the trifecta of 'civilisation' which Europeans felt it their duty to inculcate.[20]

As the British became more familiar with Africa, they became more and more confirmed in their belief in their own superiority and of the inherent inferiority of Africans.[21] This even extended to a disbelief that Africans themselves could be responsible for their own art and musical instruments, which must therefore have been brought to them by a superior northern race in the distant past.[22] Early commercial failures in trying to establish large scale plantation farming; an impression that Africans were barbarous and unreformable, borne out by reports of the cruelty of enemies such as the 'bloody' king of Benin; and the limited scale of conversions to Christianity were the counterpoint to an increasingly expansionist and triumphant global Britannia which reinforced British self-belief. The British came to believe that Africans were unable to govern themselves and needed imperial leadership which it was their duty to provide.

This hardening of racial attitudes even extended to the church and missions, which had initially encouraged indigenous participation in the governance and priesthood of their enterprise. The removal of a bishopric from an African and his replacement by a European in 1891 led to the resignation of many Africans from the church, and in Uganda the Church Missionary Society decided that it would be preferable that 'the English-speaking race may have the honour in leading the way in a policy of Christian Imperialism'.[23] Methodist ministers also faced complaints from their flock that they were patronising and had racist attitudes.[24]

Above all the British came to think of Africans as childlike. They were intellectually undeveloped and did not have the capacity for higher reasoning. Like children they could be happy and entertaining, but they also needed discipline and a firm hand to make them behave appropriately. 'Like children they are subject to sudden bursts of anger' and 'must be made to feel they are dominated by a just and strong man' according to one observer. Even soldiers were described as 'mere children in the hands of native officers', but as loyal and reliable when under firm British leadership.[25]

It was perhaps this conceptualisation of Africans that led Europeans to the habitual use of violence in dealing with them.

Beatings in both a formal and informal context were common. An officer who was in Uganda at the same time as Thruston and also commanded Sudanese troops kept a diary in which he meticulously recorded the physical corrections he meted out. These could be spontaneous outbursts on his part such as a fit of anger in which the officer broke his umbrella over his servant's back because he had failed to keep the fire alight, or 'letting fly with stick and boot' at 'ten damned niggers' who had come into his tent at night to shelter from the rain. More premeditated cases include flogging his cook for not boiling water before putting it in his bottle, and having two servants held down and given 12 lashes each with a rhinoceros-hide whip for leaving his tent door open during a rainstorm. Although flogging had been abolished in the army in 1881, on one occasion after a soldier called Rajat Faragella had left his post to eat a banana this officer 'let him off lightly' with 25 lashes and then drew a sketch of the scene.[26]

Figure 12: The punishment of Pvt. Rajat Faragella

Sir John Ponsonby was atypical in his drawing the scene but not in his actions. For all his sympathy towards the men under his command, Thruston too reverted to beating a sailor who refused to row in a storm, and 'clouted the leader over the head' when his troops were hesitant about proceeding.[27] Shouting at servants and porters was another routine practice either with or without accompanying physical violence. Officers supply wry accounts of this intimidatory behaviour such as Thruston who 'exhausted my vocabulary of abuse', or his colonel who gave the Bugandan king 'such a dressing down' that he would not forget it in a hurry.[28] The colonel later expressed mild surprise when he learned that his servants would rather he beat them than shout at them as they could not stand the sound of his voice.[29]

Did the British beat their employees out of a sense of racial superiority, or because they were angry and frustrated, or because they were themselves beaten, or some combination of all three? These are not questions which are easy to answer or can be answered, but there is a difference in degree between the sadistic pleasure taken by Colonel Ponsonby and the occasional and involuntary eruptions of Thruston. Nevertheless, the environment in which both Ponsonby and Thruston found themselves was one which allowed them to act in ways they would not have, and would not have been allowed to act in Britain itself. We cannot be blind to the reality that violence in its many forms is inextricably entwined with any imperial mission. Indeed, it remained integral to the institution of British governance in its Empire to the very end, even into the 1950s in Kenya and Malaya.

And what of the porters and servants? What did they make of the physical and verbal abuse to which they were subjected? Of course, we don't have any written accounts from them and those left by the Europeans tend to portray them as recalcitrant and stupid, comparable to animals. This does not mean however that these African men were entirely passive, that they were simply acted upon and were not themselves actors, that they had no agency or choice in their role.

Their first choice was whether to be employed by Europeans at all. It wasn't easy to get porters and prolonged negotiations through middle men were necessary. Although this was often a surprise and a source of frustration to Europeans, the reluctance of Africans to travel months from home into unknown and possibly hostile territory is understandable. Death rates were high with incidences of smallpox, death from snake bites, and even cases of porters being stung to death by bees all recorded in travellers' diaries.

Having secured porters, Europeans could not be confident that all the men they had engaged would turn up for the journey. One traveller recounted how despite every detail having been arranged when it came to the point of departure,

> *A good many men were absent, and others paraded late; some objected to their loads, while others energetically seized a box or a bale and vanished into the surrounding jungle.*[30]

After only a few days this transport experienced the 'desertion en masse' of 23 men. Posting Indian sentries to prevent further desertions proved ineffective. Sir John Ponsonby recorded the desertion of three of his porters after one month even though (or because) they had been paid in advance.[31] A missionary wrote, 'alas how often has the African traveller to write in his journal that his men have bolted; he is only fortunate if they do not take some of his valuables with them'.[32] In other words the porters were not slaves, nor signed-on soldiers and could and did unilaterally withdraw their labour.

Additionally, there are multiple examples of African servants subverting or offering informal resistance to their masters – the privilege of servants through the ages. A colonel despaired of his servants being unavailable as they were 'gossiping' with their friends elsewhere; another man found his servants putting a laxative in his tea, and occurrences of petty theft were common.[33] The missionary described above whose porters had bolted, wrote of an occasion when he sent his 'boys' ahead to erect his tent, only to arrive and find they were asleep rolled up in the canvas of the unpacked but unerected tent.[34] Servants also seem perhaps not to have understood orders, or alternatively delighted in wilfully misinterpreting them. Europeans were struck again and again by what they deemed the stupidity of those employed by them, and their inability to follow the simplest instruction without close oversight. One colonel literally oversaw the laying of every brick of his house which would stray far from his design without his personal attendance. Even when he pegged out the ground his labourers erected buildings elsewhere.[35] Given that they were employed as day labourers, rather than this being a sign of stupidity it was perhaps a ploy on their part to prolong their employment and showed a cunning which passed the colonel by.

Perhaps the final word should go to Captain Thruston who, compared to his European peers, took a typically idiosyncratic view of porters,

> *My own experience is that they are certainly wicked, lazy and stupid, but no more than many other classes, African and European. ...Out of a hundred probably fifteen are rascals, who will run away with their advance of pay at the first opportunity; another fifteen are impostors, who are not porters at all, and who cannot carry a load, but*

who will fall sick and will not try to get well again; the remaining seventy will be very decent men, not particularly honest nor truthful, but patient, strong, and enduring, who will stand a great deal of unnecessary bad treatment, and who, moreover if well fed and justly treated, however severely, will show a considerable amount of devotion.[36]

*

Christian missionaries stood to one side of this violence which was never an intentional instrument of their proselytising. But even so, the introduction of Christianity resulted in a civil war between Protestant and Catholic factions in Uganda as will become apparent.

The work that the missionaries had set themselves was extremely challenging and the high hopes with which they left the mother country could soon be crushed. The official report of a Scottish mission in 1894-96 recorded that medicine had not attracted converts even when it was effective, and that children would only come to school if they were paid. Worse than this, those that did soon left as they did not like the discipline or food. The leader of the mission begged to be transferred to a healthier highland climate (now Kenya) and outlined how his colleagues were suffering from dysentery and fever, while he himself was malnourished and showed signs of 'nervous waste'.[37] The average life expectancy of missionaries in west Africa was only two years.[38] Missionaries were undoubtedly brave and well-meaning people many of whom literally sacrificed themselves for Christ. However, although unintentional and inspired by philanthropic and benevolent sentiments, profound cultural and societal mutations nevertheless occurred as the result of the British and European missionary and colonial presence which were to have ramifications far into the future.

8: ANNEXATION

The world into which the Ugandan missionaries stepped was by no means an isolated one cut off from the rest of the world or knowledge of it. Europeans were not the first foreigners to encounter its inhabitants, and the local rulers were a lot more prepared for their arrival than the Europeans credited.

Arab traders had lived in the region for upwards of thirty years, and maintained trade links with the coast and across the Indian ocean under the dominance of the Omani Empire. Slaves and goods from this region had been traded since the late eighteenth century. There was also contact northwards with Egypt and Sudan, and the former had tried to establish Buganda as a protectorate before the arrival of Europeans on the scene.

The kingdom of Buganda was one of the most impressive and populous states in Africa. It was described in an official report to the Westminster parliament as 'an ancient kingdom of considerable stability which has been ruled for several hundred years by a single dynasty'. It had a strongly centralised government with an extensive and elaborate administrative hierarchy. 'A traveller entering Uganda is at once struck by the apparent intelligence, the decent clothing, the graceful manners, and the general air of superiority of this country… On every side are seen signs of nascent civilisation', according to an earlier report.[1] It was fertile too with extensive banana plantations which were used for food and brewing, and large herds of cattle which were a store of wealth as well as food. Travellers were struck by the well-maintained roadways and bridges. Henry Morton Stanley reported that the king could summon an army 125,000 strong. These troops were used to raid neighbouring kingdoms and seize cattle and ivory, with the neighbouring kingdom of Bunyoro being the main target. In terms of standard of living Buganda was not a poor place. There were periodic outbreaks of disease which could be devastating, but this was not unusual even in Europe at the time. Indeed, a comparison with the living conditions of the poorer parts of Britain would probably be to the latter's disadvantage.

The king of Buganda welcomed the Christian missionaries to his court, but shrewdly would not allow them to travel beyond the capital. He reasoned that having subjects of a Christian great power present in his kingdom was an effective counterweight to the threat of invasion by Muslim Egypt. His fears in this regard arose as Egypt had come under British pressure to curb the slave trade and had seen this as an opportunity to pursue a policy of southward expansion for commercial gain. While the king himself practised Islam, he allowed and encouraged members of his court to convert to Christianity and would subsequently do so himself, which led to the immediate conversion of the majority of his subjects.

Bunyoro, while smaller, was more heavily populated than Buganda and grew a wider variety of crops including sweet potatoes. It too was recognised as one of the strongest kingdoms in Africa ruled over by King Kabalega. In contrast to neighbouring Buganda, Kabalega was highly suspicious of Europeans and foresaw, not incorrectly, that if they were admitted to his territory there would be no getting rid of them. He had ample time to reflect on his wisdom in later years when he was made a prisoner by the British and exiled from his lands. Kabalega positioned himself as the friend of Islam, encouraging and supporting Islamic factions within Buganda and tacitly aligned himself with Egypt. Both kings were using outside religions and their associated nations as a tool to bolster their own power and mutual enmity.

While missionaries had imagined themselves setting forth to convert simple heathens in virgin spiritual pastures, or as bringing the benefits of their superior civilisation to an inferior and backwards people, the reality was that they were being tolerated and played by the regional indigenous political powers. The kings were a lot smarter than the British anticipated, or were able to give them credit for given their racial perspective. Missionaries were therefore mixed up from the outset both with internal politics and with international geo-politics.

The situation was further complicated in Buganda by the arrival of French Roman Catholic missionaries, two years after the Protestants, who competed with them for influence and souls. Different political factions aligned and supported the different denominations, which were themselves both also in competition with Muslim leaning political factions and groups. A further layer of complication was added by the association of Protestant missions with Britain, and of Catholic missions with France and Germany. The extent to which internal political, religious and external power relations had become fused was apparent on the death of the king of Buganda and the elevation of his young successor to the throne. King Mwanga lost control of the situation and from 1884 a long civil war followed with opposing groups identified with different religions: the *Ingleza* being Protestant, and *Franza* being Catholic; names which neatly sum up the multi-layered allegiances in play.

A major cause of this instability was that Mwanga had moved against the powerful Christian factions as he saw the threat from Egypt obviated by an Islamic revolt in the Sudan which isolated Egyptian and British forces away from his borders. An overconfident Mwanga miscalculated and ordered the execution of his Christian pages who were sons of powerful regional chiefs. He also tacitly connived in the murder of Bishop Hannington whose recovered personal effects formed part of the exhibition in Oxford described earlier. Bishop Hannington was hailed as a martyr and the name of Mwanga became well known in Britain where he was presented as a hate figure against whom Britain must be avenged.

The uprising in Sudan was led by a messianic figure dubbed 'the Mahdi' who was characterised as a mad fanatic by the British. He successfully led a popular armed movement which succeeded in expelling Egyptian forces from most of Sudan. The British became involved as they had occupied Egypt in 1882 due to concerns about the security of the Suez Canal, considered the lifeline to the important imperial possession of India. British forces were sent south from Egypt to aid the retreating Egyptian army from Sudan. At this point events entered the annals of Victorian British heroic history with the defeat of General Gordon at Khartoum, who lost his life along with his entire garrison days before a relief expedition arrived to rescue them. The British response to this was to send for the Indian army and launch a counteroffensive; it was as part of this that Captain Thruston was fighting dervishes in the Sudan before his return to Uganda. Despite the death of Mahdi Muhammad Ahmad from illness, Sudan continued to be independent until reconquered by the British led by Lord Kitchener 13 years later.

*

At this stage the British had no formal government presence or direct role in Uganda. Keeping it at arm's length, the government had however granted a charter to a private company in 1888 named The Imperial British East Africa Company. This allowed the company to make treaties with local rulers and to raise revenue in the region. One of the company's early ventures was to survey a potential route for a railway from the coast with the intention 'to carry civilisation and trade into the dark interior'.[2] This survey was led by a Major Macdonald who rapidly found himself entangled in the local conflicts and politics of the region.

The company then decided to intervene directly to try to settle these conflicts in order to smooth its commercial path and to this end despatched Sir Frederick Lugard to meet with King Mwanga. Lugard was a highly experienced officer who had served in the Second Afghan War as well as in Sudan, and would go on to become governor of Hong Kong and of Nigeria. Lugard did not so much negotiate as intimidate Mwanga into signing a hugely asymmetrical treaty which gave the company representative, who was to be permanently stationed in the capital, effective government of the country. British subjects were granted immunity from prosecution and allowed to raise taxes, conduct foreign relations, administer justice, impose customs duties and make treaties with foreign powers; even the Bugandan flag was replaced with that of the company.

Lugard then proceeded to invade neighbouring Bunyoro in pursuit of fleeing Muslims and annexed this along with Toro and Ankole so creating the modern borders of Uganda. This done, he then imposed a constitutional settlement on the newly enjoined nations which was immediately contentious as it was perceived as unbalanced in its allocation of power and resources and brought the country perilously close to a reopening of the civil war. All of this was done without referring to the company or Foreign Office in London.

It was often the case that the bounds of the British Empire expanded not because of central metropolitan direction and geopolitical ambition in London, but because the men on the spot at the periphery of Empire exceeded their mandate and presented London with a fait accompli. Sometimes this was inadvertent but it could also be deliberate. British domestic and government opinion was split on the question of Empire, over its costs, over the moral case for it, and over the need to establish formal control in particular territories. As we shall see this came to the fore later in the history of Uganda when prime minister Gladstone was outmanoeuvred by domestic political opponents over his opposition to formally incorporating Uganda into the Empire. Ambitious military officers in situ were not immune to this debate and were keen to increase their prestige and rank, pushing strongly for the imperial project. They were often able to move matters forwards without reference to their nominal masters in London. Sometimes blatantly as in this instance, but also more covertly as in the campaign in Afghanistan described earlier. In the latter case, knowledge of an imminent uprising was deliberately withheld from central authorities so that when it broke a powerful intervention could be justified and a formal annexation of territory pursued.[3]

As a by-product of his campaigning, Lugard recruited into the company's forces 1,000 Sudanese troops formerly employed by the Egyptian government who had been left unable to return home following the fall of Khartoum in Sudan to the Mahdi. This body of troops had a long history as slave mercenaries and had fought for the Ottoman Turks in Greece, in Mexico for France and in Tanganyika for Germany. They had also established independent fiefdoms of control in what is now Chad, and fought both with and against the Mahdi.[4]

Those that Lugard came across considered themselves loyal to Egypt and continued to fly the Egyptian flag but no longer received pay from that quarter or indeed from any other. The fact that they had not been paid for so long gives some indication that they must have been sustaining themselves in some other way, and indeed they existed as traders, slavers and soldiers. They captured the local population as slaves – mainly women and children - traded these slaves for ivory, and then ivory for guns. They were thus independent, Islamic armed-gangs which terrorised the local population and represented everything the British missionaries deplored and sought to counter by inculcating civilisation and Christianity. There are parallels with more recent groups such as Boko Haram in northern Nigeria, or the Lord's Resistance Army operating in northern Uganda.

Lugard promised the Sudanese armed men that he would pay them at the same rate as they were due from the Egyptians, and that they could continue to fly the Egyptian flag as a mark of their continuing loyalty to the khedive or sultan. He also undertook that they would not have to fight or travel north of Bunyoro. In other words, they became a mercenary army in the employ of a private British company.

Having collected ample looted treasures, Lugard was preparing to return home in 1890 when he learned with horror that the Imperial British East Africa Company had decided it was no longer viable, and to wind up its operations. It was spending upwards of £40,000 a year and had no revenue, nor did it anticipate any until the railroad from the coast was constructed, the cost of which it had counted on coming from the British government. When parliament declined this subsidy, the directors followed the only course of action open to them and moved to liquidate the company, and in so doing leaving a governmental vacuum in the heart of the continent.

It was not only Lugard who was horrified by this sudden loss of withdrawal and control by the British. So too was The Church Missionary Society which within the space of ten days proceeded to raise more than sufficient funds to keep the company stationed and operational for a further year while it lobbied vigorously for the British government to step in and annexe Uganda as part of the British Empire proper.[5] The Foreign Office was inundated with petitions supporting annexation from religious organisations across the land ranging from small parish meetings to those in cities attended by up to 400 people.[6] The 'Uganda Question' as it came to be called became a foremost topic in British politics with deep divisions as to whether to incorporate Uganda as a territory of the formal British Empire or not. Rather like debates around foreign aid today it ignited public opinion as the press divided and debated the issue. The Times came out strongly for annexation, but more liberal papers including The Manchester Guardian were opposed.

The British Chamber of Commerce too came out strongly for formal annexation expounding the opportunities for trade which it was claimed would result.[7] During a time of economic slump it was considered crucial for manufacturers to have access to markets to which they would otherwise be denied without British control. A telegram to the foreign secretary, Lord Rosebery, is indicative of this feeling,

> *Strong feeling among the African traders in Manchester that the government should do all possible to keep Uganda as future market for British goods. It is hoped the Government will not abandon this country to other Powers who will*

> *eventually endeavour to shut out British goods by differential duties.*[8]

A speaker at a meeting of the Manchester Chamber of Commerce pointed out how this was a national concern, going on to say,

> *Our docks and wharves, our manufacturers, bankers, brokers and merchants are all interested in the question…for the development of British East Africa will not only affect our trading community, but it will provide a new and much needed outlet for the energies of the young of this country in commercial and administrative offices, just as India and our other dependencies have done in the past.*[9]

On the other hand, there were those who were appalled at British actions in Africa and strongly opposed any further expansion of commercial interests. Similar to anti-capitalist, or anti-globalisation movements today, those on the left and certain religious groups were equally forceful in their opposition to annexation. A flavour of this appears in the opposition to the explorer Stanley's subsequent attempt to be elected to parliament. Referring to what Stanley had revealingly called 'exploration plus buccaneering', his opponents lambasted the policy of,

> *"opening up" native territories against the will of their inhabitants [which] must force on them, in the interests of a small ring of capitalists, drink which will ruin them morally and physically, and goods which they do not need, and will end in their exploitation in the manner in which the*

> *Polynesian race is being exploited today. To seven of these capitalists, under the misleading name of the British East Africa Company, the present Government has handed over the dominion of territories and populations, the real extent of which is even now unknown.....We cannot believe that you [i.e. the electors] ...will return to parliament a man...who comes before you with his hand dyed in the blood of the African, who is the nominee of a company that can only prosper at the cost of untold human suffering, who seeks its aggrandisement at the expense, if need be, of English blood and treasure'.*[10]

Despite the considerable pressure for annexation, the government recognised that the newly formed country could not realistically pay its way in the foreseeable future and that it would be a drain on the exchequer. There was consequently great reluctance by the government led by Gladstone to take on the responsibility for governing and administering Uganda There was only one thing worse than having it however, and that was not having it.

*

'The Scramble for Africa' is the name given to the rapid expansion of European powers in the African continent in the last decades of the nineteenth century. The nations of Germany, France, Italy, Belgium and Britain rushed to claim lands as their own; if not taking outright possession they sought recognition by their peers as having an exclusive claim to particular territory. This demarcation was formalised in the Treaty of Berlin in 1884 which left just two nations in the continent free of European claims of dominance: Liberia and

Abyssinia (now Ethiopia). No Africans were invited to the conference.

The British government's great fear following the company's decision to withdraw was that if it left Uganda vacant, Germany would advance from the south and fill the gap, or that similar moves would be made by France and Belgium from the west. This was made more likely by the strong likelihood of civil war erupting again in the absence of a controlling imperial power. There was also a concern that this uncertain political situation could be exploited by Muslims to the north who would sweep down crushing Christianity and the civilisation that the British had endeavoured to plant. The fear of wider Muslim revolt in the Empire was never far from the forefront of British considerations. And then there was British prestige to consider. What if this was to be the first domino to fall in the Empire if prestige was lost?

Consideration of the best course to take was hampered in Britain by a vulnerable minority government, with the circumspect Gladstone as premier who wished to avoid annexation, and his much more interventionist rival Lord Rosebery as foreign secretary. Rosebery had the support of Queen Victoria and encouraged missionary societies and industry to agitate for the formal annexation of Uganda. Characteristically, Gladstone decided that prevarication seemed the best way forwards to bridge this awkward gap in domestic politics and a commission was despatched to Uganda under Sir Gerald Portal to assess the situation on the ground and report back the best way forward. This would undoubtedly take some considerable time given the distances involved and the slow speed of travel in both directions. In theory all options were open to Portal including deciding to abandon the territory. In practice however he had secretly been briefed to ensure that Uganda remained in the British sphere of influence even if it was not formally annexed.

A small number of officers were appointed to Sir Gerald's commission of enquiry. Among them was a young captain with recent experience of fighting in Africa, and who was fluent in Arabic: Arthur Thruston.

9: DESOLATION AND DEATH

Captain Thruston was one of four Arabic speaking officers to accompany General Portal's ostensible commission of enquiry to determine Uganda's future status in the Empire. Having made the long and wearisome overland trip from Mombasa, Portal set about the task of picking up the threads where Lugard had left off. He brokered an understanding between the religious factions in Buganda, which had recently deposed and then reinstated Mwanga to his throne following a civil war, and offered an unofficial guarantee of Buganda's continuing protection by the British in line with his secret instructions.

When the king of Bunyoro, Kabalega, launched raids into Bugandan territory it was felt to be imperative that Britain followed up the words of its guarantee with actions. Colonel Colvile of the Grenadier Guards was to lead the military response to this incursion. He stated bluntly, 'I felt that I could not allow such acts of open hostility to pass unnoticed without damaging our prestige as a power whose friendship was worth counting on'. He therefore 'determined at once to march on Kabarega's (sic) capital and there dictate to him terms of peace, which would safeguard us from his aggressions in the future'; a strategy which ominously foreshadowed that to be attempted in Afghanistan four years later.[1] Colvile's outrage was partly dissimulation on his part as he had received secret orders which suggests different motives for his precipitate move to war with Bunyoro. These orders outlined that the government in London had heard rumours that the Congo Free State under the control of the Belgian king had sent officials eastwards and that he was required to protect the interests of the British in the upper Nile region and assert British rights to the territory.

Specifically, he was instructed to send emissaries and make treaties with the chiefs of the districts affected. Colvile's interpretation of his orders to make treaties as instead to make war clearly went far beyond his instructions, and his personal diaries express his concern that his actions may not be well received by the Foreign Office in London.[2]

Maj. Gen. Sir H. Colvile.

Figure 13. Colvile in later life, knighted and a major-general

Despite Colvile's resolve and adamant posturing, he faced the reality that he lacked the resources to do this. There were only eight European officers in total in his command, and around 400 Sudanese troops whose status, as we have seen, was uncertain. Moreover, he could not deploy all of these as it would leave Buganda itself exposed to strife and conflict. He meanwhile had succumbed to fever and was crippled by jiggers, insects which bore under toenails and lead to ulcers if not treated in a timely manner. The might of the British Empire was looking pretty thin and worn for the task in hand.

Colvile's solution to the conundrum was simple enough. He fell back on the well-established imperial trope of 'divide and rule' by recruiting the Bugandan military to his aid against Bunyoro. Mwanga was delighted at the prospect of an ally for what he saw as a raiding party against his traditional foe, especially one armed with a Maxim gun. Using a feint of threatening to convert to Roman Catholicism he was able to increase the pressure on Colvile to act quickly, and while the latter considered that Mwanga displayed 'extreme nervousness', and was 'wretchedly weak and utterly self-indulgent', from the king's point of view he had the British exactly where he wanted them.[3]

Mwanga's warriors were quite unlike their indigenous counterparts in India however, who were well-trained and marshalled in regiments of the queen's colours under a cadre of officers schooled in the ways of Sandhurst. In Colville's words again,

> *The position was this – eight Europeans in charge of 400 Sudanese troops, fairly disciplined, poorly armed and badly supplied with ammunition, and about fifteen thousand. wholly undisciplined savages, of whom about eighty per cent were armed with spears, fifteen percent with guns, and five per cent with modern rifles, and a large proportion of whom, if rumour is to be trusted, would have*

> *hailed with satisfaction the suppression of the white man by Kabarega.*[4]

Colvile's assessment of the troops under his command appears in his published memoirs, and we have to bear in mind that he is seeking to justify his position and actions, and burnish his own reputation. Nevertheless, the condescension is all too apparent and we are left in no doubt of his view of the indigenous troops. He is an all too apt example of the later-century Briton who approached an unfamiliar culture with the unshakeable certainty that he knew better and was in every sense superior to those around him.

This is also seen in his attitude towards the Bagandan traditional command structure which was to have a collective assembly of chiefs to make military decisions. Colvile insisted that there should be only one person in charge who would answer to him. Although this was nominally implemented, in practice the chiefs continued to negotiate both among themselves and with him throughout the campaign. Similarly, when he found himself arbitrating in local justice disputes, he was completely unable to understand the traditional way of negotiating a settlement through discussion, while he himself was also unable to impose the standards of case for the prosecution and defence that he was used to from the English courtroom.[5] Colvile set off to Bunyoro in the firm belief that he was in command, that he had a clear objective, and that this was attainable. Events were to prove otherwise.

*

The low number of white British officers and the high number of Africans in this campaign are startling but they are not especially unusual. There were very, very few British compared to the populations of their Empire. The British of necessity relied on the cooperation of subject peoples. This could be for matters as basic as having porters to carry their equipment, or guides to show them the way, or traders to sell them food and other necessities. It could also be in striking alliances with particular groups or leaders to engage them in combat with other groups. Nor need this be fixed: different groups were capable of recalibrating their interests and making alliances of their own, perhaps with other European powers, or perhaps with domestic parties opposed to the British. There was thus an ongoing political calculation made by indigenous communities as to whether to collaborate with, or accommodate, or be uncooperative towards, or outright oppose the British. The British could be recruited as allies against others competing for the same resources, or played off against other European powers. In turn the British themselves were engaged in constant negotiation with the various political interest groups they ruled over. It was a highly dynamic relationship which relied on much more than force of arms alone.

A consequence of the limited number of British personnel on the ground is that they were often very lonely. Far from home, compelled by their own code of honour to be aloof and superior to the unfamiliar population in which they found themselves; often suffering sickness ranging from diarrhoea to potentially fatal illnesses which left them debilitated for long periods; constantly facing physical dangers from insects to hostile people; the pressure to make decisions on problems while lacking the necessary information and resources to do so successfully, and in the case of Uganda in a climate they found oppressive and enervating: it is not surprising that the psychological impact could be immense. Sir John Ponsonby, whom we met earlier liberally administering beatings to his staff, confided in his diary of his desperate feelings of isolation even though he was surrounded by numerous soldiers and servants. He recorded how he longed for European company and that he had not even seen a white man for three weeks. Mail from home meant a huge amount to him and the psychological blow from the death of his dog he found to be devastating and sent him into an extended depression.[6] Even if married it was not usual to have a spouse, let alone children, near at hand, and the company of a handful of other Europeans could be a source of friction and bitterness as well as of potential support and comfort. One wrote movingly of the death of a young officer of fever,

> *Alone in the wilds… he was struck down and died without having the consolation of a man of his own race to attend him in his last moments. The sad news of the loss of this zealous and energetic officer was a great blow to the little knot of Europeans who were battling against such odds, and straining every nerve each in his own way and in his own department, to evolve peace out of disorder, and prosperity out of desolation.[7]*

This statement is clearly filtered through a racial lens, but the sentiment expressed is no less real for that.

It had not always been this way. In the early years of the British encounter with India the opposite situation had prevailed, with the British adopting the manners, dress and modes of life of Indians, marrying and raising families with them. The rise of evangelicalism and racial science, the Great Rebellion or Indian Mutiny of 1857, and the increasing numbers of Europeans in the subcontinent gradually eroded this more open and tolerant attitude until a rigid hierarchy and demarcation kept them separate and isolated from the majority of those around them.

Alcohol was often the route to dealing with these isolated circumstances. Thruston noted the 'pallid, washed-out faces of the European residents, and...their capacity for consuming alcohol in various American liquid forms of the poison'.[8] With a belief in its medicinal properties and in the frequent absence of healthy liquids to drink it was all too easy to slip into dependence. Alcohol was not the only dose that Europeans could turn to for relief as we will see.

*

As well as approximately 15,000 armed men, Colvile set off accompanied by a further 1,400 or so non-combatants including porters, servants, interpreters, craftsmen, artisans, non-fighting chiefs, and around 1,100 listed as 'followers' who were most likely women and/or slaves. He also decided to take along a large steel boat, broken down into sections and carried suspended from poles which was to prove enormously troublesome. It was far wider than the narrow pathways cut between towering reed beds, and while it could sort of surf through them going downhill, it was monstrously difficult to get uphill and slowed progress considerably. As the party approached Kabalega's city, Colvile found himself getting increasingly frustrated with his troops who fell a long way short of the standards of the Grenadier Guards and seemed to him 'more like a crowd of schoolchildren out for a holiday' who did not think war a very serious matter. They seemed to believe that 'after a pleasant little jaunt during which they would with luck surprise some Bunyoro villagers... (they would) all return home the richer by a few goats or head of cattle.' He found it incredible that the warriors carried with them birds in cages, and one even a baby. Although they were undoubtedly 'picturesque', (an epithet which could surely be applied to the Grenadier Guards), he found them 'to be a great nuisance on the line of march' as they tended to rush forward like stampeding cattle and then stop and block the way. His remonstrances to the chiefs were met by mutual complaints about the treatment they were receiving at the hands of the Sudanese troops.[9]

Colvile had correctly read the aims of his troops which was to carry out a major raid in the traditional manner, rather than to affect the takeover of a neighbouring state. However, he was unable to accept that the Baganda would not align with his own aims and that he would be unable to impose his will on them. Colvile also realised that their manner of warfare involved a large amount of theatrical posturing more than it did of violent conflict. Opposing parties would make as much noise as possible using drums and shouts, and dress as magnificently, flamboyantly and expensively as possible in order to intimidate their enemy. It was a staged manner of raiding, the rules of which were known to each side and can be interpreted as a way of minimising violence. It can be seen as a ritualised or stylised confrontation, one which potentially involved the risk of death certainly, and also winners and losers. But these added to the communal male bonding process and heightened the sense of theatrical confrontation. It was a ritual, but not an empty one. A successful outcome would be to return from battle with a large number of captured animals and slaves, and some deaths of the enemy. It was not the genocidal elimination of the enemy, nor occupation of its territory. The introduction of European technology, particularly the Maxim gun, breached these boundaries and was an early portent of the devastating loss of life which would follow in the First World War. The outcome which the Baganda envisaged then was not the overwhelmingly crushing blow on a disobedient state that Colvile sought to inflict, and he was dismayed to find on approaching the capital that rather than encountering an enemy army ready for 'a stand-up fight' as they had anticipated, they saw smoke rising from its deserted and destroyed remains as a consequence of its having been razed by the retreating Kabalega.[10]

Kabalega pursued a scorched earth policy across the fertile belt of land between his erstwhile capital and a thick forest into which he retreated and in which pursuit was impossible. Faced with this Colvile determined to surround the vast forest and starve him out, but his own forces were themselves faced with food shortages and were becoming reluctant to remain any longer. Colvile had somewhat painted himself into a corner, but still considered it absolutely necessary for British prestige, and to maintain peace in Buganda, that Kabalega's 'power should be broken, a result that could not be bought about by a mere punitive expedition.'[11] Tipped off that Kabalega's main force was nearby he mounted a covert operation to cut them off in their rear using the Sudanese troops and the Maxim gun, and was furious when he discovered that a Baganda chief had independently and without his knowledge led a party against the head of the same force. 'The usual ridiculous sort of spear-brandishing and shouting went on for some time, and then the enemy thinking that the Baganda were superior in numbers retired back into the forest before the Sudanese troops were in position to prevent them doing so.'[12] Unable to capture or defeat Kabalega and with his troops deserting, Colvile determined that permanent occupation of Bunyoro would be necessary to break Kabalega's power and ordered the construction of a chain of forts across the country. To the south of this chain he would endeavour to come to terms with the local chiefs so as to isolate Kabalega in the north of his kingdom.

While engaged in siting and building these forts, Colvile received a further tip-off about the emergence of Kabalega and his army from the forest, but declined to act on the information and left the decision whether to do so to the Baganda chiefs. They made their decision in the traditional manner and acting with promptitude succeeded in defeating his army and nearly capturing Kabalega himself. They returned in triumph with 'three thousand goats, sixty head of cattle, forty guns, ten tusks of ivory, a great quantity of ammunition, and five hundred of their countrywomen held as slaves'.[13] Colvile's wry report that had they been any better at shooting they would have killed Kabalega does not really hide his being outwitted and outmanoeuvred by the Baganda under his command.[14] Nevertheless, this was victory of a sort for him and would be claimed as such.

Colvile now returned to Kampala leaving Captain Thruston in charge of Bunyoro and its forts. Colvile subsequently despatched a second incursion into Bunyoro, which he was careful not to call an invasion, with the aim of capturing or killing Kabalega, or failing that driving him out of his kingdom and capturing his treasure. The leader of the expedition was so affected by rheumatism that he had to be carried the whole way in a hammock, which gives a good indication of the desperate shortage of officers and scant presence that the British maintained. Kabalega simply withdrew across the Nile to avoid the hammock-led force which failed to meet any of its objectives. Nonetheless, Colvile concluded that the result was very satisfactory as it had helped to reduce Kabalega's prestige.[15]

Kabalega had proved an elusive foe. British control had not been asserted over his kingdom, but it is far from clear whether it had been asserted over that of Mwanga and his kingdom either. It is difficult to determine if the British were leading and controlling the Baganda, or the other way round. As with the missionaries, the intentions of the British military expedition had been subverted and successfully co-opted by Africans to their own ends.

General Portal was invalided home sick where he died of typhoid fever the following year. The eventual and somewhat inevitable decision of his eponymous commission was the formal annexation of the whole of Uganda including Bunyoro as a British Protectorate under the control of a governor appointed by and answerable to Downing Street. The nation that had been stitched together was not a peaceful one however, nor would remain so, and the work of establishing dominance in Bunyoro was ongoing.

*

Figure 14: Sudanese Troops 1897

Captain Thruston was thus left with 400 Sudanese troops to man the forts in Bunyoro and impose control of the surrounding countryside, as well as to negotiate treaties with chiefs to the south. There was no aspect of this that he enjoyed and he began to feel increasingly disillusioned with the role he had been given and the actions he was required to undertake. He was not alone in this discontent as his Sudanese troops too were beginning to question the situation in which they had been placed. Although they had deliberately not been informed of it, their terms of engagement had been changed following their transfer from the pay of the failed Imperial British East Africa Company to the British Protectorate.[16] Their pay was derisorily low, being only a third of that of a porter, and nearly seven times less than that of their Sudanese counterparts elsewhere in the East African Protectorate. The rate of pay was in any case a theoretical matter as they had not been paid for over six months.[17] It took all of Thruston's leadership skill and language proficiency to keep them onside.

Venturing southwards from his fort he encountered a community who asked him why the British had come here, and why having a country of their own they would not leave them alone? He confessed that it was a difficult question to answer but he had heard that bad people in the neighbourhood intended to rob them and so he had come to protect them. They replied that 'we were liars, that no strangers had been near the place and that we had better be off'.[18] This refreshingly frank attitude was no impediment to the conclusion of treaties however which was the goal Thruston had been set. He described the process at some length.

> *I had a bundle of treaties which I was to make as many people as possible to sign. This signing is an amiable farce, which is meant to impose on foreign governments, and to be the equivalent of, occupation. The modus operandi is somewhat as*

> *follows: a ragged untidy European who in any civilised country would be in danger of being taken up by the police as a vagrant, lands at a native village, the people run away, he shouts out after them to come back holding out a shilling's worth of beads... Cupidity is, in end the end stronger than fear; the chief comes and receives his presents, the so-called interpreter pretends to explain the treaty to the chief. The chief does not understand a word of it but he looks pleased as he receives another present of beads; a mark is made on the printed treaty by the chief, another by the interpreter, the vagrant who professes to be the representative of a great Empire, signs his name. The chief takes the paper but with some hesitation as he regards the whole performance as a new, and therefore, dangerous piece of witchcraft. The boat sails away, and the new ally of England or France immediately throws the treaty in the fire.[19]*

Although Thruston is ironical and dismissive of the worth of the beads proffered, they were not low value items to those receiving them. Any currency relies on rarity for its value, whether that be gold, or cowrie shells or bits of paper guaranteed by a central bank. Decorative glass beads in an area that lacked them could be used for trade to secure more useful goods. It was not for their intrinsic supposed beauty that they were willingly taken, but because Thruston was handing out free money. Although portrayed as simple in accepting beads, Africans were actually acute and calculating and rapidly developed a market in which different beads had different worth. European travellers were advised what sort of bead to bring, for example: 'Red Sambai; Kiketi, blue and white; white, small, white Ukata; red and white pound'.[20] The danger to Europeans was that there was a risk of oversupply and that the value of particular type of bead could collapse, as indeed happened occasionally. Whilst Thruston regards the exchange as farcical, he does not seem to recognise that perhaps he equally was being duped as much as the other way round.

The forts needed to be provisioned and this necessitated foraging parties into the surroundings which soon came under ambushing attacks by Banyoro loyal to Kabalega. This required a response from Thruston who with a degree of reluctance and disgust was forced to 'hunt for negroes' as he put it. He had been trained for war, had never liked hunting animals let alone people, and found the type of violence he was now required to inflict to be deeply troubling. Trying to secure the hinterland he ordered the burning of villages and the destruction of crops. He ordered the torture and execution of civilians to extract information on the whereabouts of the enemy.[21] He felt himself to be nothing but 'a raider, and an ivory thief'.[22] Essentially, he found himself acting as he believed the indigenous people did themselves, leading raiding parties to seize ivory and cattle, and burning and destroying all they could in the process. This was clearly not inculcating European civilisation and he began to question what it meant to be civilised, even wondering if the less clothed a person was the more civilised they were. He fell into deep depression as in his own words he was 'worn out both mentally and physically by long marches, bad food and bad climate. I was sick of raids and bloodshed and I longed to have done with them'. He admitted to injecting himself with laudanum – an opiate – which took him 'far off, where life is ever sweet, and sorrow is not, nor winter, nor any rain or storm, and the never-dying zephyrs blow soft and cool from across the ocean.'[23]

*

In one of his forays southwards, Thruston came across another considerable body of Sudanese troops flying the Egyptian flag, who had like those encountered by Lugard also become detached from their homeland following the Sudanese uprising. Like those recruited by Lugard, they too had become embedded in the local community and profited from raiding in Belgian-controlled Congo. Thruston persuaded these unpaid and abandoned troops to enlist with the British, chiefly to prevent their being tempted by the Belgians to side with them instead. Perhaps without fully realising the scale of what he was ordering, and against Thruston's wishes, Colvile then instructed Thruston to bring all of these Sudanese into the territory of Buganda. Since these troops were Muslim and loyal to the Muslim khedive of Egypt, Thruston pretended that he was a representative of the khedive who had ordered the British to arrange the transfer of his Sudanese troops and so tricked them into making the journey. Notably, his superior officer Colonel Colvile records in his diary and reported to London that these troops were flying the flag of the Congo Free State not the Egyptian flag. He was no doubt trying to bolster his case for having overstepped his orders in establishing what he referred to as 'effective occupation' of the country.[24]

Like the British who travelled with hundreds of porters, the Sudanese soldiers did not travel lightly. But rather than taking their chattels, provisions and all the other paraphernalia essential to a British officer, they took with them their wives, children and slaves. There were therefore approximately 10,000 people who would have to make a long trek through territory which occasionally had hostile residents. It took five days to ferry them in the steel boat across the Nile, and their food started running short by the eighth day. After five days without food the weaker women and children began to die, and very soon the deaths were in the hundreds per day as they endured 18-mile marches with no water or food available to them. Thruston fell ill with malaria and was confined to his tent suffering extreme sensations of heat and cold in his delirium. At the next river crossing only 5,000 were accounted for of those who had set off. Thruston was unable to explain their whereabouts but reckoned 1,000 had probably died, and the remainder had perhaps deserted and headed off elsewhere. By the time the travellers reached their destination in Buganda the total had decreased by another 2,000, and Thruston recorded that for some weeks the road was strewn with the bones of those that had died. He witnessed flocks of birds pecking at the corpse of a young girl, and a hyena running off with a man's leg. The outcome of this catastrophe for the forces under Colvile's command in Buganda was the addition of '300 well-armed and fairly well-trained soldiers, about 50 worn out creatures, and about 1,000 young men amongst the slaves who could be enlisted'.[25]

The presence of so many slaves and the acceptance by the British authorities of their status seems surprising given that Britain had passed a law abolishing slavery throughout its Empire in 1833. It remains a proud boast of some that this was 32 years before the U.S.A. followed suit and was done without a civil war. Yet here we have a situation where the leader of the Sudanese personally had 150 slaves, all of whom had been captured through raiding.[26] The number of slaves far outnumbered the Sudanese soldiers and they were treated appallingly, not least by the Sudanese soldier's wives, according to Thruston. Colvile explicitly endorsed the retention of captured women as slaves, and another officer regarded captured people as 'really not far from the status of cattle and equally indifferent to a change of ownership'.[27]

This tolerance of slavery was not unknown to the government in London. The Aboriginal Protection Society in Britain repeatedly passed on to the government reports of slavery including that General Portal connived in the capture of slaves by his Sudanese troops, that these troops violated women and subjected them to 'frightful, horrible and indecent treatment', and that they forcefully circumcised boys. The official response was that things were certainly not ideal but given the resources available at the time were the best that could be expected.[28] The subsequent expansion of the British presence did not resolve matters however, and the continuance of slavery under the British flag became sufficiently well known for it to be raised in parliament on multiple occasions. British courts upheld the principle of slavery in the territory and on one notorious occasion returned a ten year old slave girl to her master.[29] In 1899 it was believed there were 140,000 slaves on the East African Protectorate islands of Zanzibar and Pemba alone.[30] In fact, what was termed 'domestic slavery' was officially sanctioned in British East Africa as being something 'which might properly be extended to loyal and peaceable Mohammaden populations'.[31] It has been suggested that British reticence to act more forcefully in this matter may have been driven by the need to avoid inciting Muslim revolt as it was believed that slavery was integral to Islam.[32] Other contemporary observers thought that The Anti-Slavery Society and similar pressure groups portrayed an exaggerated version and argued that slavery in East Africa was in no way comparable to that on sugar plantations in the United States; it was more like serfdom in medieval times and was therefore not inappropriate for the stage of development of the Africans concerned.[33] Slavery was not finally made illegal in British East Africa until 1909 although continued in parts into the 1920s.[34]

Once returned from Buganda to his fort in Bunyoro, Thruston launched an unauthorised raid in which he nearly captured Kabalega, and although he failed to do so he did secure some objects of symbolic significance to the king including two brass spears and a brass tripod which it was understood were the consecrated regalia of Kabalega. He arranged for their immediate despatch to Colvile in Uganda 'as an addition to his collection of curiosities'.[35] The raiding party also captured 300 cattle, and a large quantity of cloth and ivory with which they returned. Additionally, Thruston left a letter written in Arabic calling on Kabalega to negotiate a truce. Whether it was the letter, the capture of his material wealth and symbols of office, or the impact that smallpox was having on his followers, the outcome was that Kabalega negotiated a truce with his British foes.[36]

The impact of the long running war with the British occupiers was devastating for the kingdom. Without informing the Foreign Office, nor receiving permission to do so, Colvile annexed two of Bunyoro's most fertile and productive provinces and transferred them to Buganda. These lands were then awarded to Bagandan chiefs for their support in the war which they had waged on Britain's behalf. The effects of war and the British policy of destruction of villages and crops forced widespread emigration from Bunyoro and by the end of the century travellers would describe it as a virtually deserted wasteland. 'The desolation on all sides was most depressing' recorded one observer, 'The little gardens and plantations were rank with weeds and completely deserted, and the few wandering natives we met looked half starved… no food of any sort was obtainable'.³⁷ Malnutrition and greater susceptibility to disease were the inevitable outcomes and Bunyoro suffered a catastrophic drop in its fertility rate from which it would not recover.³⁸

Thruston was unsurprisingly exhausted and requested to be relieved of his post to return home. His wish was granted as in the words of Colvile, Thruston was 'worn out by the almost incessant marching and the mental strain of his difficult command'. It was Colvile himself however who was to return home first. He had been worn down by the climate and recurring illnesses. Longing for leave to return home he retreated further into himself, giving his time to handicrafts, and designing and building a house with a flower garden which gave him great comfort. He became emotionally attached to his pet monkeys and eschewed human company becoming increasingly irascible with his staff and loathing the paperwork which required his time. He recognised that his mental state was a contributory factor to his physical illnesses but was unable to overcome either, and eventually succumbed to a fever from which he nearly died and had to be carried in a hammock the 800 miles to Mombasa for the sea journey back to England. Captain Thruston followed him some months later, glad to be leaving and intending never to return. Two years later he would be back.³⁹

*

Captain Thruston returned to England ashamed at what the British and he himself had done in Uganda. He was equally disgusted at what he found in England. He found the climate vile, the people dirty and rude, society tedious, artificial and insufferable, and he struggled with what he termed the restrictions of a hideous civilisation. He no longer felt at home anywhere and after a period in north west India, and then fighting against the Islamic dervishes in Egypt, in 1897 he accepted the post of second in command of the Sudanese troops in Uganda he so admired, now known as the Ugandan Rifles.[40]

He had not been away from Uganda for long but a lot had changed in his absence. He was particularly struck on his arrival by the large number of Arab traders and Hindu entrepreneurs who had established businesses in Entebbe. The Indian presence on the coast had been considerable for some time and it was noted as early as 1865 that the value of Indian traders' business far outstripped that of all other European and U.S.trade combined. The inward migration was new however, and bore out the British imperial desire for Africa to be an 'America' for their surplus population in the sub-continent, as well as being a testament to the entrepreneurial flair of the Indians who seized this opportunity.[41] Britain felt it important that the 'richest portion of East Africa should be open to Indian enterprise under the British flag' in the words of an official report, and Britain continued to encourage this emigration, although their attitude towards Indians was not overall a positive one.[42] Evelyn Waugh, the novelist, considered that all Britain had achieved in the region was to make it safe for Indians to dominate trade and commerce; he regretted that the British had introduced a Hindu rather than Christian culture and thought that this was a worse outcome than if it had stayed Muslim.[43] British settlers in the Protectorate came to resent the Indian presence and lobbied Churchill as under-secretary of state for the colonies that 'the Asiatics should have no place in the country whatsoever'.[44] Churchill, whose views on Indians could be remarkably chauvinistic and sometimes considerably worse than that, was not unsympathetic to this plea. Although outwardly espousing a policy of racial equality, he constructed policies which made it impossible for British Indians to settle in the highland region of Kenya which remained de facto white only.[45]

The number of Indian trading entrepreneurs were however insignificant compared to the number of Indians who were employed as labourers, and often effectively in a situation of bonded labour akin to slavery. They were particularly associated with the construction of the railway from Mombasa to Lake Victoria which had commenced in 1895 but quickly ran into difficulties due to labour shortages. Indentured Indian labour first began to be used in 1896 and at its peak there were 19,000 Indians working on the line who had mostly come from the Punjab. They were recruited by gangmasters and signed on for a minimum number of years but had to repay the costs of their transport to the territory and administrative fees. The debt was mutual to the whole gang recruited and was not void on death, when it passed to remaining members of the gang. The scope for exploitation was enormous, especially on the plantations which later drew heavily on this labour supply. Many labourers found that their debt increased and that they were in lifetime bondage, unable to repay their debt and given only a fraction of the wages due to them to live on. Around a quarter either died or were invalided home during their tenure whilst working on the railway. Those that completed their term and then returned home were often no longer fit to work. A medical report from 1900 assessed 75% of those on a homebound ship as being broken in health with a large number having untreated jiggers. Although a few returned with significant savings, the majority were penniless and sometimes could not even afford the return overland journey to their village.[46] The 600 mile long railway was completed in

1901 at a cost of the lives of over four indentured labourers per mile.[47]

Forced labour was also to be a feature of the British Empire in the Second World War. In Tanganikya (Tanzania) 84,500 people were conscripted to work on plantations producing raw materials such as rubber held to be vital for the war effort, and in Nigeria 100,000 were conscripted to work in open cast tin mines.[48] An unintended consequence of this was that a lack of agricultural labour led to rural starvation.[49]

The situation to which Thruston returned in Bunyoro was calmer, but there was great resentment there at the preference given by the British to Buganda. Buganda represented only 18% of the population of the new Uganda but received preferential treatment from the British, including the annexation to it of the most productive lands in Bunyoro. It would continue to be favoured with investment and legal preference at the expense of the north and east of the country until independence.[50] King Mwanga of Buganda had also become resentful of the British and led a rebellion which was ultimately unsuccessful, leading to his deposition and to the placing by the British of his young son on the throne - who was aged five.

The greatest immediate threat to the British in Uganda was not to come from Bunyoro or Buganda however, but from the Sudanese troops under British command.

*

Following the abandonment of the country by the Imperial British East Africa Company, and the withdrawal of the ill General Portal, the Protectorate was by default under the leadership of Major Macdonald who had initially come to the country in the employ of the Imperial British East Africa Company as a surveyor to identify the best route for a railway to the interior. Macdonald seems to have been an abrasive character. Colonel Colvile confided in his diary of his loathing for the man, and thought that Macdonald was so irritating it was making him ill.[51] Moreover, it is difficult to characterise MacDonald as anything other than an Islamaphobe. He felt keenly the precarious position of Christianity in the country and in wider Africa, and associated Islam with despotism, slave trading, and the threat of invasion by the Mahdi from Sudan in the north. Robberies and murders by Muslims were common occurrences, he thought, and 'through their own idleness and recklessness they had allowed the country they held to deteriorate'.[52] He hated the leader of the Sudanese in Uganda, Selim Bey, who was otherwise widely respected, not least by his men. MacDonald had Bey arrested, believing him to be in league with foreign Islamic powers and spreading sedition amongst the Sudanese troops. Matters were further inflamed by the death of Selim Bey while in custody. Accusing the remaining Sudanese officers of lacking loyalty, and not believing their protestations to the contrary he had the whole garrison assemble and then trained a Maxim gun on them and ordered them to lay down their arms, which they duly did.[53] When he left the country at the end of his term he took satisfaction that it had been his 'good fortune to crush once and for all the last great effort made by the Mohammeden barbarism to drive European influence, missionary enterprise and civilisation from the land'.[54]

Macdonald's assessment of the Sudanese troops could not be further from that of Thruston who described them thus,

> *Possibly they are not heroes - heroes are not required; but in endurance, subordination, patience and cheerfulness, they are a model to be admired and imitated in every army in the world. They*

> *would march 20 miles a day, or more, through long tangled grass reaching over their heads, through swamps and jungles, and at the end go foraging, sometimes for many miles, to fetch food. Crime and punishment were almost unknown; they worked at parade, at agriculture, or at house-building, from sunrise to sunset, and they did so cheerfully and well for their monthly payment of some 4 shillings worth of calico (cloth).*[55]

Unlike Thruston, Macdonald was unable to speak Arabic which further exacerbated the gulf between him and the men under his command. Matters came to a head when they were ordered to go on an expedition with him to Fashoda in the extreme north of the Protectorate on the border with Sudan, and to do so without their wives, families and slaves. It will be remembered that Lugard had promised that they would not be required to operate northwards, and while the terms of their employment had been changed with the demise of the Imperial British East Africa Company, they had not been told of this. Moreover, their pay was in arrears, and they had been on multiple forced marches in recent months while their comrades had not been deployed. They also resented that the newer, young British officers placed over them no longer had the ability to speak their language. They were especially incensed about the order to leave their wives behind (they were polygamous) as to do so would leave the women without any support and was contrary to long standing practice. This is one of the rare occasions when we hear the voice of the Africans rather than Europeans in the historical record. Sergeant Janna Bilal testified,

> ..*we thought we were going very far and would not return for some time. We wished to return to Kampala to bring our women and children whilst the expedition remained here, as many of us have several children who would not be looked after on the road if they were left to follow, even under a European. We are both badly paid and badly fed.*[56]

Although this seems self-evidently sufficient reason for their grievance, subsequent enquiries suggested that the troops acted as they did with the knowledge that Europeans had recently been killed by Africans in the Congo, and in the belief that a wider, even global, Muslim revolt was in hand as foretold in a Quranic passage.[57] This perception is important not necessarily for explaining the Sudanese mutiny, but the reaction to it of the Europeans involved. With the Great Rebellion in India in mind they were ever fearful of wider insurrection. Thruston's attempts to quell the source of the mutiny came to be framed in this light as an attempt to prevent the mutineers from crossing the Nile and spreading unrest further eastwards; and specifically to safeguard European women – atrocities committed against the latter at Lucknow had shocked the British public and policy-makers and memory of those events remained a central totem of Empire.[58] In the eyes of the British involved, the revolt was not about pay and conditions but it represented a spark which threatened a calamitous end to their presence in Africa and even the wider Empire.

Despite repeated requests by the Sudanese for Macdonald to meet with them to discuss their grievances, he refused to do so, and the 300 Sudanese troops who were assembled ready to accompany his expedition began to desert and then formed a more significant and wider mutiny. Their complaints were about specific grievances, but they also pointed out that the

British ruled in Uganda only because they themselves enforced their rule, while they were treated like donkeys. They accused Europeans of 'eating the country', devouring it for their own greed.[59]

On hearing of the mutiny Thruston immediately decided to ride to the fort at Lubwa to which the mutineers were heading, and persuade the troops there to remain loyal. He was ideally placed to do so having been characterised by one fellow officer as a man of courage, tact and extensive knowledge of the Sudanese language and customs who was 'if not exactly worshipped by his men, (was) at any rate greatly respected and thoroughly popular'.[60] Thruston's reception was everything he could have expected and the garrison swore loyalty to him.

Figure 15. The engagement at Lubwa.

It was at this point that things started to go wrong. A party of mutineers who were not known to Thruston were let into the fort in the small hours of the morning and placed him, and the commander of the fort called Wilson, in chains, each with an iron slave collar around his neck. They were shortly joined in their confinement by the unfortunate Scottish captain of a steam boat who had arrived to deliver two Maxim guns previously ordered by Thruston. The latter did not have a military rank and the rebels therefore seemed to be targeting all Europeans. The symbolism of chaining them in slave collars must have made a powerful impression on those who saw or subsequently heard of the incident.

The arrival of Macdonald outside the fort led to failed negotiations to release the prisoners. Macdonald demanded that the mutinous men return to their duty – namely the expedition they objected to – and insisted that the officers among them would have to face disciplinary action. Things then briefly descended into farce with the arrival of a group of previously ultra-loyal Bagandan Muslims who it was feared were coming to join the rebels. When they were about 200 yards from the British position they 'began an act of defiance to wriggle their bodies as they do at a dance in a very obscene and suggestive manner.'[61] They then dispersed. An armed clash ensued between the protesting troops and those loyal to the British which included Sikh troops from the Indian army. This hardened Macdonald's attitude still further and when representatives from the fort came to offer up the prisoners if he would guarantee the lives of the mutineers and enquire into their grievances, he refused and demanded unconditional surrender. The three prisoners were then taken from their confinement and shot.

It was to be three more months before the mutineers vacated the by now besieged fort which they had no difficulty in defending with the aid of the captured Maxim gun. Evacuating unopposed across Lake Victoria, they marched northwards and were still attacking and being attacked by the British one year later.

*

Accounts of Thruston's death vary and are based on hearsay. The later versions stretch credulity with a portrayal of him as an heroic, even Christlike figure, who gave a noble final speech before he lay down his life for his troops. Pictured as the epitome of late Victorian, Anglo-Saxon manhood he was said to have shown no signs of fear, nor to beg for mercy, but instead to have ordered the officer who had led the mutiny to shoot him himself, and not instruct his troops to do so on his behalf, and then, this speech completed, to have placed the muzzle against his own head. Attempts to rescue some credibility or prestige from this disaster included the reflection that his bravery in the face of death was a salutary lesson to the Sudanese of the courage of Englishmen.[62] In another account, his final words are recorded as follows:

> *If you are going to shoot me, do so at once, but I warn you that many of my countrymen will come up, and that if you do this thing you will all have reason to regret it.*[63]

Again this - surely imagined - account of his last words paints Thruston as calm, courageous and rational, but he is also made to stand as a motif for the wider forces of Empire which stand behind him.

His body was initially left outside the fort for some weeks before being disposed of in the lake from where it was eventually recovered. The remains were taken to Kampala where he was buried in The Church Missionary Society cemetery, the celebrations for the queen's birthday having to be delayed for the occasion.[64] As well as his name on the memorial in Oxford, a large monument and plaque was erected to him near the fort at Lubwa where he died, and a memorial plaque placed in St

Paul's Cathedral. All of these were paid for with money raised by his fellow officers.

In the ensuing official report into the mutiny, Major Macdonald was absolved of all responsibility and there was a strong belief by some that a cover up of the extent and causes of it had taken place. Reaction against the report may well account for the generous funding of the multiple and expensive memorials to Major Thruston.

King Mwanga fled to German controlled territory following his unsuccessful rebellion and then formed an alliance with Kabalega in an attempt to regain his throne. Both were captured in 1898 and exiled to the Seychelles where Mwanga died in 1901. Kabalega was granted release in 1923 but died on his return journey before again setting eyes on his homeland and erstwhile kingdom.

Figure 16. Kabalega (left) and Mwanga on board ship heading into exile. Kabalega's arm was injured during his capture and subsequently amputated.

Just twenty years after the arrival of the first missionaries, the once mighty state of Buganda with its strong central administration and centuries old dynastic rule had been all but destroyed. New borders had been created and historically antagonistic peoples bought together into one state, a state which disproportionality favoured Buganda at the expense of Bunyoro and its Islamic members; which favoured the south and east against the west and north. The once strong rival kingdom of Bunyoro, which had been coveted by the khedive of Egypt, had been reduced to a depopulated wasteland. There had been no successful economic development, no railways, no educational or medicinal transfer beyond that associated with voluntary missionary activity, and widespread environmental destruction had been perpetrated through war and the unsustainable harvesting of ivory from elephants. So complete had been the implosion of traditional society that a British government report in 1901 argued that the native Ugandans could expect no civil rights nor entitlement to large land ownership as they contributed nothing to their society. The author blithely stated, 'Of course, there remain in these countries enormous tracts of fertile soil which the government may deal with freely, and hand over to European settlers and capitalists without any enquiry to native rights or aspirations at all.'[65] In the words of one historian, the British had progressed from asking, to demanding, to commanding.[66]

The world that the British helped create has echoed down the years with disastrous consequences. Today about a third of Uganda's population is Catholic, a third Protestant, a fifth follow local religions, and the remainder are Muslim.[67] The country remains bitterly divided along religious-ethnic lines. The first prime minister after independence, Milton Obote, believed that Bagandan dominance was an impediment to national unity, and in 1966 deposed the president, who was also king of the Baganda. In 1971 he himself was ousted by Idi Amin, a notoriously brutal dictator, and a Muslim from the north who was a member of the Nubi, a group associated with, and partially descended from the Sudanese soldiers who had enforced British rule. He had served in the successor to the Uganda Rifles, the King's African Rifles. Amin addressed another source of ethnic tension and expelled all of the originally Indian population from Uganda, the majority of whom came to settle in Britain. The offspring of one was made home secretary in 2019. The Lord's Resistance Army, a pitiless northern breakaway group continues to cause misery today. This is a long way from the Lord's work which the original missionaries set out to achieve.

In other words, political and armed conflict continues to run along the fissures created by the religious, ethnic and regional forms created under British occupation and rule. The traditional internal structures of the indigenous societies and their forms of governance were fatally undermined, and those that replaced them did not prove strong enough to cope with the competition between rival groups contained within the newly created national borders. Major Thruston would no doubt consider that his cynical and independent view on the benefits of British rule had been amply borne out.

*

Major Thruston's name is not entirely forgotten in Uganda. In 2022 the memorial erected where he was killed was restored with the aid of grant from the U.S. government to mark Black History Month. Now styled the Luba-Thruston Fort Memorial it commemorates not the death of the colonial Thruston at the hands of mutineering Sudanese troops, but the memory of the men, women and children who passed through the site as slaves. The commonality of the experience of slavery of those in Uganda and the U.S.A. was highlighted by the minister of tourism at its unveiling. There is no reference to Thruston on the accompanying plaque.

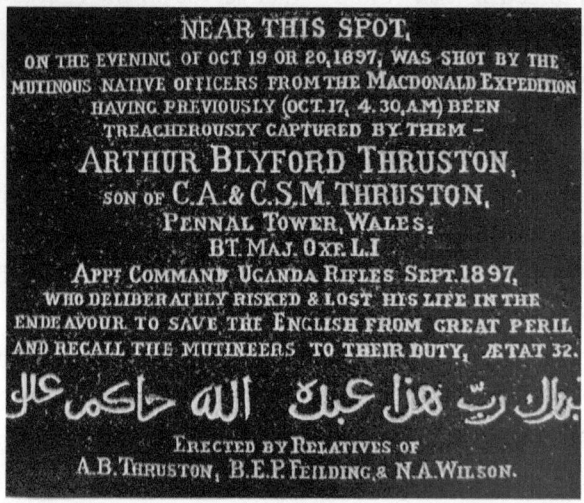

Figure 17. *The original memorial plaque placed at the fort at Lubwa in Uganda*

Figure 18. *Thruston wearing the Star of Africa*

10: REMEMBERING

The incidents traced here in Uganda and Afghanistan were just two of the small wars with which Britain was engaged in 1897-98. It was also involved in fighting in what is now Zimbabwe, Crete and Benin in west Africa, and the following year it would be fighting in China, South Africa and Sudan. The frequency of such conflicts was not new, 47 years previously the anti-imperial campaigner Ernest Jones had characterised the British Empire not as popularly claimed as that on which the sun never set, but as that on which the blood never dried.

In a way the conflicts in Afghanistan and Uganda then were both routine imperial conflicts; just part of the many small wars fought under Queen Victoria's reign which have been characterised as the noughth world war. There are many parallels between the two conflicts outlined here. Both were being fought for territory that the British did not even set out with the intention of claiming directly for themselves. Both featured irregular units: the Afghan Rifles, a paid mercenary group operating with British guns and ammunition and under British officers, but not part of the regular army; and the Ugandan Rifles, a unit of Sudanese soldiers who had initially been recruited as a mercenary force by a private British company, and then co-opted under British military command. Both of these bodies of troops had specific complaints which they felt were not being addressed: the Pashtuns around taxes, transgressions onto their land and the treatment of women; the Sudanese regarding pay, onerous duties and also the treatment of women.

The British response to these complaints was similar too. They believed that the underlying cause was connected with

Islamic resistance, and feared wider unrest spreading in their Empire as a result. In both cases there was also an underlying geo-strategic concern with neighbouring European power: with Russia in the case of Afghanistan; and with Germany, Belgium and France in the case of Uganda. In both cases the British faced guerrilla warfare which they were unable to successfully counteract. In the conflict waged with Bunyoro they fell back on the same tactics employed in Maidan: the destruction of crops and villages, the laying waste of fertile lands, a collective punishment against the whole population which mainly affected the innocent. This was a policy that would be continued in the South African War the following year, with the added refinement of introducing concentration camps for the local inhabitants to try to isolate guerrilla support and supplies.

In both Uganda and Afghanistan there were myriad, often conflicting factors of religion, ethnicity and gender in play. The British conception of identity was informed by their racial and imperialistic intellectual grounding. They believed that those who belonged to the same tribe, or subset of a larger tribe, were bound together and owed loyalty to their chief. They believed that peoples' identity was fixed by the group to which they belonged - or at least to which they were mentally assigned by the British. They saw other societies reflected back through their own conceptions of hierarchy, race and nationality. Thus, the concept of loyalty was something on which the British laid great stress. They saw it as an absolute value which could not be diluted or rescinded, rather like the oath which members of the Wehrmacht took to Hitler in subsequent years. Loyalty to the queen and flag was at the centre of British self-identity and formed the centrepiece of heroic imperial narratives such as the accounts of the storming of the Dargai Heights, or as expressed in the speeches at the unveiling ceremony of the Tirah Monument outlined in the introductory chapter. It was a concept that stretched back in British history and was taught as such – the swearing of fealty to the king on his accession or before battle.

The source of identity and loyalty was not so clear from the perspective of the people over whom the British ruled and who they tried to fit into categorised boxes. We have seen how the concept of tribes could be loose and fluid before the arrival of Europeans, and the hierarchical nature that Europeans perceived with power flowing down from chiefs was also often more notable for its absence. The Afridi and Orakzai met to discuss matters and reach conclusions in communal jirgahs, not from the dictats of any one chief. The Bagandan troops similarly had a bottom-up or collective method of reaching decisions much to the chagrin of Colonel Colvile. The Sudanese troops too had a collective palaver before they decided to desert and then mutiny.[1] All of these people had agency, they were not unthinking followers of manipulative leaders, of mad mullahs with an agenda which was hidden from them. They were not childlike in their simplicity nor lacking in strategic decision-making capacity as European understanding supposed.

It is worth considering further the loyalty and identity of the Sudanese troops. They were Muslims but not devout; pledged to the Egyptian khedive and still flying the Egyptian flag despite having been self-sustaining and detached from Egyptian command and support following the rising of the Mahdi; but they then transferred this obeisance to British command. They felt themselves to be superior to the people they were living among and captured them as slaves, but were joined in their revolt by Muslim Baganda. Nor did all the Sudanese join in the mutiny with some declining to do so when invited, and some surrendering their arms to their British officers when ordered to do so. Their identity and loyalty was far from fixed in the cultural way that the British assumed and perceived. It was a much more transactional process, a calculation about what would best serve their interests at a given time. The same is surely true of the king of Buganda, Mwanga, who changed his religion with startling frequency between Islam, Catholicism and Protestantism, depending not on his spiritual conscience but on which outside power he was courting at the time. The Afridi and Orakzai also were capable, were even masters of switching allegiances as circumstances changed. There was a fundamental cultural blind spot in the British approach to governing its imperial people which the regularity of revolt against them did not seem to change.

In terms of gender, it is more difficult to gain a perspective. Women are very much on the margin of the written accounts from the time, and the male roles are often portrayed in an uber-stereotypical way given the circumstances of the military authors and the conditions they were in. However, women are not entirely absent from the story. The British of course had a woman as their paramount chief, and she was not just a figurehead, but was actively supportive of imperial policy siding with Foreign Secretary Rosebery in the interventionist camp against her prime minster. Kabalega's mother was also a powerful queen who featured in councils to discuss military and political strategy. Less exalted British women feature in accounts in both Afghanistan and Uganda. There were some British wives in the forts in the Khyber Pass when they were initially attacked, and with the atrocities of the Great Rebellion fresh in their minds, British men were strongly motivated by chivalrous motives to protect and rescue them.[2] The narrative around Major Thruston's death also points up his desire to prevent the rebels crossing into territory where they would threaten European women. There is an unexpressed but very real sense of the threat of the violation of white women by coloured men here, and the underlying fear of white men losing control. Women too were given as the reason in both uprisings. The Sudanese wanted to take their wives with them, and the Afridis wanted their women returned to them. These women were not placed on the same imagined exalted level by their menfolk as the Europeans; they were wanted by the Sudanese for practical reasons as they were effectively their support staff who cooked for them, but there was also a concern that they would be unprovided for and unprotected if they were left behind as had been ordered. Although largely characterised as passive subjects in this history, this does not imply a simple binary division with men. There was a very obvious difference maintained between white and other women, and Sudanese wives were observed as being especially brutal to their locally-sourced female slaves.[3]

At an individual level British identity too could be conflicted. Lt. Col. Thomsett had a very poor view of Indians in general whom he tended to treat with suspicion and contempt, yet he admired and developed a friendship with a fellow Indian surgeon, and even expressed a fondness for his punkah coolie. Major Thruston committed atrocities and what would now be termed war crimes in the service of his country, but suffered terribly for it both mentally and physically, and his ultimate allegiance was arguably to the troops under his command rather than his queen.

It is also not clear at a more collective level to what extent those who fought under British colours considered themselves British or loyal to Britain. Most of the troops fighting in these two campaigns were not British. In Uganda the vast majority were not enlisted soldiers but warriors drawn from the civilian population when called to do so by their king. In Afghanistan the regiments were vertically divided along ethnic and racial lines and their loyalty or potential disloyalty was always uppermost in British officers' minds, particularly after the Great Rebellion. Afridis enlisted in the British-Indian army for instance were excluded from participation in the conflict.

One of the most striking divisions though has to be in terms of class. The social gulf between officers and privates was enormous reflecting the widely unequal world of Victorian Britain. The conditions under which the troops and officers lived were starkly different with respect to standards of accommodation, transport and rations. Even in death the difference was preserved with the Tirah Memorial being headed up not by those who were killed in action, followed by those who died of wounds, and then of disease, but starts with the commissioned officers who died of 'disease on active service'. No privates are listed as dying of disease in this way and they bring up the rear of remembered names as simply 'died of disease'. Even the cause of death is socially ordered around class.

If the various nationalities and groups in conflict had contingent and difficult to define identities and loyalties however, they did have unity of purpose. For the Banyoro and Pashtuns these were wars for sovereignty. To a greater or lesser extent all were fighting for control of territory in order to remain the dominant power in it. Kabalega perhaps gives the clearest expression of this wish to retain control and sovereignty of the borders of his kingdom. He was, and remained, emphatically opposed to European incursion into his territory and fought a tenacious guerrilla campaign over many years to retain it. Mwanga had a different approach, co-opting and accommodating Europeans, especially the British to bolster his position and secure modern weapons. The Afridi and Orakzai adopted a mixture of the two approaches, both cooperating with, and opposing the British occupiers; but fundamentally like their African counterparts, as they so clearly stated to the emir of Afghanistan, they wished to retain control of their lands and not cede them to British rule. The Sudanese militias too arguably came to the realisation that they need not be beholden to the British and act as their enforcers, but could be their own masters in the territory they occupied. This was certainly the view of some of the British who identified Sudanese officers as having conceived a plot to expel them and establish a Muslim kingdom in Uganda.[4]

British motives were different. They were not fighting to defend their national sovereignty nor national territory against an external aggressor. Their homeland was not threatened. Britain was the external aggressor and fought to protect its Empire in all its facets: as an economically valuable space which enriched Britain; as a geopolitical space which had to be defended from other European imperial powers; as an 'uncivilised' space in which it was the British and European duty to create the conditions where civilisation and its ineffable partner Christianity could thrive; and as a perceived virgin space where settler colonies could alleviate population pressures in the home country.[*] To retain control of this imperial space Britain fought using largely foreign troops, paid for by foreign countries, so as to deny independence and

---

[*] If not empty then as inhabited by people who were so racially inferior as not to deserve them. Winston Churchill encapsulated this view when he said '... I don't apologize for the takeover of America by the whites from the red Indians, or the takeover of Australia from the blacks. It is natural for a superior race to dominate an inferior one'.

sovereignty to the nations and peoples it had incorporated into its Empire.

It is all the more extraordinary therefore that 16 years after the end of the Ugandan and Afghanistan uprisings; after denying their sovereignty and independence and crushing the small nations of Bunyoro and Buganda, and attempting to do the same to the Pashtuns, in 1914 the British prime minister could stand in the House of Commons and justify the decision to launch a war against an aggressor state with these words:

> ..we are fighting to vindicate the principle which, in these days when force, material force, sometimes seems to be the dominant influence and factor in the development of mankind, we are fighting to vindicate the principle that small nationalities are not to be crushed, in defiance of international good faith, by the arbitrary will of a strong and overmastering Power.[5]

And so, Britain entered the First World War to protect Belgian sovereignty, while denying it to the countries and peoples of its own Empire. Twenty-one years after the end of this calamitous war Britain again declared war on Germany, this time over the question of Polish independence and sovereignty.

Thus, Janus-like, Britain simultaneously conceived of itself as an imperialist power denying sovereignty and freedom to the nations of its empire, while also launching into war as a defender of national freedom and sovereignty. This is as jarring as it is strange.

*

British imperial wars continued after those of 1897/8 outlined in this narrative. In 1899 imperial forces were fighting in

China and in South Africa, in 1901 in west Africa, and in 1903 in Tibet. It was part of a continuing pattern therefore when in 1914 a west African Muslim soldier in the British Gold Coast regiment named Alhaji Grunshi fired the first shot in another imperial conflict. This one however was to dwarf its predecessors and would not end until 1918 after the deaths of some 8.5 million combatants.

Britain itself was never threatened with invasion during the First World War, in the same way as it had not been in the preceding colonial wars. Nor initially were the territories of its Empire directly threatened. Sergeant-Major Grunshi was part of a force which had crossed the border and marched into the German colony of Togoland. He was not defending the British Gold Coast against invasion. Similarly, the British imperial troops pouring into Europe were not defending Britain from invasion. The threat to Britain's interests was more indirect, being in large part driven by fear of German rivalry as an emerging great power which could threaten the Empire and control of the resources which flowed back to Britain. Britain was fighting with and for its Empire, not in defence of the home island nation. Britain thus fought the 1914-18 war in Europe and elsewhere as an imperial power drawing on the full strength of its Empire to engage the enemy. Alongside the British themselves over 3 million soldiers and labourers from the Empire were directly engaged in the war.[6] The material resources of Empire were also deployed towards the war effort including coal, oil, wood, ores, cotton and wool. It was a war moreover which extended far beyond Europe. As in previous imperial wars Britain was fighting with foreign troops, financed by its imperial territories, to defend its imperial possessions. The overlap and parallels between the 1914-18 war and the two campaigns recorded on the Tirah Memorial even extend to the bodies of troops which were deployed. In France, Iraq, Italy and Macedonia the Oxfordshire Light Infantry fought alongside the 9th Gurkha Rifles, the 45th Sikhs, the Bengal Sappers and Miners, and the 27th Bombay Light Infantry. All of these units served with them in the Peshawar column of 1897.

The outcome of the conflict was that Britain emerged with its Empire not only intact but even enlarged following the Treaty of Versailles when some German colonies were transferred to it, including Togoland where Alhaji Grunshi had fired the opening shot of the global war. Britain remained determined to hold onto this Empire and this would become a source of distrust and conflict between Britain and its allies in the subsequent Second World War under the leadership of its prime minister who remained a committed imperialist. For different reasons neither the U.S.A. nor the Soviet Union shared Churchill's passion for the British Empire. America itself had of course been a previous colonial possession and fought for its independence. The freedom it saw itself fighting for did not align with Churchill's vision for a post war world and this became explicit with the signing of the Atlantic Charter in 1942 which committed to people having the right to choose their own form of government. Communist Russia had no reason to support the continuation of what it saw as a capitalist hegemony which exploited the poor.

The Second World War can be considered in many ways as a continuation of the First. The Oxfordshire Light Infantry reappear in familiar role fighting in Burma, north Africa and Italy alongside three of the colonial units that formed the Peshawar column in the Tirah campaign. After 1939 when faced with the invasion of large parts of its Empire in the east, and the catastrophic defeat at Singapore by the Japanese who sought to establish their own empire, Britain fought to regain and retain its imperial possessions, enlisting millions of Indians and other colonial men in order to do so. Again, Britain itself was not invaded and despite popular perception it is arguable whether it was threatened in this way at all. It has been argued that Germany lacked the landing craft to mount a British invasion even if it wanted to.[7] It was Britain that declared war on Germany, not the other way round, and Hitler had indicated that he sought accommodation with Britain whereby it would retain its Empire in return for Germany having a free hand in continental expansion. Britain went to war over the German invasion of Poland, to protect Polish sovereignty, despite Poland being an autocratic state which had joined with Germany in the invasion of Czechoslovakia. Britain's ostensible concern for the independence and sovereignty of nations did not however extend to the nations of its Empire.

More provocatively, Nazi German war aims can be seen as the logical extension of, or response to those of imperial Britain itself. Germany sought *lebensraum*, living space, for its surplus and supposed racially superior peoples to the east, as Britain had done in Africa and elsewhere in the previous century and continued to do in the twentieth century. Like Britain it achieved this aim by invading and occupying sovereign territories and then imposing despotic military regimes. And like Britain, it sought alliances with other states and peoples to secure this end. Of course, the scale and methods of Germany's genocidal practices remain unparalleled, but genocidal practice was not unknown in the British Empire. In Australia for instance where aborigines were literally hunted to extinction in Tasmania, or as experienced by indigenous populations in North America and Canada. Even during World War Two in Bengal, famine killed an estimated three million people while the British pursued a policy of shipping grain out of the region to Europe, a policy justified by Churchill on the grounds that 'the starvation of underfed Bengalis is less serious than that of sturdy Greeks'. He was presumably referring to the most effective allocation of resources for the aim of securing victory, but his antipathy to Indians cannot be ignored in this context.

On the other hand, Britain did not set out with a masterplan to conquer the world. The British Empire emerged over a long period and was imposed in different places at different times and for different reasons. Many Britons also believed deeply that theirs was a benevolent undertaking, seeking to bring their version of civilisation (and Christianity) to non-civilised peoples; not as being a people charged with the deliberately genocidal task of destroying civilisations. Nevertheless, slavery was ignored in Uganda and enforced labour deployed in pursuit of this civilising mission. There are uncomfortable parallels between the forced labourers working in quarries in Nigeria during the Second World War and the forced French and Russian labourers toiling in Germany during the same period. Tactics of scorched earth, torture and collective punishment were used by Germany in Russia after 1943. These methods were also a central feature of the British campaigns in Uganda and Tirah as we have seen, and collective punishment would continue to be used by the British after 1945 in Kenya and Malaya. Even if British imperial aims were benevolent, it is indisputable that the means it employed were not. Whatever its intentions, Britain's role as a violent imperial aggressor is undeniable.

Despite the narrative of the Allies fighting for good against the evil of the Axis nations, the distinction between European colonial powers was not always so clear cut to nationalists in the British Empire. In 1940 for instance the president of the Congress Party stated that 'India cannot endure the prospect of Nazism and fascism, but she is even more tired of British imperialism'.[8] Some Indian prisoners of war were sufficiently antipathetic to Britain that they joined with the Japanese to form an Indian National Army to fight for Indian independence. Even white colonial troops' dedication to Empire was limited, with a significant mutiny of New Zealand troops in 1943 who refused to return to the European theatre of war. At war's end the Allies had rid Europe and Japan of fascism, but the struggle for freedom was far from finished in the east of the European continent, as it was in the territories of the British Empire.

11: FORGETTING

The circumstances of the dedication of the monument in the city of Oxford to the fallen of 1914-18 were very different to those of the unveiling of the Tirah Monument 21 years previously. In contrast to the unanimous pride which all were able to take in the Tirah Monument, the memorial erected at the top of the broad thoroughfare of St Giles had a long and difficult inception. Although everyone agreed that something should be done to mark the death and sacrifice of those who had died, what it was that should be done was the source of much bitterness and reveals a city and country which was not at all united in pride at victory after a long war, nor even in grief at the tremendous losses and hardships which had been endured.

Oxford's mayor initially called a public meeting at which he floated the idea of a museum to remind future generations of the sacrifice made. This met with outright derision as many thought that Oxford already had a surfeit of museums which no one visited anyway. What they pressed for strongly was a memorial hall where friendly societies, trades unions and other working men's organisations could meet. Others backed the idea of a memorial hall but suggested it should incorporate a gym and swimming baths. Other suggestions were for working men's cottages to be built, for homes for invalids, for a children's hospital, for a beautiful public garden, and for a significant donation to the local John Radcliffe hospital. Although the latter had wide support, some argued that hospitals should not rely on charity and one speaker suggested that they might even be organs of the state within the next 50 years. The initial public meeting descended into outright acrimony with the mayor criticised and accused of deliberately holding the meeting during working hours so as to exclude working class people. It was also pointed out that there were no serving, nor ex-servicemen on the committee considering the matter.[1]

Figure 19. Proposal for memorial design, 1920

After the donation of a site by one of the colleges, a level of agreement was reached that a monument should be built with all excess funds channelled to some of the good causes suggested. The college had inadvertently helped matters along by not allowing a building to be erected on the site, and the vicar of the adjoining church was also opposed to any monstrosity being erected which would diminish the stature and setting of his church. £5,000 was the agreed Maximum to be spent on the memorial. A hiatus occurred while a referendum was held as to whether to site the memorial at the end or in the middle of the intended road. There then came the decision as to what form the monument should take and further division ensued. A Captain Chevallier argued that to have a statue of a soldier would be 'the worst sort of militarism', and there was agreement that they did not want a statue of a soldier in 'gumboots and a tin hat'. This was a reference to an earlier monument erected elsewhere in the city to the fallen of the South African or Boer War of which more later. One design amongst other floated was for an elaborate bronze figure in a chariot with outspread wings, folding drapery, a fallen sword and raised wreath. Another suggestion (fig. 19) was for an angel with outstretched wings holding a wreath and sword.

However, the reality was that even if they had wanted this, they could not afford it. Despite the high hopes with which they had begun, two years later it was becoming clear that funds were not forthcoming for an elaborate monument nor would there be any excess funds for good causes. The envisaged design for the monument was now described as 'at least... simple and delightful', and it was rather feebly argued that it was not the cost nor the artistic merit which was important, but the sentiment behind it. Further ongoing arguments were about whether to have the names of those who served, or only those who had died, either on the monument, or elsewhere, or not at all. After a late disagreement about whether the monument should take the form of a cross or a religiously neutral cenotaph, the final design was approved at a cost of £1,400. However, the committee had managed to secure only half of this and so organised a house-to-house collection to make up the shortfall, but this was not well supported. There began to be doubt as to whether there would be a memorial of any sort at all. Even eight days before the dedication and unveiling they were still appealing for the final £100.[2]

Figure 20. The agreed design, 1920.

As a collective act of remembrance the monument had failed to win the support of the community in the way that was intended. The final form that it took excluded all those who had preferred another option, particularly those on the left who preferred a more practical and utilitarian commemorative legacy. By favouring some values, it ignored others, and rather than bringing the community together, the process of deciding how to mark the end of the 1914-18 war divided it further. Oxford was not alone in this trauma. The commemoration of the war was to prove hugely divisive in towns and villages throughout the land. It was not unusual for protests and objections to be mounted during the unveiling and dedication ceremonies to memorials, with many feeling that those who had the means to pay for the memorials were calling the shots while ignoring the wishes of the great majority.[3]

This contestation about the appropriate way of remembering those who had died continued at a national level after the erection of the various monuments, memorial halls, parks and gates that were commissioned, and found expression in the annual Remembrance Day ceremonies on 11th November. To many people personally, the reminder of their grief on this day was unbearable and best avoided. To others however, it was an empty show of words which was not only meaningless, but offensive. The Great War was followed by an economic slump which in a time before the welfare state was devastating for many, especially ex-servicemen. In 1922 two thirds of the total number of unemployed were ex-servicemen, a further 100,000 were disabled and there were some 60,000 suffering from severe mental illness as a result of their wartime experiences.[4] Many believed that while plenty of money had been available to fight the war, there was none available to help those who had served in it now that they needed it. For instance, the two-minutes' silence ceremony was interrupted by ex-servicemen in Liverpool and Dundee protesting at the lack of support for living survivors.[5] Furthermore, attitudes differed around the day itself. Some thought it should be a solemn occasion for reverenced memory of the dead, while others thought it should be a day of celebration for victory and survival. The early years of the post-war period were marked on November 11th in part by riotous joy and drunkenness among reconvening comrades.[6] There was also a concern at the increasing military nature of memorial services and ceremonies, with even the prince of Wales expressing his regret at this turn of events and calling for a more civilian focus to be restored.[7] Public acts of remembering can also therefore be about power - who has the right to remember, who has the right to decide what to remember – and so can be a source of controversy.[8] People staking claims to the most appropriate or correct version of remembering were also staking claims to the ascendancy of their point of view, and to control of the narrative of the past.

The almost passive tone of the majority of the monuments erected throughout the kingdom in the wake of the Great War with their simple and unadorned stonework and eschewal of victorious symbolism such as winged figures in chariots, took a lead from The Cenotaph designed by Sir Edwin Lutyens for Whitehall for the occasion of a victory parade at the conclusion of the Treaty of Versailles in 1919. This first appeared as a plaster and wooden structure and there was no plan for it to become a permanent monument in stone. In a deliberately intentional way, it was and is a blank and empty space. Such memorials have a neutrality about them which speaks of the compromises people had to make to accommodate their conflicting views. They allow for the projection onto them of different conceptions of the past, of different ways of remembering, and they serve this purpose into the present day.

The international political background to this is important, as these competing claims as to how best, or most appropriately, to remember the past war were taking place in the shadow of the Russian revolution of 1917. Similar attempts at socialist revolution or transition had been made in Germany, and the dangers of militant labour were keenly felt by those in authority. The question arose of as to 'for whose benefit had the war been fought?' Pressures from the left and from the working class for a different remembering, one that did not endorse the triumphalist, militarist narrative were subversive and unwelcome in some quarters. As divisions emerged over the peace settlement of the Treaty of Versailles in 1919, previously secret diplomatic papers were uncovered, and reports of disagreements among the high command emerged. Consequently, a more cynical view of the war took hold. This is reflected in the literature and poetry of the time and forms part of the school curriculum to this day. Britain was no longer felt to be a land fit for heroes; ceremonies of remembrance lapsed.[9]

This is a long way from the simple and unified consensus which surrounded the earlier unveiling ceremony for the Tirah Memorial outlined in the Introduction. To be sure, there are other reasons for the different contemporary reception of the two monuments. The first affected a tiny proportion of the local population, and a far-away war which generated an occasional paragraph in the newspaper was not of immediate concern to most. The Tirah Monument was commissioned and paid for by officers of the regiment, not by the public and did not need public agreement on the form it should take. Nevertheless, it was recognised as a public war memorial, proudly referred to as such, and inaugurated by the civic and religious representatives of the city. This was very a different and more ambitious act of commemoration than previous regimental memorials which had taken the form of plaques in churches or the cathedral, in common with the practice elsewhere. In comparison to the Tirah campaign, the First World War was clearly of a much greater magnitude, shockingly so, and left only a handful of communities without any dead from the fighting. It also impacted the civilian population in ways that previous wars had not done, such as through shortage of food, in the huge shift in society as women were recruited to work in factories and on farms, and in the aerial bombing of civilians in the capital and coastal towns. However, the greater scale of the impact of the war also makes the scale of the conflicts around how to remember it all the greater. In other words, more people cared more deeply and were therefore more divided about the 1914-18 memorial than they ever were about the Tirah Memorial.

*

The process of memorialisation was much less fraught following the Second World War as the monuments were already in place to which further names could be appended. There were also far fewer military deaths compared to the previous conflict. Additionally, the nascent welfare state offered a fresh start for the nation, and avoided most of the problems faced by returning servicemen and women in the previous war, or at least offered hope where none was available in the previous post-war period. However, the question of what was being remembered again became pertinent.

There was no doubt in anyone's mind in 1945 that Britain had fought the war as part of, and along with its Commonwealth and Empire. People said as such. Churchill in his address to parliament following victory in Europe, stated, 'we ... from our united Empire, maintained the struggle single-handed for a whole year until we were joined by the military might of Soviet Russia'. The leader of the opposition, Atlee, similarly told an audience that, 'We were not alone. We had the other countries of the British Commonwealth and the peoples of Empire'.[10] In 1946 Britain conceived itself as 'alone' in the sense of its Empire alone, not as the island nation all by itself.

However, coexisting with this imperial pride in Empire and its strength, wartime propaganda had made much of the idea that Britons were fighting for the values of democracy and national freedom, and against the authoritarianism practised by Germany and Japan. This was clearly difficult to reconcile with national self-identity when Britain itself continued to deny democracy and oppress national freedom, and to operate authoritarian regimes based on racial superiority within its Empire. There was a fundamental contradiction here at the heart of what was being remembered. Had the combatants died to defend the Empire or for freedom?

As the years passed, a different memory of the Second World War emerged. The role of Empire, and of Britain's place in the imperial heart of it, was gradually backgrounded and then forgotten. Britain's conception of its role in the war shifted from it having been an international imperial partnership fighting alone, to an island-nation fighting alone, and consequently, to a national rather than international or imperial narrative. The memory faded of the millions of Asian, African and Commonwealth soldiers, sailors and air crew who had fought in the war.[11] Along with the First World War it became to be remembered primarily not as a global war of empires, but as a European war of nation states. The focus shifted also towards one more centred on the experience and sufferings of civilians in Britain itself. In short, the collective memory of both world wars became narrower and more nationalistic.

Several factors can explain this. Firstly, the British turned out not to be very good at Empire after all. The idea of British invincibility and supposed natural racial superiority was comprehensively destroyed by the Japanese success in the far east which culminated in the fall of Singapore. After the war, India was hurriedly dumped into independence with tremendous bloodshed in 1947, and was followed by much of the rest of the Empire through the 1950s and 60s. While some liked to believe that Britain had 'granted' independence as if it were hers to give, or a benevolent gift now that colonies were capable of self-government thanks to her tutelage, the reality was that Britain could no longer afford to keep these overseas territories and could no longer successfully maintain control over them in the face of fierce local demands for freedom. As well as regularly fighting Afghan revolts, Britain was engaged in fighting independence movements in Somaliland, Malaya, Egypt, Kenya and Cyprus. Then in 1956 in a major humiliation Britain was forced to withdraw an invasion force launched against Egypt to secure the Suez Canal. There could be no doubt in anyone's mind that the U.S.A. was now the world's foremost power and Britain was decidedly no longer the international power it liked to suppose.

Secondly, the effects of aerial bombing and the suffering of civilians were much greater in the Second World War than previous wars and this led to an inward focus on the national and civilian experience of war as a shared experience. The legacy of this in post-war Britain was a chronic housing shortage along with rationing which continued until 1954. People were understandably more concerned with domestic shortages and conditions than with imperial possessions.

Additionally, the dropping of the Soviet Union as a lionised ally forced the adoption of a different narrative of remembering the war. As the western perception of the communist empire transitioned to it being the epitome of authoritarianism and the overwhelming threat to the free world with the same global ambitions as fascism, then by definition 'we' must have the opposite characteristics and ambitions. Building on wartime propaganda and heavily influenced by American perspective, Britain transitioned to defining itself as a nation which stood for and fought for freedom and democracy. This is a curious twist as in reality what the British and their colonial troops had been fighting for in so many theatres of the war was to protect territories in which those were the exact values that Britain actively suppressed. For example, during the 1939-45 war British authorities killed thousands of protestors in India and imprisoned the majority of members of the Congress Party who were campaigning for freedom from British rule.[12] In the 1914-18 war gathering of more than five people required police permission. In northern Rhodesia striking workers were shot by the military and police in 1940, as they were in Bermuda in 1942.[13] These were not expressions of the national values espoused in war-time propaganda as worth fighting for. Meanwhile nationalists in the constituent parts of Empire were acutely aware of the pledge that Britain had signed up to in the Atlantic Charter of 1941 which affirmed 'the rights of all peoples to choose the form of government under which they will live'. This was a choice they were denied by the British.

*

Fighting for freedom and democracy is a version of ourselves that we can all like and buy into. It represents and forms a memory of ourselves at our best. It gives us common values and a shared narrative around which we can coalesce. Remembering Empire is altogether more unpleasant and difficult. To a greater or lesser extent, it requires us to acknowledge and remember the darker side of our past, and recalls an image of our national selves we would rather avoid, and from which we would rather be disassociated. Put simply, rather than being a source of pride, the Empire has become an embarrassment for modern Britain, an unacknowledged foul smell for which no one wants to take responsibility and everyone hopes will soon disappear. The dominant memory-narrative now is that 'we' fought for freedom and democracy, not that we fought to maintain their absence from our Empire using troops to whom we denied these same freedoms and rights. Britain has sloughed off the memory of its imperial past, like a snake shedding its skin, to emerge in the national collective memory as guiltless and innocent of its history. There is thus projected back onto the 1914-18 Oxford memorial, as with its peers elsewhere, a sanitised nationalistic version of wars fought in the cause of national freedom and democracy. The Tirah Monument by contrast indubitably stands for everything opposed to those values and sits uncomfortably at the heart of a modern city. It remembers wars fought by an imperial power against national freedom and popular rule, the imperial power being Britain. Although both memorials were erected to commemorate imperial wars, the respective perception of them has changed because we have rewritten our history, or rewired our remembering of the events they commemorate.

It was Professor Sir John Seeley, the author of 'The Expansion of England', who first expressed the view that the British had acquired their Empire in a fit of absence of mind. This characterisation, as if the Empire were the product of the eccentric bumbling of an elderly relative, or a bit of accidental shop-lifting, does a disservice and downplays the motivation and zeal of those who have been portrayed in this book. It is though perhaps true to say that the absent-minded British seem to have lost their memory of their Empire, along with the Empire itself. There is a tacit amnesia around the Empire, an unsaid agreement that it happened a long time ago, a long way over there, and needn't concern us. It is best left unacknowledged, unremembered and ignored. This is the fate of the Tirah Memorial.

12: RECKONING

You can see why it caught his eye. It's about the size of an iPad - but as thick as a house-brick. It is covered with a material that is almost like a carpet in its texture and has a rich, brightly coloured design. It looks a bit like a present wrapped up with a rug rather than wrapping paper. When he opened the covers he would not have been able to understand a single word of the flowing Arabic hand-writing inside; he was cold, he was in danger of being killed by a sniper at any moment, and he and his colleagues were subject to constant attacks - yet even so, he paused to pick it up and place it in his pocket or pack before destroying the building where he found it.[1] This book must have clearly meant a lot to the 35 year-old officer of the Gordon Highlanders who took it in such circumstances, and then carried it with him through the harrowing retreat via the Bara valley back to Peshawar and so to his home in Scotland. It was prize loot, potentially worth good money, or if nothing else a useful souvenir of his time in the mountains of the north west frontier to show to his friends on his return.

Today, the book is stored in the Bodleian Library in Oxford where it is listed in the catalogue as 'Koran in Arabic, beginning incomplete, colophon in Persian, probably Afghanistan, 19th century'.[2] An additional note relates that it was placed in the library by Ampleforth Abbey in 1996 as part of the archive of Lady Elizabeth Lewis and her family. Lady Lewis died in 1931. The catalogue also records that it was acquired by the owner before her in 1897, but gives no further information as to who this was or how it had been acquired.

And yet this is no great mystery because tucked into the back page is a handwritten note which reads simply:

Taken out of a Mohammaden Musjid in the Bara Valley (Afridi, Tirah) at Sandana on 10th December 1897. A Haldane. Gordon Hylanders.

A musjid or masjid is a mosque and the man who took it went on to become General Sir Alymer Haldane. Following his time in the Tirah, Haldane went on to fight in the South African War of 1899-1902 where he was captured and planned the escape of himself and Winston Churchill. Luck was not on his side on this occasion and while he failed to get away, Churchill did and as a result secured the fame for which he so longed. Twelve years later Haldane was commander of the British Expeditionary Force in the First World War when British propaganda made much of the 'frightfulness' of Germany's shelling of churches and cathedrals in the countries it invaded. He was then by no means an exceptional European in his actions on that day in December 1897 when he destroyed a religious building.

Sandana today is situated in the Khyber Pakhtunkhwa province of Pakistan, a country which did not exist until 1947 when the British created it as part of their calamitously executed withdrawal from India. There is now a road through the Bara valley but the settlement at Sandana remains a remote place where the memory of war is all too recent. In 2012 the population fled to safety following military operations as part of the 'war on terror' against the militant group Lashkar-i-Islam and have only recently begun to return. In June 2023 the school there was reopened with an initial intake of 50 pupils including seven girls. The challenges and lack of opportunities for young people remain immense however. Additionally, basic infrastructure is lacking. Recent moves to address this include reconstruction of the irrigation channels which were destroyed in the recent military campaign - just as they had been in 1897.[3]

There have been no calls for the return of the Quran - the whereabouts of which remained previously unknown - but it does raise the question of what would be the correct response if there were such calls. The looting of civilian property during warfare had been proscribed by 15 states including Britain in 1874, but this was never ratified; in 1880 a meeting of international lawyers in Oxford nevertheless affirmed this as a principle of international law. The latter became the basis for the more well-known Hague convention signed in 1899. While looting was not strictly illegal under international law at this stage, which in any case applied only to so-called civilised nations, there was nevertheless an awareness that it was unethical. It remained the norm in military campaigns however, and indeed is not unknown to this day. There is then arguably a good claim that the Quran belongs in the Bodleian Library despite it being property which was stolen using force. That said, the University of Oxford has a published policy outlining how it reacts to calls for reparation of objects found in its collections. This is something to which it is sympathetic providing that there is clear evidence of the object having been looted and there is a surviving or remaining community to where it could be returned. These criteria seem to be met, however the choice is not the University's to make as the Quran remains the property of the trust which holds the assets of the Catholic monks at Ampleforth Abbey. The trust has not responded to enquiries in this regard. It is salient that this particular Holy Book was seized at the same time and in the same circumstances as the Benin Bronzes which are now being repatriated to Nigeria so the question of to whom it belongs - and where it belongs - is perhaps wider than just its legal status.

It is not the only object related to the Tirah Memorial's wars which is in Oxford. The Pitt Rivers Museum has a number of items including King Kabalega's royal throne-stool, his sceptre, several royal spears, a regal sword, and a variety of artefacts used in royal ceremonies connected with milk obtained from sacred cows.[4] These objects were donated to the museum in 1921 and were apparently obtained shortly beforehand by a retired missionary on his return from an ethnological expedition financed by a wealthy individual with an interest in mythology and religion. The aim of the expedition was to find 'details of the social anthropology which would be of value to science and to the Government, especially in regard to customs relating to land tenure, marriage, inheritance and birth'.[5] Additionally, the Reverend Roscoe had been tasked by the government, rather than his sponsor, with investigating 'native secret societies'.[6] He wrote extensively on the social practices he witnessed and was a prolific photographer. Although he was not welcomed everywhere or by everyone, he tried to interview older people to understand the traditional customs which he believed were lapsing.

The king of Bunyoro was particularly accommodating to his enquiries and re-enacted rituals for his benefit and provided old men who he could interview about past customs and rituals. Roscoe did not share a common language with those he interviewed and relied on both him and his interviewees speaking a common third language. Nowhere in his writings does Roscoe say how he acquired the many objects he collected although he does give space to describing arrangements for their transport home.[7] These items then do not appear to be looted objects.

It is striking from reading Roscoe's account how exaggerated and colourful a picture emerges of traditional practice compared to contemporary accounts from a few decades earlier when the first Europeans encountered Bunyoro. For instance, in a public lecture delivered on his return to Britain, Roscoe described how the king was not allowed to die of natural causes and so would poison himself in old age or infirmity. Every one of his sons then had to fight to the death until there was only one remaining who would then be crowned as the king. Several of the king's wives and court officials were clubbed to death and buried with him, and others voluntarily poisoned themselves so as to be able to join them in the grave.[8] Yet had Roscoe read Speke's account published in 1864 of his meeting with the king of Bunyoro (and he surely must have done) then he could not have failed to notice that rather than having fought his brothers to the death, the king's brothers were very much alive.[9] This is corroborated in the recorded traditional oral history of Bunyoro which recounts how in 1869 on the death of the king, his brothers gathered to choose a successor.[10] Similarly while Speke describes numerous meetings with the king including at the British campsite, Roscoe describes a deity-king whose day was so entirely taken up with ritual that he had no time to leave his palace or stray from his proscribed routine.[11]

His lurid descriptions of barbaric and primitive practices extended to his published report on the expedition. Very elaborate royal ceremonies were described by Roscoe in which the slightest mistake could lead to instantaneous death for the offending courtier – such as touching the king's teeth with the fork while he was being fed meat.[12] This again seems odd as other European witnesses attest that the king's lower incisors and his eye teeth had been removed when he was a child.[13] Roscoe further described how the royal cows and objects connected with them were holy; even to look at the king drinking his milk was an offence; and the king survived on a diet consisting solely of improbably liquid milk and four morsels of meat a day. The throne-stool was never left unattended and two of the king's wives slept at its side. In his lecture Roscoe further painted the Africans he encountered as alien and peculiar with the claim that cattle were so important to them that although he had never witnessed anyone lamenting the loss of a child, he had known a man strangle himself at the death of one of his cows.

Was Roscoe deliberately painting an exaggerated picture of the people he encountered? A tale of primitive savagery in the dark heart of Africa with elaborate rituals and beliefs - such as those which were of interest to Roscoe's sponsor, or would appeal to the preconceptions of his audience. Or were the men interviewed by Roscoe perhaps embellishing their stories and telling him what he wanted to hear? Were they even having a laugh at his expense? Above all though, the reader is left wondering why, if the artefacts Roscoe describes, including the throne-stool, were such venerated and holy relics, their keepers then allowed him to take them with him to England? Perhaps the king was prompting his elderly subjects to boost their tale and thereby the value of the artefacts which were under negotiation. Perhaps they were not even what they were purported to be. If so, they would not be the last fake antiques to fall to a gullible buyer.

Whatever the provenance, Bunyoro would like their royal throne-stool back. It is one of 279 objects identified by the regional government of Bunyoro which they are seeking to locate and negotiate for their return. The eight-legged stool is said to be 700 years old and was the symbol and seat of power of the Bunyoro kings. In 2021 the deputy prime minister of Bunyoro maintained that the throne was looted by Colonel Colvile's troops in 1894 and cast doubt on the idea that there could be have been more than one such distinctive stool.[14] The source for this claim is the traditional oral history of Bunyoro which was written down in 1901. In this version which corroborates that of Thruston, Kabalega narrowly escaped capture by Thruston's raid, but rather than his regalia being captured as Thruston says, the traditional history says that they were destroyed apart from the royal throne-stool, two royal spears and a large symbolic ritual drum. These were then sent by Thruston to Colonel Colville who took them back to England with him.[15] In this reading the stool was therefore part of the 'specially consecrated' regalia which Thruston wrote about having seized in a raid. Thruston himself detailed the regalia as being 'two brass spears, and a brass tripod' but this does not preclude there having been more objects taken, as Thruston's brother writing after Thruston's death mentions two leopard skins (which were the only items of loot which Thruston kept for himself), and two standards being seized. He corroborates the account of the 'sacred regalia' having been sent to Colvile.[16] Thruston also wrote that 'all of [Kabalega's] household goods fell into our hands'.[17] Colvile too wrote of Thruston having captured 'all Kabarega's household goods including the trebly consecrated insignia of royalty, the famous brass and iron sceptre and copper spear'.[18] It seems highly probable then that the royal stool was amongst the household items seized by Thruston and then despatched to Colvile.

Things become a little murkier as recent claims for the stool's restitution maintain the looted throne had nine not eight legs, and the University has identified that part of its Bunyoro collection was donated not by Roscoe, but by a Ugandan doctoral student in the 1930s.[19] Notwithstanding these interjections, the Pitt Rivers Museum has come to the conclusion that the stool it has is not Kabalega's throne and that there has been a major misunderstanding. In 2014 the director of the museum said that the stool was,

> ..*part of the collection made by the Reverend John Roscoe in Bunyoro in 1919-1920, and is not to be confused with the stool looted by Col.Henry Colville in 1894, the whereabouts of which appear to be unknown.*[20]

The only problem with this explanation is that the display notice attached to the stool in the Pitt Rivers Museum identifies it as 'Throne (Nyamalo) of King Kabarega'. Until recently it was similarly listed in the catalogue of the collection. Moreover, Roscoe the donor of the object also identified it as Kabalega's throne and captioned it as such in a published photograph in his report of his expedition.[21]

Figure 21. Pitt Rivers display of Bunyoro royal artefacts. The throne-stool is bottom left.

We are left with the strange situation where the Reverend Roscoe believed he was obtaining the royal throne, where the Pitt Rivers Museum listed and displays the stool as the throne previously belonging to Kabalega, and where the government in Bunyoro believes that their royal throne is in the Pitt Rivers Museum; and yet the museum maintains that this is not the throne claimed by Bunyoro, that it was not looted but properly acquired, and that therefore its return cannot be countenanced.

Cambridge University takes a less legalistic line in its approach to the Ugandan objects in its care. In a pilot project a few dozen of the many hundreds of objects donated by the Reverend Roscoe which it has in its collection were returned to Uganda in 2022. Although this is a new initiative, some sacred objects from the University's collection were were previously returned to the Ugandan National Museum in 1961 and 1962 at the time of Uganda's independence. Dr Peterson, the leader of the project explained that 'we want to put these objects back in the hands of the people that made them meaningful'. His counterpart Rose Mwanga, Ugandan commissioner for museums, expanded 'We want them to live again not only as museum pieces but as part of Uganda's public culture...... Bringing these items back will also help people come to terms with their own collective memory, (and) celebrate their rich histories and identities'.[22]

The current king of Bunyoro who is a grandson of Kabalega visited the Pitt Rivers Museum to view his ancestral throne in 2011. Although unknown in Britain, Kabalega is seen as an iconic freedom fighter in the land of his birth where the king or omukana remains the titular head of the regional government and is regarded as an hereditary unifying figure above party politics. Unlike his predecessors he has not been crowned on the traditional throne - which may or may not be in the Pitt

Rivers Museum. In 2013 the king formally asked for the return of the throne, and then five years later the matter was referred by his government up to the national Ugandan government who engaged with the British high commissioner to try to secure its return. While saying that the British government was not responsible for museums' collections, the high commissioner agreed to pursue the matter with colleagues in London. There has been no reported progress since.[23]

Whether it is the throne or just a remarkably similar stool, and whether it was looted or sold in a fair manner, the throne-stool in the Pitt Rivers Museum clearly has cultural and political significance for today's Bunyoro. It is difficult to think that anyone would miss the regal stool, or even notice its absence from these shores.

Bunyoro's claims for reparation run wider than the symbolic return of the royal stool however. In 2004 a group of Bunyoro formed a speculative association and attempted to sue the United Kingdom for reparations of £500 million for atrocities committed during the invasion of 1893. In 2014 further claims were lodged relating to an alleged 2.4 million deaths during the war of 1891-99, and the violation of land ownership rights when the British ceded parts of the kingdom to King Mwanga's Buganda.[24] The claim rested on the principle that the British are directly responsible for Bunyoro's tragic trajectory which continues into the modern day.

The fact that events such as these happened a long time in the past is often put forward as a reason to avoid engaging with the question of restitution and recompense. But by definition all crimes and events happen in the past. The pertinent point is not how long-ago controversial events happened but how concrete the consequences are for those living today. It would be absurd to seek compensation from the modern state of Italy for the depredations of the Roman army because there are no people living today who are recognisably adversely affected as a result of these past actions. But when the events under consideration are within a few generations of the present then a different calculus must surely apply, and indeed does. In 2022 industrialised nations agreed to recompense developing nations for historical emissions which led to global climate change; and on a more individual level, the untangling and restitution of Jewish assets continues 75 years after the Holocaust. It is against this background that Bunyoro's claim for reparations must be assessed.

Kabalega's throne is just one object of the many that museums and other institutions are being asked to return. The Benin Bronzes join human remains and other legacies of Empire which are being repatriated. Britain has begun to consider and address wider claims for reparations. It has settled claims by those it tortured in the 1950s during the Kenyan Mau Mau risings, while denying any legal responsibility for doing so in case it establishes a precedent and opens the floodgates to more claims. Likewise, the monarch has been exact in expressing regret for past sufferings caused by the British state, but not going so far as to apologise which would be to implicitly admit responsibility and open up the route to reparation. The Dutch king has been less reticent. In 2023 he apologised for the Dutch role in slavery in south east Asia with these words,

> *I ask forgiveness for this crime against humanity.*
> *As your king and as a member of the government,*
> *I make this apology myself.*

The question of imperial responsibility is not entirely clear cut however. For example, the British were after all aided by Bagandan and Sudanese warriors in warfare and looting in

Bunyroro, and we have seen how Britain usually relied on local cooperation in securing and acquiring its Empire.[25] Even so, not being responsible for everything is not the same as being responsible for nothing. Britain surely bears at least some if not a major share of the responsibility for the legacy of its Empire. The two examples of Empire detailed in this book show that the British were not guiltless or innocent. Nor is this assessment a projection of contemporary moral standards into the past. British people at the time deplored the actions that were taken in their name, from the opium wars to the vainglorious militarism and atrocities that were committed. They said so, and organised against it in their civic societies and churches to oppose and try to prevent the worst excesses of imperialism.

*

No single individual has as many representations in portraits and sculptures in the University of Oxford as Cecil Rhodes. Rhodes was an ardent imperialist who built an immense fortune principally through diamond mining in South Africa. In his will he left money for the establishment of a secret society to bring about the governance of the world by the British race, a cause to which he maintained he had dedicated his life. He believed it was the mission of Englishmen to colonise every piece of fruitful land they could inhabit. His will was subsequently toned down somewhat and the requirement for a secret society replaced by the foundation of a trust to finance 'young colonists, to give breadth to their views, for their instruction in life and manners, and for instilling in their minds the advantage to the Colonies as well as to the United Kingdom of the retention of the unity of the Empire'. He was a controversial figure at the time - there was a campaign to deny him an honorary degree - and concerns expressed when the bombshell news of his bequest to the University became known after his death. He left £100,000 to Oriel College and the remainder of his £4 million fortune to the trust which bears his name.[26]

In recognition of his munificence Oriel placed a life-sized statue of him on the front of a new building erected with his benefaction where it remains overlooking the High Street. It has recently come to symbolise a wider debate around decolonisation and the culture wars. A body of students rallying under the 'Rhodes must fall' banner have called for the removal of the statue, a move agreed to and then rescinded by the college where it is located. The intervention of the relevant secretary of state then followed, disallowing any change at all – even to the extent of affixing an explanatory plaque to the facade. The students' demands are wider than just the question of a statue and its perceived offensive qualities, but extend to questioning the Eurocentric and colonialist assumptions and underpinnings of large parts of the curriculum as they see it.[27] To their detractors they are seen as attempting to erase or rewrite history, and to deny the more positive legacy that has resulted from Rhodes' gift. Thus are the culture wars fought.

This is not the first statue on the High Street to cause dissension. During the religious controversies of the seventeenth century a fiercely protestant leading-townsman called John Nixon complained that people were genuflecting before the recently erected statue of Mary the Virgin located on the porch of the church of that name on the High Street.[28] There is also a precedent for the removal of a statue from the same road. In 1950 a memorial to the 142 men who died serving in the South Africa or Boer War placed at the far end of the street was removed to make way for a roundabout just

48 years after the end of the war in which they had served. This broke the solemn pledge made at the unveiling ceremony that it was 'a sacred possession, and would be handed down for many years in the City of Oxford amongst the beautiful buildings and historic houses', and be 'always prominent before the citizens'.[29] In 1966 it was moved again and continued its peregrinations in 2008 and can now be found in the environs of the nearby town of Abingdon.

The fact that the statue of Rhodes has come into focus after decades of it being ignored suggests that the amnesia around the British Empire might be beginning to dissipate. It is time that the British woke up to the legacy of their Empire as it is all too live an issue in the many parts of the world where they imposed themselves. First among these must be China, no longer a weak power that can be bossed around and ordered to open up to free trade, including in addictive narcotics, by the shelling of Beijing by a gunboat. This is an event of which very few British people are aware, but which forms a core part of Chinese education and was the subject of a phenomenally successful epic-heroic film which reached an even wider domestic audience. The current president of China is committed to reversing 'the century of humiliation' that sprang from the events the film outlines. Another major power that has always taken a dim view of the British Empire, even to the extent of rebelling and declaring its independence from it, was similarly offended when in 2016 Boris Johnson then mayor of London described its president, Barak Obama, as having 'an ancestral dislike of the British Empire' due to his 'part-Kenyan heritage'. More recently still, the coronation of a new queen has led to the revival of calls for the return of the Koh-I-Noor diamond which adorns one of the royal crowns. It was taken from its last owner, the eleven year-old Maharajah

Duleep Singh by the British East India Company in 1849.

Whatever the rights and wrongs of reparations, and of returning objects which were often looted or coerced from their owners, it seems clear that ignoring the past is no longer tenable. It is one thing for the British to pretend their Empire never happened, or at least the unmentionable bits of it, but it is another when their rivals, markets and allies are clamouring for the return of artefacts, for apologies and compensation. Britain has never really faced up to its imperial past, has never reckoned honestly with the role it played in the world and the consequences of this.

It does not have to be this way. Germany has fully addressed its role in the Second World War and its own colonial past. In an often painful, divisive and difficult process over many decades, it has admitted responsibility for atrocities, apologised and made compensation, and continues to do so. A museum to Jewish victims of the Holocaust is shortly to open in the Greek city of Thessaloniki which has been partly funded by a 10m Euro contribution from the German government. Even more significantly in 2021 it agreed to pay 1.1 billion Euros in compensation to Namibia in recognition of the genocide against the Herero people between 1904-1908. Reparations are about more than just finance however. Perhaps more importantly they are also about accepting responsibility for past transgressions, for acknowledging rather than denying the more egregious aspects of our past. In the very centre of its capital city is a significant monument to those who died in the Holocaust, and monuments to victims of Nazi oppression are to be found throughout the country. In contrast, although Britain has a memorial prominently located on London's Park Lane to animals that suffered during wartime, it has no memorial to victims of Empire. This surely is a serious omission and is emblematic of the wider denial of an often-shameful imperial past.

While we naturally prefer to remember the parts of our nation's past that we are proud of such as the fight against fascism, we should not lose sight of the parts that we find uncomfortable or abhorrent. We should make more of an effort to remember things that are forgotten. It is only by recognising that we are capable of doing great wrong as well as right that we can avoid doing so again in the future.

*

There are alternatives to removing statues that are found distasteful and offensive. They don't have to be torn down by a mob, or removed by the vote of a committee. They can be given context by placing contrasting or opposing statues to accompany them, or by affixing explanatory text. The process of recognising changing historical perspectives does not need to be binary.

As for the Tirah Memorial, it could perhaps become once more a monument to remembering rather than a monument to forgetting which is what it has become. For instance, it could be framed with memorials to the colonial troops who fought alongside their British counterparts: the Sikhs, Bengalis, Punjabis and Nepalese Gurkhas, many of whose descendants are now also British and form part of the fabric of the nation. Perhaps too, a monument to the Banyoro, Baganda, Orakzai and Afridis whose villages and lives were laid waste by imperial forces might be considered. If that is too ambitious, a clean and brush up is long overdue, renovation of the names would not be out of place, and some notice boards explaining what it is and why it is there would be a valuable step forward. It wouldn't be everything. But it would be a start.

AFTERWORD

Shortly before completing this book, protests broke out across Iran driven by the death of a young woman who was not wearing the required religious dress. A vigil was held next to the Tirah Memorial and photographs of Mahsi Amini and other victims of the Iranian regime were placed on its steps along with candles and flowers. An accompanying poster called for freedom for Kurdistan and Balochistan. The latter is a region crossing the territories of Iran, Pakistan and Afghanistan. On the other side of the memorial three scaffolders in high-viz clothing were having their sandwiches. All three wore turbans and were Sikhs. None of the protestors nor the builders were aware of the memorial's origin or significance, yet it seemed more relevant than ever, showing as it does the extraordinarily interconnected nature of our world.

ACKNOWLEDGMENTS

I am grateful to the archivists and librarians who helped me navigate the way through their collections, particularly during the period of restrictions relating to the Covid virus. The staff at county record collections in particular stand out for the courteous way they deal with members of the public while operating under tight financial constraints.

My thanks are due to Dr. Sebastian Pender for his early advice and help in focussing the narrative. I am immensely grateful to Dr. Sudhir Hazareesingh for his guidance and review of the manuscript, as well as for his generous endorsement of what is a merge work compared to his prodigious and scholarly output. My thanks too to Henry Eliot, who among his many other qualities has a remarkable ability to spot typographical and grammatical errors. Those that remain are entirely my responsibility. My gratitude to Kim remains boundless - not least for her many cups of tea and for putting up with me.

NOTES

Introduction

1. 'Unveiling Ceremony', *Jackson's Oxford Journal*, (1900), July 7th., p. 8. Mockler-Ferryman, A. F., 'The Oxfordshire Light Infantry Chronicle', (London:1900), (pp. 307-14).
2. Toye, Richard, *Churchill's Empire: The World That Made Him and the World He Made*, (London:2010), pp. 31-34.
3. Hernon, Ian, *Britain's Forgotten Wars: Colonial Campaigns of the 19th Century*, (Stroud:2003), p. 450.
4. David B. Edwards, 'Mad Mullahs and Englishmen: Discourse in the Colonial Encounter', *Comparative Studies in Society and History*, 31 (1989), 649-50.
5. Edgerton, David, 'The Nationalisation of British History: Historians, Nationalism and the Myths of 1940', *The English Historical Review*, 136 (2021), 950-85.
6. Jeffery, Keith, 'The Second World War', in *The Oxford History of the British Empire: Volume IV: The Twentieth Century*, (Oxford:1999), pp. 306-28 (p. 319).
7. Ibid. p. 312.
8. Killingray, David and Plaut, Martin, *Fighting for Britain: African Soldiers in the Second World War*, (Woodbridge:2012), p. 8.

1. The North West Frontier

1. Thomsett, Richard Gillham, *With the Peshawar Column, Tirah Expeditionary Force*, (London:1899), p. 39.
2. Ibid.
3. Ibid. p. 82.

4. Mackenzie, John, 'Tirah 1897', 2002-2011, https://www.britishbattles.com/north-west-frontier-of-india/tirah-1897/, Accessed: 23/10/2022.

5. Thomsett, *With the Peshawar Column*, p. 78.

6. Hutchinson, H.D., Colonel., *The Campaign in Tirah, 1897-98*, (London:1898), p. 37.

7. Ibid.; Johnson, Robert, *The Afghan Way of War: Culture and Pragmatism : A Critical History*, (London:2014), p. 160.

8. Agha, Sameetah, 'The Tirah Campaign', in *Queen Victoria's Wars : British Military Campaigns, 1857-1902*, ed. by Stephen M. Miller (Cambridge:2021), pp. 240-59 (p. 256).

9. Ibid. p. 253; Courtney, William, 'The Tirah Campaign', *Fortnightly Review*, 63 (1898), 390-400, 391; Mills, H. Woosnam, *The Tirah Campaign: Being the Sequel to the Pathan Revolt in North-West India*, (Lahore, India:1898), p. 37.

10. Thomsett, *With the Peshawar Column*, p. 78.

11. 'Oxfordshire Soldier on War: Thrilling Letter from the Indian Frontier', *Oxford Chronicle and Reading Gazette*, (1898), 29th Jan., p. 2; Thomsett, *With the Peshawar Column*, p. 75.

12. Warburton, Robert Sir, *Eighteen Years in the Khyber, 1879-1898*, (England:1900), p. 18.

13. Ibid.; Soldiers of Oxfordshire Museum Woodstock, Davies, H.R., 'Diary of Major General H. R. Davies', A collection of letters from 1897 and a diary of Major General H R Davies, (13th May 1896-15th Jan 1898) covers time of Tirah Expedition, plus Mention in Dispatches, certificates, a red hardback address book and newspaper cutting., SOFO.6128. Aug. 30th.

14. Tharoor, Shashi, *Inglorious Empire: What the British Did to India*, (London:2017), p. 9.

15. Ibid. p. 4.
16. Ibid. p. 6.
17. Beckert, Sven, *Empire of Cotton: A Global History*, (New York:2014), p. 45.
18. Cain, P.J., 'Economics: The Metropolitan Context', in *The Oxford History of the British Empire: The Nineteenth Century, Vol.Iii*, ed. by Andrew Porter (Oxford:1999), pp. 31-52 (p. 35).
19. Tomlinson, B.R., 'Economics and Empire: The Periphery and the Imperial Economy', in *The Oxford History of the British Empire: The Nineteenth Century: Vol. Iii*, ed. by Andrew Porter (1999), pp. 53-74 (p. 69).
20. Buxton, Julia, *The Political Economy of Narcotics: Production, Consumption and Global Markets*, (London:2006), p. 9.
21. Emdad-ul Haq, M., *Drugs in South Asia: From the Opium Trade to the Present Day*, (Houndmills:2000), p. 20.
22. Lin, Imperial Commissioner at Canton, 'Letter to Queen Victoria', 1839, https://sourcebooks.fordham.edu/mod/1839lin2.asp, Accessed 10/2/2020.
23. Rimner, Steffen, *Opium's Long Shadow: From Asian Revolt to Global Drug Control*, (Cambridge, Massachusetts:2018), p.6.
24. Bauer, Rolf, *The Peasant Production of Opium in Nineteenth-Century India*, (Leiden:2019), p. 39.
25. Trocki quoted in ibid. p. 34.
26. Moore, Robin, J., 'Imperial India, 1858-1914', in *The Oxford History of the British Empire: The Nineteenth Century: Vol. Iii*, ed. by Andrew Porter (Oxford:1999), pp. 422-46 (p. 441).

27. Hurd, John M., 'Railways', in *The Cambridge Economic History of India: Vol. II: c.1757–c.1970*, ed. by Dharma Kumar and Meghnad Desai (Cambridge:1983), pp. 737-61 (p. 738).
28. Omissi, David E., *The Sepoy and the Raj: The Indian Army, 1860-1940*, (Basingstoke:1994), p. 3.;Tharoor, *Inglorious Empire*, p. 23.
29. Omissi, *The Sepoy and the Raj*, p. 45.
30. Thomsett, *With the Peshawar Column*, p. 207.
31. Omissi, *The Sepoy and the Raj*, p. 232.
32. Ibid.

2. A Good Thrashing

1. Slessor, Arthur Kerr, *The 2nd Battalion Derbyshire Regiment in Tirah*, (London:1900), p. 107.
2. Callwell, C. E., *Tirah, 1897*, (London:1911), p. 9.
3. Slessor, *The 2nd Battalion* pp. 3-4.
4. Agha, pp. 240-41.
5. Zeidan, Adam, 'Anglo-Afghan Wars', 2021, https://www.britannica.com/event/Anglo-Afghan-Wars, Accessed: 23/4/2021; Atwood, Rodney, 'The Second Afghan War, 1878–1880', in *Queen Victoria's Wars: British Military Campaigns, 1857–1902*, ed. by Stephen M. Miller (Cambridge:2021), pp. 126-45 (p. 131).
6. Zeidan, 'Anglo-Afghan Wars'.
7. Toye, *Churchill's Empire: The World That Made Him and the World He Made*, p. 39.
8. Seeley, John Robert Sir, *The Expansion of England: Two Courses of Lectures*, (England:1883).
9. Seeley, J. R. and Gross, John, *The Expansion of England*, (Chicago ; London:1971), pp. 240-43.

10. Tripodi, Christian, *Edge of Empire: The British Political Officer and Tribal Administration on the North-West Frontier 1877-1947*, (Farnham:2011), p. 12.

11. Ibid.

12. Hutchinson, *The Campaign in Tirah, 1897-98*, p. 226.

13. Tripodi, *Edge of Empire*, pp. 3-4.

14. Quoted in Kiran, Nirvan, *21 Kesaris: The Untold Story of the Battle of Saragarhi*, (New Delhi:2019).

15. Sections of the authorities were aware of the imminent threat but did little to counter it or warn higher echelons of command in the belief that it would strengthen the case for the 'forward' policy. See Agha, Sameetah, 'Sub-Imperialism and the Loss of the Kyber: The Politics of Imperial Defence on British India's North West Frontier', *Indian Historical Review*, 40 (2) (2013), 307-30.

16. Eg. 'The Cause of the Rising', *Henley & South Oxford Standard* - (1897), Sep. 10th.

17. Mills, *The Tirah Campaign*, p. 45.

18. Tripodi, *Edge of Empire*, p. 241.

19. Thomsett, *With the Peshawar Column*, pp. 2-3.

20. Mills, *The Tirah Campaign*, p. 2.

21. Condos, Mark, '"Fanaticism" and the Politics of Resistance Along the North-West Frontier of British India', *Comparative Studies in Society and History*, 58 (2016), 717-45, 744.

22. Ibid. pp. 744-45.

23. Quoted in Edwards, David B., 'Mad Mullahs and Englishmen: Discourse in the Colonial Encounter', *Comparative Studies in Society and History*, 31 (1989), 649-70, 654. Churchill was later to change his view, or at least his account of it, and ascribe the cause to the forward policy.

24. Johnson, Robert A., 'The 1897 Revolt and Tirah Valley Operations from the Pashtun Perspective', Cultural and Geographic Reseach Tribal Analysis Center, 2009, https://tribalanalysiscenter.com/PDF-TAC/The%201897%20Revolt%20and%20Tirah%20Valley%20Operations.pdf, Accessed: Feb. 21st 2023.

25. Edwards, pp. 652-53.

26. Atwood, p. 247.

27. Surridge, Keith, 'The Ambigous Amir: Britain, Aghanistan and the 1897 North-West Frontier Uprising', *The Journal of Imperial and Commonwealth History*, 36 (2008), 417-34.

28. Hutchinson, *The Campaign in Tirah, 1897-98*, p. 19.

29. Ibid. p. 51.

30. Holdich, T. H., 'Tirah', *The Geographical Journal*, 12 (1898), 337-59, 348.

3. Struggling On.

1. Thomsett, *With the Peshawar Column*, p. 97 ff.

2. Johnson, *Afghan Way*, p. 160.

3. Holdich, p. 338.

4. Slessor, *The 2nd Battalion* p. 161.

5. Plowden, F.H., 'The Battalion on the Frontier', *Chronicle of the Oxford Light Infantry*, (1899), 243-71, 267-70.

6. Booth, Philip, *The Oxfordshire and Buckinghamshire Light Infantry*, (London:1971), p. 83.

7. Courtney, p. 399.

8. Soldiers of Oxfordshire Museum Woodstock, Crutch, Charles, 'Photocopies of a Diary Written by Charles Crutch (3130) Relating to the Tirah Expedition of 1897.', SOFO:6130.

9. Agha, p. 250.

10. Courtney, p. 399.

11. Plowden, p. 266.
12. Thomsett, *With the Peshawar Column*, p. 123.
13. Plowden, p. 263.
14. Shadwell, Leonard Julius, *Lockhart's Advance through Tirah.*, (New York (State):1899), pp. 254-55.(New York (State):1899), pp. 254-55.
15. Mills, *The Tirah Campaign*, p. 120.p. 120.
16. Courtney, p. 399.
17. Davies, 'Diary of H. R. Davies'. Aug. 25th.
18. Memorandum no 5 in ibid.
19. Ibid.March 19th.
20. Davies In a letter to his father writes that Crowhurst is the only one with very dangerous wounds. Ibid.; cf. Frith (unsigned letter) writes that Crowhurst was unscathed in Soldiers of Oxfordshire Museum Woodstock, 'Photocopies of Letters from Fred Evelegh During the Tirah Expedition, India, Jan 1898-Nov 1899'.
21. Mockler-Ferryman, A. F., 'The Oxfordshire Light Infantry Chronicle', (London:1897), (p. 108).
22. Soldiers of Oxfordshire Museum Woodstock, Davies, H.R., 'A Collection of Letters from 1897 Plus Mention in Dispatches, Certifcates, a Red Hardback Address Book and Newspaper Cutting.', SOFO.6128.
23. 'Letters from Fred Evelegh'.
24. Crutch, 'Diary', (p. 44).
25. Ibid. p. 74.
26. Quoted in Coughlin, Con, *Churchill's First War: Young Winston and the Fight against the Taliban*, (London:2013), p. 187.
27. Crutch, 'Diary', (p. 39).
28. Coughlin, *Churchill's First War*, p. 216.
29. Davies, 'Diary of H. R. Davies'. Oct. 20th.

30. Crutch, 'Diary', (p. 80).

31. Mills, *The Tirah Campaign*, pp. 214-16.

32. Mockler-Ferryman, 'Oxfordshire Light Infantry Chronicle 1897', p. 97.

33. Soldiers of Oxfordshire Museum Woodstock, '5pp Typescript of Record of Service Covering the Tirah Expedition, 1897', SOFO.2766.

34. Coughlin, *Churchill's First War*, p. 188.

35. Mockler-Ferryman, 'Oxfordshire Light Infantry Chronicle 1897', p. 100.

36. Crutch, 'Diary', (p. 45).

37. Slessor, *The 2nd Battalion* p. 174.

38. Ibid. p. 175.

39. Hernon, *Britain's Forgotten Wars*, p. 448.

40. Mills, *The Tirah Campaign*, p. 61.

41. Ibid. p. 68.

42. Ibid. pp. 61-62.

43. Ibid. p. 67.

44. Spiers, Edward M., *The Scottish Soldier and Empire, 1854-1902*, (Edinburgh:2022), pp. 125-26. Wilkinson, Glen, R., 'Purple Prose and the Yellow Press: Imagined Spaces and the Military Expedition to Tirah, 1897', in *Negotiating India in the Nineteenth-Century Media*, ed. by David Finkelstein and Douglas M. Peers (Basingstoke:2000), pp. 253-76 (pp. 256-62).

4. Unbeaten

1. Thomsett, *With the Peshawar Column*, p. 213. James, Lionel, *The Indian Frontier War: Being an Account of the Mohmund and Tirah Expeditions, 1897*, (London:1898), p. 173.

2. James, *The Indian Frontier War*, p. 173.

3. Holdich, p. 347.
4. James, *The Indian Frontier War*, p. 149.
5. Mills, *The Tirah Campaign*, p. 114.
6. Slessor, *The 2nd Battalion* p. 119.
7. Thomsett, *With the Peshawar Column*, p. 166.
8. 'The Medical Arrangements for the Tirah Expeditionary Force', *The Lancet (British edition)*, 151 (1898), 52-54.
9. Slessor, *The 2nd Battalion* p. 177.
10. Ibid. p. 134.
11. Gabriel, Richard A., *Between Flesh and Steel: A History of Military Medicine from the Middle Ages to the War in Afghanistan*, (Washington, District of Columbia:2013), p. 159.
12. Cartwright, Frederick F. and Biddiss, Michael D., *Disease & History*, (Stroud:2000), p. 109.
13. Gabriel, *Between Flesh and Steel*, p. 159.
14. Chakrabarti, Pratik, *Medicine and Empire : 1600-1960*, (Basingstoke:2014), p. 112.
15. Cartwright and Biddiss, *Disease & History*, p. 119.
16. Chakrabarti, *Medicine and Empire : 1600-1960*, p. 104.
17. Spiers, *The Scottish Soldier and Empire, 1854-1902*, p. 113.
18. Jenkins, Stephanie, 'Oxford War Memorials: Tirah Campaign, Bonn Square', http://oxfordhistory.org.uk/war/tirah_campaign/index.html, Accessed: 15th Feb., 2022.
19. Tripodi, *Edge of Empire*.
20. Quoted in Slessor, *The 2nd Battalion* p. 136.
21. Callwell, *Tirah, 1897*, p. 184.
22. Shadwell, *Lockhart's Advance through Tirah.*, pp. 266-75. pp. 266-75.
23. Callwell, *Tirah, 1897*, pp. 186-206.
24. Ibid. Thomsett, *With the Peshawar Column*, pp. 146-48.

25. Churchill, 'The Tirah Campaign: Striking Letter from Mr Winston Churchill', *The Times of India*, (1898), May 23rd p. 6. Quoted in Hernon, *Britain's Forgotten Wars: Colonial Campaigns of the 19th Century*, p. 448.

26. Chamberlain, Neville, 'The Occupation of Tirah', *Saturday review of Politics, Literature, Science and Art*, (1897), November 6th.

27. Slessor, *The 2nd Battalion* p. 174.

28. 'Abroad', *The Speaker : The Liberal Review*, 16 (1897), Dec. 18th., p. 674.

29. Quoted in Slessor, *The 2nd Battalion* p. 176.

30. 'The North-West Frontier', National Army Museum, https://www.nam.ac.uk/explore/north-west-frontier-india, Accessed: July 7th., 2022.

31. Johnson, *Afghan Way*, pp. 172-73.

32. Mills, *The Tirah Campaign*, p. 235.

33. Johnson, *Afghan Way*, p. 171.

34. Chakrabarti, *Medicine and Empire : 1600-1960*, p. 103.

5. Foundations

1. 'Unveiling Ceremony', Jackson's Oxford Journal.

2. Flanders, Amy and Colclough, Stephen, 'The Bible Press', in *The History of Oxford University Press: Volume Ii: 1780 to 1896*, ed. by Simon Eliot (2013), pp. 356-401.

3. 'Industries', in *A History of the County of Oxford*, ed. by William Page (London:1907), pp. 225-77.

4. 'Barrows & Co.', Grace's Guide, 2017, https://www.gracesguide.co.uk/Barrows_and_Co, Accessed: Sep. 29th 2022, ; 'Barrows & Stewart', Grace's Guide, 2020, https://www.gracesguide.co.uk/Barrows_and_Stewart, Accessed: Sep. 29th 2022,

5. Oxford Record Office Oxford, Launchbury, G.T., 'John Allen & Son (Oxford) Ltd. 1868-1952. A History of over 80 Years of Progress', Extracts from Allen's Activities, Oxfo 681.7 Alle.

6. Baggs, A.P. and others, 'Witney Borough: Economic History, the Industrial Revolution in Witney C.1800-1900', in *A History of the County of Oxford*, ed. by Simon Townley (London:2004), pp. 99-97.

7. Oxfordshire Record Office Oxford, 'Early's of Witney Financial Records and Diaries', B1/2/A7/1.B1/2/C1/1 ibid.

8. Ibid.B1/2 /A7/1

9. Eliot, Simon, *The History of Oxford University Press. Volume II, 1780 to 1896*, (Oxford:2014), p. 725.

6. African Pearl

1. Thruston, Arthur Beyford, *African Incidents, Personal Experiences in Egypt and Unyoro*, (London:1900), p. 219.

2. Kasfir, Nelson, *The Shrinking Political Arena: Participation and Ethnicity in African Politics with a Case Study of Uganda*, (Berkeley; London:1976).

3. Thruston, *African Incidents*, p. 79.

4. Ibid. p. 107. Portal, Gerald Herbert, 'Africa No. 7: Report by His Majesty's Special Commissioner on the Protectorate of Uganda', (London:1901), p. 9.

5. Beachey, R. W., 'Macdonald's Expedition and the Uganda Mutiny, 1897-98', *The Historical Journal*, 10 (1967), 237-54, 253.

6. 'Africa No. 15: General Report on the Uganda Protectorate for the Year Ending March 31, 1903', (London:1903), p. 17.

7. Portal, Gerald Herbert, 'Africa No. 2: Reports Relating to Uganda', (London:1894).

8. Cartwright and Biddiss, *Disease & History*, p. 159.

9. Ibid.

10. Thomas, Jonathan York, 'The Role of the Medical Missionary in British East Africa, 1874-1904', (Thesis (D.Phil.), University of Oxford, 1982), p. 4.

11. Ibid. p. 302.

12. Colvile, H. E., *The Land of the Nile Springs: Being Chiefly an Account of How We Fought Kabarega*, (London; New York:1895), p. 26.

13. Thomas, p. 12.

14. Roscoe, John, *Preliminary Report of the Mackie Ethnological Expedition to Central Africa*, (London:1921), p. 312.

15. 'Society for the Propagation of the Gospel', *Jackson's Oxford Journal*, (1884), Feb. 7th., p. 7.

16. Portal, 'Report on Protectorate of Uganda', p. 7.

7. Mission Fever

1. 'Oxford Diocesan Missionary Loan Exhibition', *Jackson's Oxford Journal*, (1899), 28th Oct., p. 8.

2 Ibid.

3 Ibid.

4 Ibid.

5 Ibid.

6. Oliver, Roland Anthony, *The Missionary Factor in East Africa*, (London:1965), p. 13.

7 Stanley, Henry M., 'New African Expedition', *The Daily Telegraph*, (1875), Nov. 15th, p. 5.

8. 'Church Missionary Society', *Jackson's Oxford Journal*, (1885), 14th Feb., p. 6.

9. 'Oxford Diocesan Missionary Loan Exhibition', Jackson's Oxford Journal.

10. Oliver, *The Missionary Factor in East Africa*, p. 212. Tiberondwa, Ado K., *Missionary Teachers as Agents of Colonialism: A Study of Their Activities in Uganda, 1877-1925*, (Lusaka:1989). Wild-Wood, Emma, 'Bible Translation and the Formation of Corporate Identity in Uganda and Congo 1900-1940', *Journal of African History*, 58 (2017), 489-507.
11. Weber, Eugen, *Peasants into Frenchmen: The Modernization of Rural France, 1870-1914*, (London:1979), pp. 486-93.
12. 'British and Foreign Bible Society', *Jackson's Oxford Journal*, (1890), Oct. 25th., p. 6.
13. Tiberondwa, *Missionary Teachers as Agents of Colonialism* p. xiv.
14. Portal, 'Report on Protectorate of Uganda', p. 18.
15. McCaski, T.C., 'Cultural Encounters: Britain and Africa in the Nineteenth Century', in *The Oxford History of the British Empire: The Nineteenth Century: Vol. III,* ed. by Andrew Porter (Oxford:1999), pp. 665-89 (p. 677).
16. Kasfir, *The Shrinking Political Arena*, p. 92.
17. Amone, Charles and Muura, Okullu, 'British Colonialism and the Creation of Acholi Ethnic Identity in Uganda, 1894 to 1962', *Journal of Imperial and Commonwealth History*, 42 (2014), 239-57.
18. Kasfir, *The Shrinking Political Arena*, p. 100.
19. McCaski, p. 685.
20. Oliver, *The Missionary Factor in East Africa*, pp. 9-11.
21. McCaski, pp. 674-77.
22. Portal, 'Report on Protectorate of Uganda', p. 1.
23. Porter, Andrew, 'Religion, Missionary Enthusiasm, and Empire', in *The Oxford History of the British Empire: The Nineteenth Century: Vol. III.,* ed. by Andrew Porter (Oxford:1999), pp. 223-45 (p. 238). McCaski, pp. 674-77.

24. McCaski, pp. 674-77.

25. Mockler-Ferryman, A. F., 'The Story of the Uganda Mutiny', *Macmillan's Magazine,* 78 (1898), 308-20, 316. Thruston, *African Incidents*, p. 87.

26. Derbyshire Record Office, Colvile, Henry Edward Sir, 'Military Correspondence and Papers', D461/5.

27. Thruston, *African Incidents*, pp. 65, 161.

28. Ibid. Colvile, 'Military Correspondence'. April 8th.

29. Colvile, 'Military Correspondence'. July 16th.

30. Macdonald, James Ronald Leslie, *Soldiering and Surveying in British East Africa, 1891-1894*, (London:1897), pp. 10-12.

31. Bodleian Libraries Oxford, Ponsonby, John, 'Sir John Ponsonby's Diary of Military Expedition through British East Africa to the Congo, 1898-99 : With a March through Naivasha and Mumias to Unyoro Where He Commanded Sudanese Troops in the Uganda Mutiny. [Microform]', Micr. Afr.597. Feb. 20th.

32. Ashe, Robert Pickering, *Two Kings of Uganda; or, Life by the Shores of Victoria Nyanza; Being an Account of a Residence of Six Years in Eastern Equatorial Africa*, (unknown:1889), p. 11.

33. Colvile, *The Land of the Nile Springs,* July 2nd; Macdonald, *Soldiering and Surveying*, p. 24.

34. Ashe, *Two Kings of Uganda*, p. 13.

35. Colvile, 'Military Correspondence'.

36. Thruston, *African Incidents*, p. 130.p.

37. Bodleian Libraries Oxford, 'British East Africa (Uganda), 1886-1910', Archive of the Anti-Slavery Society, MSS. Brit. Emp. s.22/G4.

38. 'Church Missionary Society', Jackson's Oxford Journal.

8: Annexation

1. Portal, 'Report on Protectorate of Uganda', pp. 1,15. Portal, 'Reports Relating to Uganda', p. 15.
2 Macdonald, *Soldiering and Surveying*, p. 316.
3. Agha, Sub-Imperialism.
4. Leopold, Mark, 'Legacies of Slavery in North-West Uganda: The Story of the 'One-Elevens'', *Africa*, 76 (2006), 180-99, 182-83.
5. Low, D. A., *Buganda in Modern History*, (London:1971), p. 56.
6. Ibid. pp. 61-78.
7. Gregory, J. W., *The Foundation of British East Africa*, (London:1901), p. 238.
8. 'Archive of the Anti-Slavery Society'.
9 Ibid.
10 Clipping from Daily News, July 5th, 1892 in ibid.

9. Desolation and Death

1. Colvile, *The Land of the Nile Springs* p. 70.
2. Colvile, 'Military Correspondence'. Feb. 11th.
3. Colvile, *The Land of the Nile Springs* p. 55.
4. Ibid. pp. 98-99.
5. Ibid. p. 62.
6. Ponsonby, 'Sir John Ponsonby's Diary'. June 11th ff.
7. Macdonald, *Soldiering and Surveying*, pp. 209-10.
8. Thruston, *African Incidents*, p. 100.p.
9. Colvile, *The Land of the Nile Springs* pp. 95, 97-98.
10. Ibid. pp. 114, 17.
11. Ibid. p. 119.
12. Ibid. pp. 142-43.
13. Ibid. p. 188.
14. Ibid.
15. Ibid. pp. 258-63.

16. Mockler-Ferryman, *Ugandan Mutiny*, p. 311.
17. Thruston, *African Incidents*, p. 294.p.
18. Ibid. pp. 159-60.
19. Ibid. pp. 170-71.
20. 'Africa No. 2: Papers Relating to Recent Events in the Uganda Protectorate : [in Continuation of "Africa No. 2 (1898)]', (London:1898), p. 3.
21. Thruston, *African Incidents*, pp. 214,18-19.
22. Gregory, *The Foundation of British East Africa*, p. 248.
23. Thruston, *African Incidents*, p. 224.
24. Colvile, 'Military Correspondence'. Jan. 19th.
25. Thruston, *African Incidents*, pp. 180-88.
26. Ibid. p. 168.
27. Doyle, Shane, *Crisis & Decline in Bunyoro: Population & Environment in Western Uganda 1860-1955*, (London : Oxford : Kampala : Athens, Ohio:2006), p. 71.; Colvile, 'Military Correspondence'. Jan. 10th.
28. Bodleian Library Oxford, 'Lugard's Behaviour in Uganda, 1890-1893 and N.D.', Papers of Frederick Dealtry Lugard, Baron Lugard of Abinger, MSS Brit. Emp. s.44.
29. 'Debate in the House of Commons: East African Protectorate and Uganda', in *Hansard*, (1899), pp. 693-725 (pp. 718-19).
30. Ibid. p. 704.
31. 'Correspondence Respecting the Status of Slavery in East Africa and the Islands of Zanzibar and Pemba, C-9502, Africa No. 8 ', (London:1899), p. 26.
32. Ahmad, F., 'Slavery in the Ottoman Empire and Its Demise: 1800-1909.', *CHOICE: Current Reviews for Academic Libraries*, 34 (1997), 1861, 85.
33. Gregory, *The Foundation of British East Africa*, pp. 257-59.

34. McCaski, p. 683.
35. Colvile's diary ends abruptly shortly after this incident and there is no record of him receiving this despatch.
36. Thruston, *African Incidents*, pp. 227-32.
37. Doyle, *Crisis & Decline,* p. 87.
38. Ibid. pp. 134-63.
39. He left in March 1895 and returned in April 1897.
40. Thruston, *African Incidents*, pp. 98, 228, 234.
41. Oliver, *The Missionary Factor in East Africa*, p. 1.
42. Portal, 'Report on Protectorate of Uganda', p. 7.
43. Waugh, Evelyn, *Remote People*, (London:1991), p. 203.
44. Quoted in Toye, *Churchill's Empire: The World That Made Him and the World He Made*, p. 117.
45. Ibid. pp. 154-55.
46. Tinker, Hugh, *A New System of Slavery: The Export of Indian Labour Overseas, 1830-1920*, (London:1993), pp. 175-79.
47. Anand, Anita, *The Patient Assassin*, (New York:2019), p. 131.
48. Jeffery, p. 312.
49. Brown, Carolyn A., 'African Labor in the Making of WW II', in *Africa and World War II*, ed. by Judith A. Byfield, et al. (New York:2015), pp. 43-67.
50. Thruston, *African Incidents*, p. 287.
Haynes, Jeffrey, 'Religion, Ethnicity and Civil War in Africa: The Cases of Uganda and Sudan', *Round Table (London),* 96 (2007), 305-17, 310-11. Acker, Frank van 'Ethnicity and Institutional Reform: A Case of Ugandan Exceptionalism?', in *Politics of Identity and Economics of Conflict in the Great Lakes Region,* ed. by Ruddy Doom and Jan F. J. Gorus (Brussels:2000), pp. 149-74 (p. 150).
51. Colvile, 'Military Correspondence'.March 28th.

52. Macdonald, *Soldiering and Surveying*, pp. 220-21.
53. Ashe, R. P., *Chronicles of Uganda*, (London:1894), pp. 404-05.
54. Macdonald, *Soldiering and Surveying*, p. 322.
55. Thruston, *African Incidents*, p. 235.
56. Wild, J. V., *The Uganda Mutiny, 1897*, (Kampala:1954), p. 18.
57. Beachey, pp. 245-46; 'Papers Relating to Recent Events in the Uganda Protectorate ', p. 8.
58. Thruston, *African Incidents*, p. 305.
59. Kline, Craig G., 'British Protestant Missionary Societies During the Early Stages of British Administration in Uganda : 1895-1907', (Thesis (M.Litt.)--University of Oxford, 1975), p. 40.
60. Mockler-Ferryman, *Ugandan Mutiny*, p. 314.
61. Wild, *The Uganda Mutiny, 1897*, p. 33.
62. Mockler-Ferryman, *Ugandan Mutiny*, p. 316.
63. Wild, *The Uganda Mutiny, 1897*, p. 39.
64. 'Papers Relating to Recent Events in the Uganda Protectorate '. Africa No. 1.
65. Portal, 'Report on Protectorate of Uganda', pp. 8,14.
66. McCaski, p. 688.
67. Haynes, p. 310.

10. Remembering

1. Wild, *The Uganda Mutiny, 1897*, p. 18.
2. Mills, *The Tirah Campaign*, p. 14.p. 14.
3. Thruston, *African Incidents*, pp. 182-83.
4. Wild, *The Uganda Mutiny, 1897*, p. 5.
5. Asquith, House of Commons, August 6th 1914.
6. 'The Commonwealth and the First World War', National Army Museum, https://www.nam.ac.uk/explore/

commonwealth-and-first-world-war#:~:text=In%20
1914%2C%20the%20Germans%20and,in%20the%20First%20
World%20War, Accessed: Sep. 24th, 2023.
7. Hitchens, Peter, *The Phoney Victory: The World War II Illusion*, (London:2018), pp. 119-20.
8. Jeffery, p. 314.

11. Forgetting

1. 'Oxford War Memorial: Numerous Suggestions', *The Oxford Chronicle*, (1919), May 9th.
2. 'Oxford War Memorial', Oxford Chronicle (1921), July 1st, p. 1.
3. Abousnnouga, Gill and Machin, David, *The Language of War Monuments*, (London:2014), p. 85. Nicholls, Christine 'Europeans in East Africa', 2023, https://www.europeansineastafrica.co.uk, Accessed: July 23rd., 2021. King, Alex, *Memorials of the Great War in Britain [Electronic Resource] : The Symbolism and Politics of Remembrance*, (Oxford ; New York:1998). Ch. 3 & 4.
4 Gregory, Adrian, *The Silence of Memory: Armistice Day, 1919-1946*, (Oxford; Providence, RI, USA:1994), pp. 44-45.
5. Ibid. p. 57.
6. Ibid. p. 65.
7. Ibid. p. 100.
8. Rieff, David, *In Praise of Forgetting: Historical Memory and Its Ironies*, (New Haven, Connecticut ; London, England:2016).
9. Küchler, Susanne and Forty, Adrian, *The Art of Forgetting*, (Oxford:1999), p. 14.
10. Edgerton, pp. 959-65.
11. Ibid.

12. Satia, Priya, *Time's Monster: History, Conscience and Britain's Empire*, (London:2020), p. 212.
13. Jeffery, p. 326.

12: Reckoning

1. 'On 10th December 1897 the 2nd Division marched out of Dwatoi, the 4th Brigade in the lead heading for Sandana, the 3rd Brigade making for Karana, 3 miles short of Sandana. The fortified villages passed through on the journey were destroyed'. Mackenzie, 'Tirah 1897'.
2. Bodleian Libraries Oxford, 'Koran in Arabic, Beginning Incomplete, Colophon in Persian, Probably Afghanistan, 19th Cent. ', Dep. e. 393.
3. 'Schools in Far-Flung Areas of Bara Reopen after Nine Years', *Dawn*, (2023), June 12.
4. Pitt Rivers 1920.101.4, 1921.9.66, 1921.9.56, 1921.9.63, 1921.9.64, 1921.9.75, 1921.9.77, 1921.9.74, 1921.9.52, 1921.9.53, 1921.9.116, 1922.38.1, 1921.9.41-48.
5. Roscoe, *Preliminary Report of the Mackie Ethnological Expedition* p. 217.
6. Ibid. p. 209.
7. Roscoe, John, *The Soul of Central Africa: A General Account of the Mackie Ethnological Expedition*, (London; New York 1922).
8. 'The Bantu Tribes: The Rev. John Roscoe on Peculiar Customs', *The Manchester Guardian*, (1912), Nov. 26th, p. 12.
9. Speke, John Hanning, *Journal of the Discovery of the Source of the Nile.*, (New York (State):1864), p. 534.
10. Nyakatura, John, *Anatomy of an African Kingdom: A History of Bunyoro-Kitara*, (Garden City, N.Y.:1973), p. 108.

11. Roscoe, John, *The Bakitara or Banyoro; the First Part of the Report to the Mackie Ethnological Expedition to Central Africa*, (England:1923), pp. 90-91.

12. Roscoe, *Preliminary Report of the Mackie Ethnological Expedition* pp. 213-15.

13. Grant, James Augustus, *A Walk across Africa; or, Domestic Scenes from My Nile Journal*, (Edinburgh:1864), p. 285.

14. Atuhairwe, Robert, 'Bunyoro's Continued Push to Return Stolen Artefacts from Britain', The Albertine Journal, 2023, https://thealbertinejournal.com/bunyoros-continued-push-to-return-stolen-artifacts-from-britain/, Accessed: Sep. 1st., 2023; Kwesiga, Pascal, 'British University Holds onto Bunyoro Cultural Artefacts', Newvision, 2023, https://www.newvision.co.ug/new_vision/news/1327372/british-university-holds-bunyoro-cultural-artifacts, Accessed: July 4th., 2023; Akuma, Patience and Thorpe, Vanessa, 'Ugandan King Battles Oxford Museum over Lost Throne', *The Guardian*, June 14th 2014.

15. Nyakatura, *Anatomy of an African Kingdom*, p. 161.

16. Thruston, *African Incidents*, pp. 22-23.

17. Ibid. p. 227.

18. Colvile, *The Land of the Nile Springs* p. 283.

19. Kwesiga, 'British University Holds onto Bunyoro Cultural Artefacts'.

20. Mwijuke, Gilbert, 'The Fight for a Stool: Bunyoro Wants Its Seat of Power Back ', The East African, 2021, https://www.theeastafrican.co.ke/tea/magazine/the-fight-for-a-stool-bunyoro-wants-its-seat-of-power-back-3429808?view=htmlamp, Accessed: July 7th., 2023.

21. Roscoe, *The Bakitara*, p. 112.

22. Musinguzi, Bamuturaki, 'Cambridge University to Return Uganda's Historic Artefacts', Monitor, 2021, https://www.monitor.co.ug/uganda/magazines/people-power/cambridge-

university-to-return-uganda-s-historic-artefacts-3593386, Accessed: July 7th., 2023.

23. Mwijuke, 'The Fight for a Stool: Bunyoro Wants Its Seat of Power Back '.

24. Kiva, Fred, 'Banyoro Asked to Provide Local Evidence on UK Colonial Atrocities', ugandaradionetwork.net, 2014, https://ugandaradionetwork.net/story/banyoro-asked-to-provide-local-evidence-on-uk-colonial-atrocities, Accessed: Sep 13th., 2023.

25. Ireland and Australia are exceptions.

26. Symonds, Richard, *Oxford and Empire [Electronic Resource] : The Last Lost Cause?*, (Oxford:1991), pp. 162-66.

27. Beinart, William, 'Rhodes Must Fall', University of Oxford, 2022, https://oxfordandcolonialism.web.ox.ac.uk/article/rhodes-must-fall, Accessed: Aug. 13th, 2022.

28. Larminie, Vivien, 'Oxford in the Seventeenth Century: Kings, Parliaments, People and Press.', in *lecture at St. Giles Church, Oxford. Feb. 13th.*, (2020).

29. Jenkins, Stephanie, 'Boer War Memorial Oxford', http://oxfordhistory.org.uk/war/boer_war/index.html, Accessed: Oct. 20th., 2021.

BIBLIOGRAPHY

Primary Sources

Oxford, Bodleian Libraries, Papers of Frederick Dealtry
Lugard, Baron Lugard of Abinger, MSS Brit. Emp.
s.44.

_____, Koran in Arabic, Beginning Incomplete, Colophon
in Persian, Probably Afghanistan, 19th Cent., Dep. e.
393.

_____, Sir John Ponsonby's Diary of Military Expedition
through British East Africa to the Congo, 1898-99:
With a March through Naivasha and Mumias to
Unyoro Where He Commanded Sudanese Troops in
the Uganda Mutiny. [Microform], Micr.Afr.597.

_____, Journal by Cyril Punch, MSS.Afr.s.1913.

_____, British East Africa (Uganda), 1886-1910, Archive
of the Anti-Slavery Society, MSS. Brit. Emp. s.22/G4.

Oxfordshire Record Office, Early's of Witney Financial
Records and Diaries, B1/2/A7/1.

_____, John Allen & Son (Oxford) Ltd. 1868-1952. A
History of over 80 Years of Progress, Oxfo 681.7 Alle.

London, Welcome Collection, Typescript Diary Formed of
Extracts from Letters by Surgeon Captain Alfred E.
Master, Army Medical Service, Re Campaigning with
the Queens Regiment against the Afridi Tribes on the
North-West Frontier of India (the Tirah Campaign),
RAMC/185.

Matlock, Derbyshire Record Office, Sir Henry Colvile,
Military Correspondence and Papers, D461/5.

Woodstock, Soldiers of Oxfordshire Museum, 5pp Typescript

of Record of Service Covering the Tirah Expedition, 1897., SOFO.2766.

_____, Photocopies of Letters from Fred Evelegh During the Tirah Expedition, India, Jan 1898-Nov 1899,

_____, Photocopies of a Diary Written by Charles Crutch (3130) Relating to the Tirah Expedition of 1897., SOFO:6130.

_____, Diary of Major General H. R. Davies, 13th May 1896-15th Jan 1898., SOFO.6128.

_____, A Collection of Letters from 1897 Plus Mention in Dispatches, Certificates, a Red Hardback Address Book and Newspaper Cutting., SOFO.6128.

Printed Primary Sources

(Allahabad), Pioneer, *The Rising on the North-West Frontier Being a Complete Narrative* (Allahabad: 1898).

Ansorge, William John, *Under the African Sun; a Description of Native Races in Uganda, Sporting Adventures and Other Experiences* (New York (State): 1899).

Anti-slavery Society (Great Britain), and Anti-slavery and Aborigines Protection Society (Great Britain), 'The Anti-Slavery Reporter and Aborigines' Friend', (London: 1842).

Ashe, Robert Pickering, *Two Kings of Uganda; or, Life by the Shores of Victoria Nyanza; Being an Account of a Residence of Six Years in Eastern Equatorial Africa* (unknown: 1889).

———, *Chronicles of Uganda* (London: 1894).

Austin, H. H., *With Macdonald in Uganda: Narrative Account of the Uganda Mutiny and Macdonald Expedition in the Uganda Protectorate and the Territories to the North* (London: 1903).

Callwell, C. E., *Tirah, 1897, Campaigns and Their Lessons* (London: 1911).

Colvile, H. E., *The Land of the Nile Springs: Being Chiefly an Account of How We Fought Kabarega* (London; New York: 1895).

Courtney, William, 'The Tirah Campaign', Fortnightly Review, 63 (1898), 390-400.

Grant, James Augustus, *A Walk across Africa; or, Domestic Scenes from My Nile Journal* (Edinburgh: 1864).

Haldane, Aylmer, *A Soldier's Saga; the Autobiography of General Sir Aylmer Haldane* (Edinburgh: 1948).

Her Majesty's Stationery Office, Great Britain. Foreign Office, Papers Relating to Uganda: [in Continuation of "Africa No. 4 (1892)."], Africa (Great Britain. Foreign Office) ; 1892, No. 8 (London: 1892).

———, Further Papers Relating to Uganda: [in Continuation of "Africa No. 3 (1893) :" C. 6853.]. (London:1893).

———, Africa no. 2: reports relating to Uganda 1894

———, Correspondence Respecting the Retirement of the Imperial British East Africa Company, (London:1895).

———, Report on Military Operations against Kabarega, King of Unyoro. (London: 1896)

———, Great Britain. India Office, Military Operations on the North-West Frontiers of India. Papers Regarding the British Relations with the Neighbouring Tribes of the North-West Frontier of India, 1897-98 (England: 1898).

———, Papers Relating to Recent Events in the Uganda Protectorate: [in Continuation of "Africa No. 2 (1898)].

———, Report by Her Majesty's Commissioner in Uganda on

the Recent Mutiny of the Soudanese Troops in the Protectorate. (1898: London).

———, Preliminary Report by HM Special Commissioner on the Protectorate of Uganda. (1900: London).

———, Africa No. 1: papers relating to recent events in the Ugandan Protectorate [in continuation of Africa no. 10 (1898)]

———, Correspondence Respecting the Status of Slavery in East Africa and the Islands of Zanzibar and Pemba, C-9502, Africa No. 8 (London:1899).

———,'Debate in the House of Commons: East African Protectorate and Uganda', in Hansard (1899), pp. 693-725.

———, Africa No. 6: Preliminary Report by HM special commissioner on the Protectorate of Uganda 1900

———, Africa no. 7: report by his majesty's special commissioner on the Protectorate of Uganda 1901

———, Africa no. 15: General report on the Uganda Protectorate for the year ending March 31, 1903

Hutchinson, H.D., Colonel., *The Campaign in Tirah, 1897-98* (London: 1898).

James, Lionel, *The Indian Frontier War: Being an Account of the Mohmund and Tirah Expeditions, 1897* (London: 1898).

Kagwa, Apolo, and Kiwanuka, M. S. M., *The Kings of Buganda, Historical Texts of Eastern and Central Africa* (Nairobi: 1971).

Lugard, Lord Frederick J. D., *The Rise of Our East African Empire (1893) : Early Efforts in Nyasaland and Uganda* (2 Volume Set) (1893).

Macdonald, James Ronald Leslie, *Soldiering and Surveying in British East Africa, 1891-1894* (London: 1897).

Mills, H. Woosnam, *The Tirah Campaign: Being the Sequel to the Pathan Revolt in North-West India* (Lahore, India: 1898).

Mockler-Ferryman, A. F., 'The Story of the Uganda Mutiny', Macmillan's magazine, 78 (1898), 308-20.

———., ed., *The Oxfordshire Light Infantry Chronicle* (London: 1895).

———, ed., *The Oxfordshire Light Infantry Chronicle*, (London: 1897).

———, ed., *The Oxfordshire Light Infantry Chronicle*, (London: 1898).

———, ed., *The Oxfordshire Light Infantry Chronicle* (London: 1899).

———, ed., *The Oxfordshire Light Infantry Chronicle* (London: 1900).

Nyakatura, John, *Anatomy of an African Kingdom: A History of Bunyoro-Kitara* (Garden City, N.Y.: 1973).

———, *Aspects of Bunyoro Customs and Tradition* (Nairobi: 1970).

Plowden, F.H., 'The Battalion on the Frontier', *Chronicle of the Oxfordshire Light Infantry* (1899), 243-71.

Portal, Gerald Herbert, (1894: London), Reports Relating to Uganda.

———, (1901: London), Report by His Majesty's Special Commissioner on the Protectorate of Uganda.

Portal, Gerald Herbert, and Rodd, Rennell, *The British Mission to Uganda in 1893, Ed. With a Mem. By R. Rodd. With the Diary of R. Portal* (Lond.: 1894).

Roscoe, John, Preliminary Report of the Mackie Ethnological Expedition to Central Africa (London:1921).

———, *The Bakitara or Banyoro; the First Part of the Report to the Mackie Ethnological Expedition to Central*

Africa (England: 1923).

———, *The Soul of Central Africa: A General Account of the Mackie Ethnological expedition* (London; New York 1922).

———, *Twenty-Five Years in East Africa* (Cambridge: 1921).

Shadwell, Leonard Julius, *Lockhart's Advance through Tirah.* (New York (State): 1899).

Slessor, Arthur Kerr, *The 2nd Battalion Derbyshire Regiment in Tirah*, Derbyshire Campaign Series 5 (London: 1900).

Speke, John Hanning, *Journal of the Discovery of the Source of the Nile.* (New York (State): 1864).

Stanley, Henry M., *Through the Dark Continent: Or the Sources of the Nile around the Great Lakes of Equatorial Africa and Down the Livingstone River to the Atlantic Ocean* (London: 1878).

Thomsett, Richard Gillham, *With the Peshawar Column, Tirah Expeditionary Force* (London: 1899).

Thruston, Arthur Beyford, *African Incidents, Personal Experiences in Egypt and Unyoro* (London: 1900).

Warburton, Robert Sir, *Eighteen Years in the Khyber, 1879-1898* (England: 1900).

White, E.D., 'Narrative of Events in the Bara Valley and Khyber Pass, 1897-98', in The Oxfordshire Light Infantry Chronicle, ed. by Mockler-Ferryman, A.F. (London: 1898), pp. 81-106.

Wylly, H. C., *From the Black Mountain to Waziristan: Being an Account of the Border Countries and the More Turbulent of the Tribes Controlled by the North-West Frontier Province, and of Our Military Relations with Them in the Past*, Military Text-Books (London: 1912).

Willis, Alice, *The Heights of Dargai: And Other Poems* (London: 1929).

Newspapers

Al Mayadeen, https://english.almayadeen.net/news, (2023)
Dawn, https://www.dawn.com (2023)
Jackson's Oxford Journal (Oxford, 1884, 1885, 1890, 1899)
The Daily Telegraph (London, 1875)
The Henley and South Oxford Standard (1897)
The Banbury Advertiser (1899)
The Bicester Herald (1898)
The Express Tribune https://tribune.com.pk (2010)
The Guardian, (London, 2014, 2019, 2023)
The Henley & South Oxford Standard, (Henley-on-Thames, 1897)
The Liberal Review, (London, 1897)
The Manchester Guardian (1912)
The Oxford Mail, (Oxford, 1900)
The Oxford Chronicle (Oxford, 1919-1920)
The Oxford Chronicle and Reading Gazette (1898, 1919-21)
The Scotsman, (Edinburgh, 1898)
The Times, (London, 1897-98)
The Times of India, (India, 1898)

Secondary Sources

'The Commonwealth and the First World War', National Army Museum, <https://www.nam.ac.uk/explore/commonwealth-and-first-world-war#:~:text=In%201914%2C%20the%20Germans%20and,in%20the%20First%20World%20War> [Accessed Sep. 24th 2023].

'The Medical Arrangements for the Tirah Expeditionary Force', The Lancet (British edition), 151 (1898), 52-

54.

'The Tirah Expeditionary Force', The Lancet (British edition), 151 (1898), 953.

'The Campaign in the Tirah', Nature, 59 (1899), 315-16.

'The Baganda. An Account of Their Native Customs and Beliefs by John Roscoe', Journal of the Royal African Society, 11 (1912), 365-66.

'Barrows & Co.', Grace's Guide, (2017) <https://www.gracesguide.co.uk/Barrows_and_Co> [Accessed Sep. 29th 2022].

'Barrows & Stewart', Grace's Guide, (2020) <https://www.gracesguide.co.uk/Barrows_and_Stewart> [Accessed Sep. 29th 2022].

Abousnnouga, Gill, and Machin, David, *The Language of War Monuments*, (London: 2014).

Acker, Frank van 'Ethnicity and Institutional Reform: A Case of Ugandan Exceptionalism?', in Politics of Identity and Economics of Conflict in the Great Lakes Region, ed. by Doom, Ruddy and Gorus, Jan F. J. (Brussels: 2000), pp. 149-74.

Agha, Sameetah, 'Sub-Imperialism and the Loss of the Kyber: The Politics of Imperial Defence on British India's North West Frontier', Indian Historical Review, 40 (2) (2013), 307-30.

———, 'The Tirah Campaign', in *Queen Victoria's Wars: British Military Campaigns, 1857-1902*, ed. by Miller, Stephen M. (Cambridge: 2021), pp. 240-59.

———, 'Roots of Afridi Insurgency in British India's North-West Frontier: 1849-1897', Small Wars & Insurgencies, 34 (3) (2022) 546-570.

Ahmad, F., 'Slavery in the Ottoman Empire and Its Demise: 1800-1909', CHOICE: Current Reviews for Academic

Libraries, 34 (1997), 1861.
Ali, Tariq, *Winston Churchill: His Times, His Crimes* (London: 2022).
Allen, Charles, *Soldier Sahibs: The Men Who Made the North-West Frontier* (London: 2012).
Alpers, Edward A., *Ivory and Slaves: Changing Pattern of International Trade in East Central Africa to the Later Nineteenth Century* (Berkeley: 1975).
Amone, Charles, 'Ethnicity and Political Stability in Uganda: Are Ethnic Identities a Blessing or a Curse?', Ethnopolitics Paper (2015).
Amone, Charles, and Muura, Okullu, 'British Colonialism and the Creation of Acholi Ethnic Identity in Uganda, 1894 to 1962', Journal of Imperial and Commonwealth History, 42 (2014), 239-57.
Anand, Anita, *The Patient Assassin* (New York: 2019).
Andrews, P. W. S., and Brunner, Elizabeth, *The Eagle Ironworks, Oxford: The Story of W. Lucy and Company Limited* (London: 1965).
Appiah, Anthony, and Gates, Henry Louis, Jr. *Encyclopaedia of Africa*. 'Buganda and Baganda' (Oxford, 2010).
Atwood, Rodney, 'The Second Afghan War, 1878–1880', in *Queen Victoria's Wars: British Military Campaigns, 1857–1902*, ed. by Miller, Stephen M. (Cambridge: 2021), pp. 126-45.
Baggs, A.P., Chance, Eleanor, Colvin, Christina, Cooper, Nicholas, Crossley, Alan, Day, Christopher, Selwyn, Nesta, Williamson, Elizabeth, and Yates, Margaret, 'Witney Borough: Economic History, the Industrial Revolution in Witney C.1800-1900', in *A History of the County of Oxford*, ed. by Townley, Simon (London: 2004), pp. 88-97.

Bala, Poonam, *Medicine and Colonial Engagements in India and Sub-Saharan Africa*, (Newcastle upon Tyne: 2018).

Balachandran, G., *India and the World Economy 1850-1950*, (Delhi; Oxford: 2005).

Banham, Robert, 'The Workforce', in *The History of Oxford University Press: Volume II: 1780 to 1896*, ed. by Eliot, Simon (2013), pp. 174-225.

Barthorp, Michael, *The Frontier Ablaze: North-West Frontier Rising, 1897-98* (London: 1996).

———-, *Afghan Wars and the North-West Frontier 1839-1947* (London: 2002).

Bauer, Rolf, *The Peasant Production of Opium in Nineteenth-Century India* (Leiden: 2019).

Beachey, R. W., 'Macdonald's Expedition and the Uganda Mutiny, 1897-98', The Historical Journal, 10 (1967), 237-54.

Bean, Philip, and Melville, Joy, *Lost Children of the Empire* (London: 2018).

Beattie, John, *Bunyoro: An African Kingdom,* (New York; London: 1960).

Beckert, Sven, *Empire of Cotton: A Global History* (New York: 2014).

Beinart, Peter, 'A Kingdom Preserved: Buganda's Entrance into the British Empire, 1875-1900' (Thesis (M.Phil.), University of Oxford, 1995).

Beinart, William, 'Rhodes Must Fall: The Uses of Historical Evidence in the Statue Debate in Oxford 2015-2019) <https://oxfordandempire.web.ox.ac.uk/article/rhodes-must-fall-uses-historical-evidence-statue-debate-oxford-2015-6> Accessed: 24th July 2022.

Boorman, Derek, *At the Going Down of the Sun: British First*

World War Memorials (York: 1988).

Booth, Philip, *The Oxfordshire and Buckinghamshire Light Infantry* (London: 1971).

Bowen, Claire, and Hoffmann, Catherine, (eds.), *Representing Wars from 1860 to the Present: Fields of Action, Fields of Vision*, (Leiden: 2018).

Brown, Carolyn A., 'African Labor in the Making of WW II', in *Africa and World War II*, ed. by Byfield, Judith A., Brown, Carolyn A., Parsons, Timothy and Sikainga, Ahmad Alawad (New York: 2015), pp. 43-67.

Buxton, Julia, The Political Economy of Narcotics: Production, Consumption and Global Markets. (London: 2006).

Cain, P.J., 'Economics: The Metropolitan Context', in *The Oxford History of the British Empire: The Nineteenth Century*, ed. by Porter, Andrew (Oxford: 1999), pp. 31-52.

Campbell, Sue, Koggel, Christine M., and Jacobsen, Rockney, *Our Faithfulness to the Past: The Ethics and Politics of Memory*, (New York: 2014).

Carey, Hilary M., *God's Empire: Religion and Colonialism in the British World, C.1801-1908*, (Cambridge: 2011).

Carpenter, Charles C. J., and Hornick, Richard B., 'Killed Vaccines: Cholera, Typhoid, and Plague', in *Vaccines: A Biography*, ed. by Artenstein, Andrew W. (New York, NY: 2010), pp. 87-103.

Cartwright, Frederick F., and Biddiss, Michael D., *Disease & History* (Stroud: 2000).

Casely-Hayford, Gus, *The Lost Kingdoms of Africa* (London: 2012).

Chakrabarti, Pratik, *Medicine and Empire: 1600-1960*, (Basingstoke: 2014).

Chaudhuri, K. N., 'Foreign Trade and Balance of Payments (1757–1947)', in *The Cambridge Economic History of India: Volume 2: C.1757–C.1970*, ed. by Kumar, Dharma and Desai, Meghnad (Cambridge: 1983), pp. 804-77.

Choudhuri, P., Poynder, F. S., and Stevens, *9 Gurkha Rifles: A Regimental History, 1817-1947* (New Delhi: 1984).

Condos, Mark, '"Fanaticism" and the Politics of Resistance Along the North-West Frontier of British India', Comparative Studies in Society and History, 58 (2016), 717-45.

Coughlin, Con, *Churchill's First War: Young Winston and the Fight against the Taliban* (London: 2013).

Cox, Jeffrey, *The British Missionary Enterprise since 1700* (New York; London: 2008).

Cross, Alan, and Russell, Phil, 'Diseases of Military Importance', in *Vaccines: A Biography*, ed. by Artenstein, Andrew W. (New York, NY: 2010), pp. 249-64.

Cuppiramaṇiya Aiyar, Ji, *Economic Aspects of British Rule in India* (Delhi: 1988).

Dickinson, Greg, Blair, Carole, and Ott, Brian L., *Places of Public Memory: The Rhetoric of Museums and Memorials* (Tuscaloosa 2010).

Dominik Geppert, and, and Müller, Frank Lorenz, *Sites of Imperial Memory: Commemorating Colonial Rule in the Nineteenth and Twentieth Centuries*, (Manchester, England: 2015).

Downs, Jim, *Maladies of Empire: How Colonialism, Slavery, and War Transformed Medicine* (Cambridge, Massachusetts: 2021).

Doyle, Shane, *Crisis & Decline in Bunyoro: Population &*

Environment in Western Uganda 1860-1955 (London : Oxford : Kampala : Athens, Ohio: 2006).

Dunbar, A. R., *A History of Bunyoro-Kitara*, East African Studies; 19 (Nairobi: 1968).

Dwyer, Philip, and Nettelbeck, Amanda, *Violence, Colonialism and Empire in the Modern World*, (Basingstoke, Hampshire: 2017).

Edgerton, David, 'The Nationalisation of British History: Historians, Nationalism and the Myths of 1940', The English Historical Review, 136 (2021), 950-85.

Edwards, David B., 'Mad Mullahs and Englishmen: Discourse in the Colonial Encounter', Comparative Studies in Society and History, 31 (1989), 649-70.

Eliot, Simon, *The History of Oxford University Press. Volume II, 1780 to 1896*, (Oxford: 2014).

Emdad-ul Haq, M., *Drugs in South Asia: From the Opium Trade to the Present Day* (Houndmills: 2000).

Etherington, Norman, *Missions and Empire*, (Oxford; New York: 2005).

Eyewitness, 'The Tirah Campaign', Eyewitness Fortnightly Review, March 1898, 63,375 (1898), 390-400.

F, E. N., 'The Mackie Ethnological Expedition to Central Africa', Nature, 106 (1920), 454-54.

Fisher, Ruth B., *Twilight Tales of the Black Baganda: The Traditional History of Bunyoro-Kitara, a Former Uganda Kingdom* (London: 1970).

Flanders, Amy, and Colclough, Stephen, 'The Bible Press', in *The History of Oxford University Press: Volume II: 1780 to 1896*, ed. by Eliot, Simon (2013), pp. 356-401.

Floud, Roderick, Humphries, Jane, and Johnson, Paul, (eds.), *The Cambridge Economic History of Modern Britain* (Cambridge, UK: 2014).

Fraser, Robert, 'Press Books Abroad', in *The History of Oxford University Press: Volume II: 1780 to 1896*, ed. by Eliot, Simon (2013), pp. 704-32.

Gabriel, Richard A., *Between Flesh and Steel: A History of Military Medicine from the Middle Ages to the War in Afghanistan*, (Washington, District of Columbia: 2013).

Gardyne, Charles Greenhill, *The Life of a Regiment, the History of the Gordon Highlanders* (Edinburgh: 1901).

Garton, Stephen, 'The Dominions, Ireland, and India', in *Empires at War: 1911-1923*, ed. by Gerwarth, Robert and Manela, Erez (Oxford: 2014), pp. 152-78.

Gerwarth, Robert, and Manela, Erez, eds., *Empires at War: 1911-1923* (Oxford: 2014).

Gilroy, Paul, *Postcolonial Melancholia*, (New York: 2005).

Gopal, Priyamvada, *Insurgent Empire: Anticolonial Resistance and British Dissent* (London: 2020).

Gordon, Michelle, *Extreme Violence and the 'British Way': Colonial Warfare in Perak, Sierra Leone and Sudan*, (London: 2020).

Gregory, Adrian, *The Silence of Memory: Armistice Day, 1919-1946*, (Oxford; Providence, RI, U.S.A.: 1994).

Gregory, J. W., T*he Foundation of British East Africa* (London: 1901).

Harrison, Mark, *Disease and the Modern World: 1500 to the Present Day*, (Cambridge: 2004).

———, *Medicine in an Age of Commerce and Empire: Britain and Its Tropical Colonies, 1660-1830*, (Oxford: 2010).

Haynes, Jeffrey, 'Religion, Ethnicity and Civil War in Africa: The Cases of Uganda and Sudan', Round Table (London), 96 (2007), 305-17.

Hernon, Ian, *Britain's Forgotten Wars: Colonial Campaigns of* the *19th* Century (Stroud: 2003).

Heston, A., 'National Income', in *The Cambridge Economic History of India: Volume 2: C.1757–C.1970*, ed. by Kumar, Dharma and Desai, Meghnad (Cambridge: 1983), pp. 376-462.

Hevia, James Louis, *Animal Labor and Colonial Warfare*, (Chicago: 2019).

Hitchens, Peter, *The Phoney Victory: The World War II Illusion* (London: 2018).

Holdich, T. H., 'Tirah', The Geographical Journal, 12 (1898), 337-59.

Holland, Robert, 'The British Empire and the Great War, 1914-1918', in *The Oxford History of the British Empire: Volume IV: The Twentieth Century* (Oxford: 1999), pp. 114-37.

Hurd, John M., 'Railways', in *The Cambridge Economic History of India: Volume 2: C.1757–C.1970*, ed. by Kumar, Dharma and Desai, Meghnad (Cambridge: 1983), pp. 737-61.

James, Lawrence, *Churchill and Empire: A Portrait of an Imperialist* (New York: 2014).

Janin, Hunt, *The India-China Opium Trade in the Nineteenth Century* (Jefferson, N.C.; London: 1999).

Jasanoff, Mayer, 'Misremembering the British Empire', <https://www.newyorker.com/magazine/2020/11/02/misremembering-the-british-empire>. Accessed: 3rd March 2022.

Jeffery, Keith, 'The Second World War', in *The Oxford History of the British Empire: Volume IV: The Twentieth Century* (Oxford: 1999), pp. 306-28.

Jenkins, Stephanie, 'Boer War Memorial Oxford' <http://oxfordhistory.org.uk/war/boer_war/index.

html> [Accessed Oct. 20th. 2021].

———, 'Oxford War Memorials: Tirah Campaign, Bonn Square' <http://oxfordhistory.org.uk/war/tirah_campaign/index.html>. [ibid.]

Jensz, Felicity, 'Missionaries and Indigenous Education in the 19th-Century British Empire. Part II: Race, Class, and Gender', History Compass, 10 (2012), 306-17.

Johnson, Robert, *The Afghan Way of War: Culture and Pragmatism : A Critical History* (London: 2014).

Johnson, Rob, 'Egypt and the Sudan, 1881–1885', in *Queen Victoria's Wars: British Military Campaigns, 1857–1902*, ed. by Miller, Stephen M. (Cambridge: 2021), pp. 187-219.

Johnson, Robert A., 'The 1897 Revolt and Tirah Valley Operations from the Pashtun Perspective', Cultural and Geographic Reseach Tribal Analysis Center, (2009) <https://tribalanalysiscenter.com/PDF-TAC/The%201897%20Revolt%20and%20Tirah%20Valley%20Operations.pdf> [Accessed Feb. 21st. 2023].

Jones, Herbert Gresford, *Uganda in Transformation, 1876-1926* (London: 1926).

Kasfir, Nelson, *The Shrinking Political Arena: Participation and Ethnicity in African Politics with a Case Study of Uganda* (Berkeley; London: 1976).

Khan, Haseen, *The Captives of Tirah* (Karachi: 2001).

Killingray, David, and Plaut, Martin, *Fighting for Britain: African Soldiers in the Second World War* (Woodbridge: 2012).

King, Alex, *Memorials of the Great War in Britain: The Symbolism and Politics of Remembrance*, (Oxford;

New York: 1998).

Kiran, Nirvan, *21 Kesaris : The Untold Story of the Battle of Saragarhi* (New Delhi: 2019).

Kiwanuka, M. S. M., *A History of Buganda: From the Foundation of the Kingdom to 1900* (London: 1971).

Kline, Craig G., 'British Protestant Missionary Societies During the Early Stages of British Administration in Uganda: 1895-1907' (Thesis (M.Litt.), (University of Oxford, 1975).

Küchler, Susanne, and Forty, Adrian, *The Art of Forgetting* (Oxford: 1999).

Leopold, Mark, 'Legacies of Slavery in North-West Uganda: The Story of the 'One-Elevens'', Africa, 76 (2006), 180-99.

Lotem, Itay, *The Memory of Colonialism in Britain and France: The Sins of Silence*, (Basingstoke: 2021).

Low, D. A., *Buganda in Modern History* (London: 1971).

Lowe, Keith, *Savage Continent* (London: 2013).

Lydon, Jane, *Imperial Emotions: The Politics of Empathy across the British Empire*, (Cambridge: 2019).

Mackenzie, John, 'Tirah 1897 <https://www.britishbattles.com/north-west-frontier-of-india/tirah-1897/> [Accessed 23/10/22].

MacKenzie, John M., *Propaganda and Empire: The Manipulation of British Public Opinion, 1880-1960*, (Manchester: 2017).

McCaski, T.C., 'Cultural Encounters: Britain and Africa in the Nineteenth Century', in *The Oxford History of the British Empire: The Nineteenth Century*, ed. by Porter, Andrew (Oxford: 1999), pp. 665-89.

McMahon, Elisabeth, *Slavery and Emancipation in Islamic East Africa: From Honor to Respectability*,

(Cambridge: 2013).

Miller, Stephen M., *Queen Victoria's Wars: British Military Campaigns, 1857–1902*. ed. by Miller, Stephen M. (Cambridge: 2021).

Moore, Robin, J., 'Imperial India, 1858-1914', in *The Oxford History of the British Empire: The Nineteenth Century*, ed. by Porter, Andrew (Oxford: 1999), pp. 422-46.

Mosse, George L., *Fallen Soldiers: Reshaping the Memory of the World Wars* (New York ; Oxford: 1990).

Mudoola, Dan M., *Religion, Ethnicity, and Politics in Uganda* (Kampala, Uganda: 1996).

Musisi, N., and Musisi, S., 'Inimitable Colonial Anxiety: African Sexuality in Uganda's Medical History, 1900-1940', in *Medicine and Colonial Engagements in India and Sub-Saharan Africa*, ed. by Bala, Poonam (Newcastle upon Tyne: 2018), pp. 131-53

Napier, D. M., *The Life of a Regiment: The History of the Gordon Highlanders. Volume IX, 1787-1994 : Events That Shaped the Regiment* (Aberdeen: 2017).

Nasson, Bill, 'British Imperial Africa', in *Empires at War: 1911-1923*, ed. by Gerwarth, Robert and Manela, Erez (Oxford: 2014), pp. 130-51.

Navarro, Vicente, *Imperialism, Health and Medicine*, (London: 2020).

Neish, Francis Hugh, *Historical Diary of the Gordon Highlanders*, (Dundee: 1914).

Nevill, H. L., *Campaigns on the North-West Frontier*, (Nashville: Fleet: 1999).

Nicholls, Christine 'Europeans in East Africa', Christine Nicholls, (2023) <https://www.europeansineastafrica.co.uk> [Accessed July 23rd. 2021].

O'Rourke, Kevin Hjortshøf, 'From Empire to Europe: Britain in the World Economy', in *The Cambridge Economic History of Modern Britain: 1807 to the Present* (Cambridge: 2014), pp. 60-91.

Offer, Avner, 'The British Empire, 1870-1914: A Waste of Money?', Economic History Review, 46 (1993). 215-238.

Oliver, Roland Anthony, T*he Missionary Factor in East Africa* (London: 1965).

Omissi, David E., *The Sepoy and the Raj: The Indian Army, 1860-1940*, (Basingstoke: 1994).

Pati, Biswamoy, and Harrison, Mark, *Health, Medicine and Empire: Perspectives on Colonial India*, (New Delhi: 2001).

Pawliková-Vilhanová, Viera, *History of Anti-Colonial Resistance and Protest in the Kingdoms of Buganda and Bunyoro, 1890-1899*, Dissertationes Orientales ; Vol. 45 (Prague: 1988).

Porter, Andrew, 'Religion, Missionary Enthusiasm, and Empire', in *The Oxford History of the British Empire: The Nineteenth Century*, ed. by Porter, Andrew (Oxford: 1999), pp. 223-45.

Porter, Bernard, *The Absent-Minded Imperialists: Empire, Society, and Culture in Britain*, (Oxford [England] ; New York: 2004).

———, British Imperial: *What the Empire Wasn't*, (London, [England] ; New York, New York: 2016).

———, *Empire Ways: Aspects of British Imperialism*, (London, [England] ; New York, New York: 2016).

Pulford, Cedric, *Eating Uganda: From Christianity to Conquest* (Banbury: 1999).

———, *Casualty of Empire: Britain's Unpaid Debt to an*

African Kingdom (Woodford Halse: 2007).

———, *Two Kingdoms of Uganda: Snakes and Ladders in the Scramble for Africa* (Daventry: 2011).

Qureshi, Sadiah, *Peoples on Parade [Electronic Resource] : Exhibitions, Empire, and Anthropology in Nineteenth-Century Britain*, (Chicago, [Ill.] ; London: 2011).

Ray, Benjamin C., *Myth, Ritual, and Kingship in Buganda* (New York:1991).

Ray, Indrajit, *Bengal Industries and the British Industrial Revolution (1757-1857)*, (New York: 2011).

Raychaudhuri, Tapan, 'The Mid-Eighteenth-Century Background', in *The Cambridge Economic History of India: Volume 2: c.1757–C.1970*, ed. by Kumar, Dharma and Desai, Meghnad (Cambridge: 1983), pp. 1-35.

Reekes, Andrew, *More Than Munich: The Forgotten Legacy of Neville Chamberlain* (Alcester: 2018).

Reid, Richard J., *A History of Modern Uganda*, (Cambridge: 2017).

Renfrew, Barry, *Britain's Black Regiments: Fighting for Empire and Equality* (Cheltenham: 2022).

Richards, J.F., 'The Indian Empire and the Peasant Production of Opium in the Nineteenth Century', Modern Asian Studies, 15 (1981), 59-82.

Rieff, David, *In Praise of Forgetting: Historical Memory and Its Ironies*, (New Haven, Connecticut ; London, England: 2016).

Rimner, Steffen, *Opium's Long Shadow: From Asian Revolt to Global Drug Control* (Cambridge, Massachusetts: 2018).

Rothberg, Michael, *The Implicated Subject: Beyond Victims and Perpetrators* (Stanford, California: 2019).

Rowe, John A., 'Roscoe's and Kagwa's Baganda - the Baganda: An Account of Their Native Customs and Beliefs. By the Rev. John Rosocoe. ', Journal of African history, 8 (1967), 163-66.

Roy, Tirthankar, *How British Rule Changed India's Economy: The Paradox of the Raj*, (Cham: 2019).

———, *The Economic History of India, 1857-2010*. (New Delhi: 2020).

Sandes, E. W. C., *The Indian Sappers and Miners* (Chatham: 1948).

Satia, Priya, *Time's Monster: History, Conscience and Britain's Empire* (London: 2020).

Saunders, Kay, *Indentured Labour in the British Empire, 1834-1920*, (London: 2018).

Seeley, J. R., and Gross, John, *The Expansion of England*, (Chicago; London: 1971).

Seeley, John Robert Sir, *The Expansion of England: Two Courses of Lectures* (England: 1883).

Simner, Mark, *Pathan Rising: Jihad on the North West Frontier of India 1897-1898* (Stroud: 2016).

Smart, Nick, *Neville Chamberlain*, (London: 2010).

Spiers, Edward M., 'Reconquest of the Sudan, 1896–1898', in *Queen Victoria's Wars: British Military Campaigns, 1857–1902*, ed. by Miller, Stephen M. (Cambridge: 2021), pp. 260-80.

———, *The Scottish Soldier and Empire, 1854-1902* (Edinburgh: 2022).

Stanley, Brian, *The Bible and the Flag: Protestant Missions and British Imperialism in the Nineteenth and Twentieth Centuries* (Leicester: 1990).

Starzmann, Maria Theresia, Roby, John R., Shackel, Paul A., and Brown, Richelle C., *Excavating Memory: Sites of*

Remembering and Forgetting, (Gainesville, Florida: 2016).

Steinhart, Edward I., *Conflict and Collaboration: The Kingdoms of Western Uganda, 1890-1907*, (Princeton, NJ: 2019).

Surridge, Keith, 'The Ambigous Amir: Britain, Aghanistan and the 1897 North-West Frontier Uprising', The Journal of Imperial and Commonwealth History, 36 (2008), 417-34.

Symonds, Richard, *Oxford and Empire: The Last Lost Cause?*, (Oxford: 1991).

Tharoor, Shashi, *Inglorious Empire: What the British Did to India* (London: 2017).

Thomas, Jonathan York, 'The Role of the Medical Missionary in British East Africa, 1874-1904' (Thesis (D.Phil.), University of Oxford, 1982).

Tiberondwa, Ado K., *Missionary Teachers as Agents of Colonialism: A Study of Their Activities in Uganda, 1877-1925* (Lusaka: 1989).

Tinker, Hugh, *A New System of Slavery: The Export of Indian Labour Overseas, 1830-1920* (London: 1993).

Tomlinson, B.R., 'Economics and Empire: The Periphery and the Imperial Economy', in *The Oxford History of the British Empire: The Nineteenth Century*, ed. by Porter, Andrew (1999), pp. 53-74.

Toye, Richard, *Churchill's Empire: The World That Made Him and the World He Made* (London: 2010).

Tripodi, Christian, 'Peacemaking through Bribes or Cultural Empathy? The Political Officer and Britain's Strategy Towards the North-West Frontier, 1901-1945', Journal of Strategic Studies, 31 (2008), 123-51.

———, *Edge of Empire: The British Political Officer and Tribal*

Administration on the North-West Frontier 1877-1947 (Farnham: 2011).

Tylden, G., 'The Uganda Rifles and Major Martyr's Nile Expedition of 1898', Journal of the Society for Army Historical Research, 34 (1956), 62-66.

Ward, Stuart, *British Culture and the End of Empire* (Manchester: 2017).

Waugh, Evelyn, *Remote People* (London: 1991).

West, Brad, War *Memory and Commemoration*, (London: 2016).

Whitcombe, Elizabeth, 'Irrigation', in *The Cambridge Economic History of India: Volume 2: C.1757–C.1970*, ed. by Kumar, Dharma and Desai, Meghnad (Cambridge: 1983), pp. 677-737.

Wild, J. V., *The Uganda Mutiny, 1897*, (Kampala: 1954).

Wild-Wood, Emma, 'Bible Translation and the Formation of Corporate Identity in Uganda and Congo 1900-1940', Journal of African History, 58 (2017), 489-507.

Wilkinson, Glen, R., 'Purple Prose and the Yellow Press: Imagined Spaces and the Military Expedition to Tirah, 1897', in *Negotiating India in the Nineteenth-Century Media*, ed. by Finkelstein, David and Peers, Douglas M. (Basingstoke: 2000), pp. 253-76.

Winter, J. M., *Remembering War: The Great War between Memory and History in the Twentieth Century* (New Haven ; London: 2006).

———, *Sites of Memory, Sites of Mourning: The Great War in European Cultural History*, (Cambridge: 2014).

———, *War Beyond Words: Languages of Remembrance from the Great War to the Present* (Cambridge: 2017).

Winter, J. M., and Prost, Antoine, *The Great War in History: Debates and Controversies, 1914 to the Present*,

(Cambridge: 2020).

Woolley, Liz, 'Industrial Architecture in Oxford, 1870 to 1914', Oxfordshire Architectural and Historical Society, (2010) <https://www.oxoniensia.org/volumes/2010/Woolley.pdf>. [Accessed: 22/10/22]

Wylly, H.C., *The Borderland: The Country of the Pathans* (Karachi: 1998).

Zeidan, Adam, 'Anglo-Afghan Wars'2021) <https://www.britannica.com/event/Anglo-Afghan-Wars>. [Accessed 14/3/21]

Ziino, Bart, *Remembering the First World War, Remembering the Modern World* (Abingdon: 2014).

INDEX

A

Abyssinia 35, 141
Acholi 121, 251
Afghanistan 6, 17, 18, 21, 23, 37, 38, 39, 40, 41, 42, 43, 47, 48, 89, 136, 143, 175, 176, 178, 180, 181, 182, 203, 219, 243, 256
Afridi 21, 41, 43, 44, 45, 46, 48, 49, 50, 52, 53, 56, 65, 66, 71, 72, 75, 76, 77, 84, 85, 86, 88, 89, 90, 91, 177, 178, 179, 180, 181, 204, 218, 243, 250
Ahmed, Lieutentant-Colonel 51
Amin, Idi 173
Ampleforth Abbey 203, 205
Amritsar 99
Animal 19, 20, 44, 55, 57, 71, 75, 76, 79, 85, 110, 126, 150, 156, 217, 257
Ankole 106, 135
Armenia 38
Aryan 42
Ashmolean Museum 96
Atlantic Charter 184, 199
Atlee, Clement 197
Australia 97, 98, 110, 181, 185, 242

B

Bagh 50, 76
Bagisu 121
Balliol College 99
Bangladesh 33
Bara 18, 50, 65, 75, 85, 203, 204, 248
Barrows & Co. 97, 250
Beads 155
Belgium 107, 140, 141, 143, 157, 182
Bellew, Henry Walter 47
Bell, W. Lance-Corporal 57, 58, 63
Bengal 18, 24, 28, 35, 65, 184, 185, 262

Benin 78, 123, 175, 205, 213
Bermuda 98, 199
Bey, Selim 165
Bhutan 35
Bilal, Janna 166
bin Laden, Osama 90
Bodleian Library 203, 205, 243
Bokhara 38
British and Foreign Bible Society 96, 117, 118
British Chamber of Commerce 138
British Gold Coast 183
Buganda 106, 107, 119, 125, 131, 132, 133, 135, 143, 145, 150, 151, 152, 153, 157, 158, 160, 164, 172, 173, 177, 178, 182, 212, 218, 246, 250, 251, 252, 255, 259, 261, 262, 263
Bulgaria 38
Bulwer-Lytton, Robert 40
Bunyoro 106, 132, 135, 137, 143, 145, 146, 149, 151, 152, 153, 160, 164, 172, 176, 182, 206, 207, 208, 209, 210, 211, 212, 213, 247, 252, 254, 255, 261
Burma 7, 33, 35, 91, 184
Butler, Pt. W. 57, 59, 63

C

Canada 74, 82, 97, 185
Carter, Lt. 59, 60, 63, 67
Catholic 96, 128, 133, 172, 205
Caucasus 38
Chad 136
Chamberlain, Neville 87, 262, 263
China 25, 28, 29, 30, 33, 81, 114, 175, 183, 216, 257
Churchill, Winston 5, 6, 41, 47, 65, 69, 71, 72, 87, 162, 181, 184, 186, 197, 204, 225, 251, 254, 257, 264
Church Missionary Society 116, 117, 123, 138, 170
Church of England 116
Clive, Robert 24
Colvile, Col. Henry Edward 143, 144, 145, 146, 149, 150, 151, 152, 157, 158, 160, 161, 165, 177, 208, 209, 237, 245
Congo 106, 143, 157, 167, 243, 265
Congress Party 187, 199
Coombe, Thomas 96

Crimean War 38
Crowhurst, bugler 59, 67
Crutch, Sgt. 64, 65, 66, 70, 244
Cyprus 198

D

Dargai 71, 176, 249
Davies, Lt. 60, 61, 62, 64, 65, 68, 69, 244
Dempsey, Sgt.-Maj. 58, 59, 60, 61, 62, 63, 68
Disease 20, 68, 79, 80, 81, 82, 109, 132, 161, 180
  cholera 109
  dysentery 79, 90, 107, 109, 128
  jiggers 145, 163
  malaria 21, 35, 81, 103, 107, 158
  measles 109
  typhoid 79, 80, 83, 103, 153
Disraeli, Benjamin 39
Durand 40

E

Early and Co. 98
East India Company 23, 24, 25, 27, 29, 31, 39, 81, 217
Egypt 6, 25, 33, 103, 105, 114, 131, 132, 133, 134, 136, 137, 157, 162, 172, 177, 198, 248, 258
Ethiopia 33, 141

F

Fante 120
Faragella, Rajat 124
Fashoda 166
Feilden, Lt. 58, 59, 68
Findlater, piper 73
First Afghan War 86
Fitzgerald 80
Forward Policy 39, 45, 225
France 25, 28, 107, 118, 133, 136, 140, 141, 155, 176, 184, 186, 259
Frank Cooper Oxford Marmalade 97
Frith, Lt. 61, 62, 63, 68

G

Germany 7, 133, 136, 140, 141, 176, 182, 185, 186, 195, 197, 204, 217
Gladstone, William 136, 140, 141
Godliman, W. 83
Gordon, General 113, 134
Great Rebellion 27, 29, 32, 35, 38, 86, 148, 167, 178, 180
Greece 46, 121, 136, 217
Grunshi, Alhaji 183, 184
Gurkha 18, 66, 184, 254

H

Hague Convention 205
Haldane, Alymer 204, 245
Hannington, Bishop 134
Hastings, Warren 24
Hindu 35, 46, 66, 111, 162
Hitler, Adolf 43, 176, 185
Hopkins, J.S. 57, 62

I

Imperial East Africa Company 137, 154, 164, 166
India 3, 6, 7, 15, 16, 18, 19, 20, 21, 23, 24, 25, 26, 27, 28, 29, 30, 31,
    32, 33, 35, 36, 38, 39, 40, 41, 42, 43, 44, 45, 46, 51, 53, 55, 56,
    61, 65, 67, 74, 78, 79, 80, 81, 82, 83, 87, 89, 90, 91, 97, 98, 99,
    105, 111, 114, 126, 131, 134, 139, 145, 148, 162, 163, 167, 169,
    173, 179, 180, 187, 198, 199, 204, 217, 243, 244, 245, 246, 247,
    249, 250, 252, 254, 256, 257, 260, 261, 262, 263, 264, 265
Indian National Army 187
Indonesia 35
Iran 25, 219
Iraq 19, 184
Islam 38, 43, 44, 46, 47, 49, 55, 91, 104, 105, 116, 132, 133, 137, 141,
    157, 159, 162, 165, 167, 172, 173, 176, 177, 178, 181, 183, 204,
    259
Italy 28, 118, 184, 212

J

Japan 7, 25, 114, 197

Jihad 47, 76, 89, 90
Jirgah 45, 84
Jones, Colour-Sergeant 62, 64, 258
Jones, Ernest 175

K

Kabalega, King 105, 132, 143, 149, 151, 152, 156, 160, 171, 178, 180, 206, 209, 210, 211, 213
Kabul 37, 39, 40, 41
Kampala 152, 167, 170, 255, 260, 265
Kandahar 37
Kenya 106, 107, 121, 125, 128, 163, 186, 198
Khan, Dost 37, 38
Khyber Pass 21, 41, 44, 45, 49, 57, 67, 89, 91, 103, 178, 204, 248
Kikuyu 107, 121

L

Lake Victoria 106, 117, 163, 169
Lewis, Lady Elizabeth 203
Livingstone, David 116, 122, 248
Lockhart, Sir William 35, 36, 49, 50, 64, 75, 83, 84, 88, 90, 248
Looting 25, 77, 78, 205, 213
Lord's Resistance Army 137, 173
Lubwa 168, 170, 174
Lucy's Ironworks 96, 97
Lugard, Sir Frederick 135, 136, 137, 138, 143, 157, 166, 243, 246
Lutyens, Sir Frederick 194

M

Macdonald, Maj. James 135, 164, 165, 166, 167, 169, 171, 244, 246, 252
Macedonia 184
Mahdi 47, 134, 136, 165, 177
Maidan 18, 49, 50, 55, 64, 75, 76, 77, 84, 89, 176
Malaya 125
Malta 33
Manchester 138, 139, 249, 254, 259, 265
Marlborough College 82, 104
Maxim Gun 44, 145, 150, 151, 165, 169

Mayor 2, 83, 189, 190, 216
Medicine 81, 109, 113, 122, 128
Methodist 123
Mexico 136
Mombasa 107, 143, 161, 163
Mwanga, King 133, 134, 135, 143, 145, 153, 164, 171, 178, 181, 211, 212
Myanmar 33

N

Newfoundland 98
New Zealand 98, 110, 187
Nightingale, Florence 81
Nubi 173

O

Obote, Milton 172
O' Dwyer, Sir Michael 99
Omani Empire 131
Opium 27, 28, 29, 30, 33, 99
Orakzai 44, 48, 88, 177, 178, 181
Oriel College 98, 99, 215
Ottoman Empire 38, 136, 250
Owen, Lt. 58, 59, 63
Oxfordshire Light Infantry 1, 18, 54, 55, 57, 64, 67, 69, 80, 83, 103, 184, 247, 248
Oxford Steam Plough Company 97
Oxford University Press 95, 96, 252, 255, 256

P

Pakistan 18, 33, 41, 89, 204, 219
Park, Mungo 109
Parr, Capt. 59, 60, 61, 62
Peshawar 17, 18, 20, 21, 35, 41, 46, 50, 51, 53, 85, 103, 184, 203, 248
Pitt Rivers 206, 209, 210, 211, 212, 240
Plowden, Col. 58, 59, 61, 63, 68, 69, 247
Poland 185
Political Officers 66, 85, 88, 89
Ponsonby, Sir John 125, 126, 147, 243

Portal, Sir Gerald 141, 143, 153, 159, 164, 247
Porters 56, 86, 107, 125, 126, 127, 147, 149, 157
Pre-Raphaelite 96
Protestant 117, 119, 128, 133, 172, 215
Punjab 39, 41, 163

Q

Queen Elizabeth I 23
Queen Victoria ix, 27, 28, 46, 91, 141, 175, 250, 251, 258, 260, 263

R

Radbourn, George 83
Railways 122, 257
Reparation 28, 35, 50, 83, 89, 205, 212, 213, 217
Rhodes, Cecil 7, 98, 214, 215, 216, 252
Romania 38
Roscoe, Rev. John 206, 207, 208, 209, 210, 211, 247, 250, 263
Rosebery, Sir Archibald 138, 141, 178
Royal Society 81
Russia 37, 38, 40, 87, 176, 184, 197
  Soviet Union 7, 184, 199
Rwanda 106

S

Samarkand 38
Sandana 204, 240
Sandhurst 82, 104, 145
Second Afghan War 135, 251
Seeley, Sir John 42, 43, 44, 200, 263
Seychelles 171
Sikh 39, 66, 75, 169
Singapore 6, 184, 198
Singh, Maharajah Duleep 39, 217
Slavery 37, 113, 114, 116, 126, 132, 136, 137, 149, 150, 152, 157, 158,
    159, 163, 165, 166, 168, 169, 174, 177, 179, 186, 213, 244
Smith, Pt. 60, 63
Sniping 51, 56, 57, 58, 76, 85
Society for the Propagation of the Gospel 110, 115, 116
South Africa 80, 96, 97, 98, 110, 175, 183, 214, 215

273

South African War 176, 204
Sovereignty 180, 181, 182, 185
Sri Lanka 33
Stanley, Henry Morton 116, 131, 139, 248, 263
Stretcher-bearers 67, 86
Sudan 33, 47, 105, 106, 121, 131, 133, 134, 135, 136, 165, 166, 175, 256, 258, 263
Sudanese troops 105, 124, 136, 144, 145, 150, 151, 153, 154, 157, 159, 162, 164, 165, 167, 173, 177
Suez Canal 134, 198
Swat valley 46

T

Tanganyika 136
Tanzania 106, 164
Tashkent 38
Tax 29, 30, 35, 46, 99
Textile 25, 26, 31, 113, 160, 166
The Daily Express 72
The Daily Telegraph 116, 249
The Times 61
Thomsett, Lt. Col. 15, 17, 18, 21, 46, 51, 52, 53, 55, 76, 78, 86, 91, 179, 248
Thruston, Arthur Blyford 99, 103, 124, 125, 127, 134, 142, 143, 149, 152, 153, 154, 155, 156, 157, 158, 160, 161, 164, 165, 166, 167, 168, 169, 170, 171, 173, 174, 179, 209, 248
Tibet 33, 183
Timour the Tarter 67
Togoland 183, 184
Toro 106, 135
Treaty of Berlin 140
Treaty of Versailles 184, 194, 195
Trench, Lt. 80

U

Uganda 103, 105, 106, 107, 110, 111, 113, 116, 117, 121, 123, 124, 128, 131, 134, 135, 136, 137, 138, 140, 141, 143, 147, 153, 160, 161, 162, 164, 165, 168, 172, 173, 174, 175, 176, 178, 180, 181, 186, 211, 243, 244, 245, 246, 247, 251, 252, 255, 256, 258, 259,

260, 261, 262, 264, 265
University, Oxford 1, 95, 96, 98, 99, 103, 115
USA 7, 19, 27, 82, 110, 158, 162, 173, 174, 184, 198, 256

V

Violence 24, 26, 123, 125, 128, 150, 156

W

Walker, Sgt. 66
Warburton, Robert 21, 22, 248
Warner, Pt. 63
Waziristan 39, 248
Whisky 17, 52, 54, 55
Wiggins, Thomas 83
Wilson, N.A. 168

Z

Zanzibar 105, 106, 113, 159, 246
Zenana Missionary Society 114

ABOUT THE AUTHOR

Duncan Taylor read politics, philosophy and economics at Oxford University and has a masters and PhD in history from the University of Bristol where he taught on the British Empire. He lives in Oxford.

www.ingramcontent.com/pod-product-compliance
Lightning Source LLC
Chambersburg PA
CBHW020136130526
44590CB00039B/193